THE CORN LAWS

THE CORN LAWS

The Formation of Popular Economics in Britain

Edited by
ALON KADISH

VOLUME V

PROVINCIAL FREE TRADE I

LEEDS, MANCHESTER AND THE LEAGUE

Routledge
Taylor & Francis Group
LONDON AND NEW YORK

First published 1996 by Pickering & Chatto (Publishers) Limited

Published 2016 by Routledge
2 Park Square, Milton Park, Abingdon, Oxon OX14 4RN
605 Third Avenue, New York, NY 10017

Routledge is an imprint of the Taylor & Francis Group, an informa business

BRITISH LIBRARY CATALOGUING IN PUBLICATION DATA
Corn Laws: Formation of Popular Economics
in Britain
I. Kadish, Alon
941.081

Set ISBN 13: 978-1-85196-410-9

ISBN13 :978-1-13875-890-2 (hbk) (vol-5)

LIBRARY OF CONGRESS CATALOGING-IN-PUBLICATION DATA
Kadish, Alon, 1950–
The corn laws : the formation of popular economics in Britain / Alon Kadish.
p. cm.
Includes bibliographical references and index.
ISBN 1–85196–410–X (set)
1. Corn laws (Great Britain) 2. Free trade––Great Britain.
3. Anti-Corn-Law League. I. Title.
HF2044.K33 1996
v. 1. Whig free trade I –– v. 2. Whig free trade II : Free trade and Irish nationalism I –– v. 3. Free trade and Irish nationalism I : James Wilson and the economist –– v. 4. Free trade and religion –– v. 5. Provincial free trade I –– v. 6. Provincial free trade II : Free trade farmers.
382.7'3'0942––dc20 98–1232
CIP

CONTENTS

ON THE

MORAL INFLUENCE

OF

FREE TRADE,

AND ITS EFFECTS

ON THE

PROSPERITY OF NATIONS:

A PAPER READ BEFORE THE LEEDS PHILOSOPHICAL AND LITERARY SOCIETY, ON THE 19TH FEBRUARY, 1830.

BY EDWARD BAINES, JUN.

LONDON:

RIDGWAY, PICCADILLY; AND BALDWIN AND CRADOCK, PATERNOSTER-ROW:

JOHN BAINES AND CO., LEEDS; AND ALL BOOKSELLERS.

1830.

Edward Baines Junior (1800–90)[1]

Edward Baines Junior was the second son of Edward Baines (1774–1848), proprietor of the *Leeds Mercury* and MP for Leeds 1834–41, and Charlotte, daughter of Matthew Talbot. Edward Baines Junior began writing for the *Mercury* in 1815. By 1818 he edited the paper, and in 1827 became its proprietor. In 1818 he helped found the Leeds Literary and Philosophical Society on the model of Manchester, Liverpool, and Newcastle, and in 1824, after attending a lecture in London by George Birkbeck and Henry Brougham to an audience of five or six hundred workers, he was instrumental in founding a Mechanics' Institute in Leeds. In 1837 he became President of the West Riding Union of Mechanics' Institutes.

Edward Baines was elected to Parliament in April 1859 and represented Leeds until 1874 when he lost his seat in the general elections in which the Liberal party was defeated. In the course of his parliamentary career he introduced bills, in 1861, 1864, and 1865, for the reduction of the borough franchise from £10 to £6. He served as member of the Schools Inquiry commission December 1864–December 1867, and was chairman of Yorkshire College, Leeds 1880–7. Baines was magistrate and Deputy Lieutenant of the West Riding and in 1880 was Knighted.

Baines' politics were largely determined by this religion. His point of departure was his father's Whiggism. In his biography of Edward Baines Senior he wrote:

> His public and political conduct was mainly governed by two principles, the love of right and the spirit of improvement. Hence he was in every thing a Reformer. Yet he did not desire change for its own sake. ... He was attached to the Whigs, because he found them the advocates of popular rights; and through life he thought it prudent to sustain that party, as on the whole likely to do best for the people. When conscientiously differing from them, however, ... he took an independent course.[2]

The issue on which the Baines' and the Whigs differed was state support for education to which the Baines', father and son, strongly objected to as contrary to the principle of voluntarism. At the age of eighty Baines explained his priorities:

[1] On Baines see *Memorial to Edward Baines, on completion of his 80th year. Public Presentation in the Albert Hall, Leeds, December 3rd, 1880*, London: Hodder & Stoughton, Manchester: J. Heywood. Leeds: Charles Goodall, [1880], Frederic Boase, *Modern English Biography* vol. iv, supplement to vol. 1 (1908), London: Frank Cass, 1965, p. 233, Michael Stenton, *Who's Who of British Members of Parliament* vol. i, Hassocks, Sussex: The Harvester Press, 1976, p. 18, and Derek Fraser, 'Edward Baines' in Patricia Hollis (ed.), *Pressure from Without in Early Victorian England*, London: Edward Arnold, 1974.

[2] Edward Baines, *The Life of Edward Baines. Late M.P. for the Borough of Leeds*, London: Longman, Leeds: Reid Newsome, 1851, p. 362.

. . . great as is the value which I attach to education, and which I wish every student in every branch of learning to attach to it, I cannot for a moment compare it to the value or the happiness of personal religion. . . . The book that transcends all books is God's own Word; and the lesson it teaches, as beyond all other lessons for time or eternity, is this – Fear God and love the Saviour![1]

Thus on free trade Baines' position was largely influenced by the changes in his alliance with the Whigs which served to bring him closer, although not too close, to the League.

[The bibliography of Edward Baines is printed on p. 57.]

[1] *Memorial to Edward Baines*, p. 36

ADVERTISEMENT.

It is a rule of the Leeds Philosophical and Literary Society, before which the following Paper was read, to exclude from its discussions the subjects of Politics and Religion; but the science of Political Economy, as distinguished from Politics, has been justly thought worthy to be treated of in the Society. This Paper, therefore, discusses none of those *specific measures* which have been designated as Free Trade measures, and of which Mr. Huskisson and Lord Wallace were the principal authors; but it examines the *general principles* of Trade, with a view to show the political and moral evils of Restrictions and Monopolies, and the political and moral benefits of absolute Freedom of Commerce. In the discussions which have lately taken place on particular measures, it has been evident that the most important errors prevailed as to general principles. An error in principle naturally leads to practical errors. It has been the author's object, therefore, to show that Freedom of Trade is best calculated to promote the prosperity of a nation, and that many of the arguments by which legislative protection and restriction have been defended, though plausible, are fallacious.

He wished also to illustrate a higher class of advantages, namely, the *Moral* advantages resulting from Free Trade. It was, indeed, the principal object of his Paper to show, that unrestricted Commerce was calculated to prevent wars, by binding the nations of the world together in the ties of mutual interest, and also to ameliorate the condition of mankind, by hastening the progress of civilization, and diffusing knowledge and truth throughout the world. On these grounds he claims for the principles of Free Trade a higher importance than would attach to them from any political or commercial considerations.

ON THE MORAL INFLUENCE

OF

FREE TRADE.

In a great trading community it is of high importance that the principles of Commerce should be well understood. It is desirable that every man should see how commerce promotes the interests of nations, and should be acquainted with the general principles that ought to guide legislation concerning it. The errors that have prevailed in former times on this subject have led to practical measures of the most mischievous nature. Yet there is no subject that admits of a more full and clear elucidation. Modern science has established the principles of trade on an immoveable basis of reasoning and experience. The investigation of those principles cannot but be fraught with interest; and in pursuing the inquiry, we shall be led, if I do not mistake, not merely to lessons of political wisdom, but to still more important views of the moral consequences resulting from sound commercial legislation.

The subject of my paper cannot fail to be interesting in this commercial town. I shall endeavour to show the benefits and blessings of Commerce, not merely in supplying the wants of men, and enriching a state, but more particularly in its Moral Influence upon mankind—in its tendency to promote pacific and friendly relations among the nations of the world, and to diffuse the light of civilization and true religion over the whole earth. I have entitled my paper "On the Moral Influence of *Free* Trade," because I intend especially to illustrate the benefits of unrestricted commerce, in opposition to all systems of commercial prohibition or restriction; and to show that the more unfettered and the more extensive is the commercial intercourse of nations, the more numerous and powerful will be their bonds of amity, and the more rapid will be the operation of trade in ameliorating the condition of the human race. I shall not enter on the question of the propriety of liberating any particular trade from its shackles, in an artificial state of things. I have now to do with general principles. But those principles may assuredly be applied to practice; and I cannot, if I would, avoid the inference, that it is the interest of all countries to establish—how quickly or gradually I do not pretend to decide—an absolute Freedom of Commerce.

Before I proceed to speak of the *Moral Influence* of Free Trade, I think myself bound to show that Free Trade is not opposed to the political interests of a nation—to the development of its natural resources, and its growth in riches and power. If I neglected this, some of my hearers, who have little considered the subject, might suppose that I was influenced by general views of philanthropy, to the disregard of the dictates of patriotism, or that I was desirous of cultivating the harmonious relations of states in opposition to their individual interests.

No principle of political economy seems to me more incontestably true than this—that the resources of a nation will be the most rapidly developed, and its prosperity built upon the surest basis, under an entire absence of interference on the part of government with its commerce or industry. Protection for person and property, and for all the operations of trade, is what every government owes to its subjects; but that kind of protection which restricts one branch of industry in order to encourage another, and which prohibits the importation of any commodity from abroad in order to promote its production at home, is not merely useless, but mischievous.

Men who are dependant on their industry for their subsistence, or who engage in production for the increase of their wealth, are far more likely to *discover* than any government can be to *dictate* to them the most beneficial mode of employing their labour and capital. Self-interest is incomparably more powerful than any other motive in sharpening the discernment and stimulating the enterprise of men. There is not a process of industry so difficult or dangerous that men will not perform it, or a corner of the earth so remote that they will not visit it, for the sake of gain. With as patient a quest as that of the bloodhound in tracking his prey, over high and low, over rugged and smooth, will man, on the scent of profit, pursue his game, when governors, who have only their eyes to guide them, would be utterly baffled. We may also safely assume that a man will not prefer foreign commerce to domestic production, unless the former is more profitable. He will prefer earning his bread in that mode which takes him to the smallest distance from his home and his friends, if he can in the same length of time obtain an equal return for his labour. If he *should* brave the risks of the deep and of foreign lands, it will be because he can more beneficially employ his industry in foreign traffic than in domestic production. Nor will he leave the earnings of his toil to enrich a stranger; he will bring it home to the last farthing, and pour it into the lap of his family and of his country. Whether, therefore, he visits foreign lands in his own person, or makes something at home which he sends abroad,—and whether the return be in money, or money's worth,—the object is to obtain the largest possible profit, and to deposit that profit under his own roof. Thus, in enriching himself, he enriches his country; and thus his country is more benefited by the employment of his energies in foreign commerce than if he had expended them in cultivating some less fruitful soil at home.

If, then, individual interest is the surest guide in the choice of a profitable employment, and if the profits earned by individuals all go to enrich the state, there is no motive to induce a wise government to control the industry of its subjects. Restrictions may shut them out from some source of gain, but cannot open any new channels. Protection, except to secure them in the pursuit of their avocations, is vain and impertinent. No trader would think of asking protection, who either was not engaged in an unprofitable pursuit, in which he ought rather to be discouraged, or who did not wish for the advantage of a monopoly at the expense of his fellow countrymen.

Some writers have inculcated the absurd notion, that foreign commerce cannot be profitable to both the nations carrying it on—for, say they, if the commodities exchanged are of equal value, neither party gains; if of unequal value, one party must lose. The reverse of this proposition, however, is the truth, for it is certain that commerce cannot be carried on unless both parties gain. No man would exchange or sell, if he did not gain by the transaction. Every nation has, or can produce, more than it wants of some commodities, and less than it wants of others : by parting with a commodity of which it has an excess, in exchange for one of which it has a deficiency, it obtains what is to it of greater value. A piece of cloth or of cutlery is of more value in Jamaica than in England, because the West Indians want it without being able to make it, whilst we can make more than we want; for a similar reason, a hogshead of sugar is of more value in England than in Jamaica. The exchange is a convenience to both parties, and therefore it is profitable to both. The error I am exposing has arisen from the practice of measuring the value of commodities in money : it has been taken for granted that if a guinea's worth of English commodities was exchanged for a guinea's worth of Jamaica produce, there would be no profit to either party. It was overlooked that cloth which is worth a guinea in England is worth much more in Jamaica, and that sugar which is worth a guinea in Jamaica is worth much more here. The *wants* of both parties are supplied by the exchange ; and what do all men toil for but the *supply of their wants?* Money is of no value but to this end.

Now that the principles of commerce are well understood, it may be thought useless to spend time in exposing so gross an error as, that a nation could continue for any length of time to carry on a losing trade. Yet this error has not only been entertained by speculative writers, but has for ages been admitted by merchants, and seriously acted upon by governments and senates. The absurd calculations that were made on what was called "the balance of trade," and of which so much was seen in the publications and heard in the parliamentary debates of the last two centuries, proceeded on this very principle—that a nation, or a body of merchants, might be carrying on a losing trade unawares, and that it required the calculations of some sage politician to apprise them of the fact. The most important commercial connexions between this and other countries have been broken off, under the notion that all the profit of the transactions went to the other party, and all the loss to ourselves—or, as it was expressed, that "the balance of trade was against us." To prevent the further progress of this supposed injury, the trade was prohibited by government; and the merchants, who had been quietly making their fortunes, were ruined in reality, to prevent their ruining both themselves and the country! Even so late as the year 1787, the wise measure of Mr. Pitt and Mr. Jenkinson, for extending our trade with France under a commercial treaty, was opposed by Mr. Fox and his party on this ground amongst others, that the trade between the two countries in the reign of James II. was very unprofitable to England, and that this losing trade was increasing so fast as to compel our government to put a stop to so alarming an evil, by wholesome restrictions and prohibitions! Those who sneer at political economy may condemn Adam Smith for having exploded this mischievous absurdity.*

The experience and common sense of merchants often convinced them of the mischief done by meddling statesmen; and the French merchants, when asked by the celebrated Minister Colbert what he could do for them, answered wisely—*Laissez nous faire*—"Let us alone."

I think I have sufficiently shown that absolute freedom of trade is most favourable to the prosperity of a nation. Further proofs and illustrations might easily be accumulated, if it were necessary; but as this is not the immediate object of my paper, I shall not dwell further on the point, except to expose the fallacy of two popular objections. The first I believe to be most extensively prevalent, though it will not bear the test of a single minute's careful consideration. It is—that by making all the articles that we want at home, and spending all our money at home, we afford fuller employment to our own population, and advance most rapidly the prosperity of the state. This is true with regard to all articles which we can make at home as cheap or as good as we can buy them abroad; but with regard to no others. In order to remove the vagueness in which the

* It is to the honour of the manufacturers of Leeds, that they petitioned at that time for the utmost degree of freedom in the commercial intercourse between England and France. Benjamin Gott, Esq. was a member of the Committee appointed to promote that object.

fallacy of the objection is concealed, let us suppose the case of a single individual in this country, wishing for a particular article of manufacture—say, a piece of ornamental jewellery. We may suppose that he could make the article himself by the expenditure of *ten* days' labour. If, at some different employment—as the manufacture of cloth—he could in *eight* days earn as much as would purchase a similar piece of jewellery made in Paris, it would be his interest to buy the article, and not to make it. The case of the Parisian may be the converse of this; it might take him ten days to make the cloth, and only eight days to make the jewellery. It is obvious that it would be a great disadvantage to the Englishman to make his own jewellery, or to the Parisian to make his own cloth. But the same principle which governs the individual ought to govern the nation. It is possible, indeed, to make certain articles at home, but it would be more profitable to buy them abroad; and by making them at home, the prosperity of the country is not advanced, but retarded. Nor is the amount of employment to our own population diminished by purchasing from foreigners. No foreigner will give us the produce of his labour, without receiving in exchange the produce of ours. If we buy, we must also sell. Our only object, then, should be to employ our labour and capital in the most productive manner, by doing which we shall best support our population and advance the prosperity of our country. The objection I am refuting, if it had any force, would apply as strongly to individual families as to nations, and would require that every family should make its own clothes, shoes, and hats, and raise its own food—a thing only attempted in the lower stages of civilization, when the advantage of a division of labour is not understood or not attainable.

The second objection which requires a brief notice, is made by some who allow the principle of Free Trade, but who contend that though it may be more advantageous to procure many commodities from other countries than to produce them at home, yet that the *safer* plan is to produce them at home; because, in case of hostilities with the country from which we obtain any article, our supply might be cut off, and thus our people inconvenienced, and perhaps our manufacturers deprived of their raw material. If this objection were well founded, England would be in a lamentable case. She depends upon other countries for the raw materials of her principal manufactures,—upon America for her cotton,—upon Saxony for her fine wool,—upon Russia for her flax,—upon Italy and India for her silk,—upon the countries of the Baltic for her timber and tow, the indispensable materials of her navy,—and upon India, Brazil, and Central America for her dyeing wares. Thus England, if the objection be valid, is the most dependant of nations, and at the mercy of every despot and republic in the world. Yet has she seen Europe and America banded against her, and has sustained a twenty years' war, without ever being seriously inconvenienced for any of the commodities she receives from abroad. The truth is, commerce is too strong and subtile to be intercepted by war; and when there is a sufficient motive for carrying it on, the edicts of governments and the barriers of custom-houses are easily evaded or broken through. Too many persons are interested in the continuance of an important branch of commerce, to allow it to be cut off. When it cannot be continued directly, it may indirectly. When the circulating fluid is checked in its course through the main artery, it takes a more circuitous channel—an anastomosing branch—which, however inadequate it seems at first to convey the flood of commerce, is soon enlarged to the requisite dimensions. Neutral nations gladly make their ports the emporiums, and their ships the carriers, for a profitable trade. Let a war come to-morrow, and let freights be raised a single pound per ton, all the ports of all neutral nations would be swept within a few weeks for vessels to supply the trade of England,—if, indeed, England were not well able to protect her own commercial marine. Even two nations at war with each other will carry on an indirect trade in defiance of their respective governments, and in general their governments wink at the practice from motives of policy. During the last war, in the height of the "continental system," a most extensive trade was carried on between England and Germany through the small island of Heligoland. During the present exclusion of American vessels from the British West Indies, the flour, timber, and provisions of the United States have reached our islands through the neutral harbours of St. Thomas's, St. Bartholomew's, and Santa Cruz. Such was the power of British commerce on Russia during the late war, that the Emperor was induced by the remonstrances of his discontented subjects to break through the doubly riveted bonds of the "continental system," and to brave the vengeance of the conqueror of Europe. In the war which followed, the power of Napoleon received its death-blow; and thus was that formidable despot vanquished no less by the influence of British commerce than by the prowess of the British arms. An anecdote is related discreditable to Dutch patriotism, but strikingly illustrative of the power of gain to bring supplies even from the midst of enemies—that when a warlike general invaded Holland, he had no prospect of succeeding in the siege of its principal cities without new supplies of the munitions of war, but that the Dutch merchants actually sold to him the means of subduing their country. How vain, then, is the apprehension that Free Trade would endanger the supplies of a nation!—and how unwise would be the policy, which should induce us to forego the advantages of commerce through this unfounded apprehension!

I do not deny that war causes great *inconvenience* to a commercial country; I shall afterwards argue from this fact, to prove that nations carrying on extensive commerce would be anxious to preserve peace; what I contend for now is, that a country would not be in danger of being deprived of any thing necessary to its people.

But there is another answer to this objection made by the friends of restriction, namely, that the tendency of Free Trade is *to prevent war.* And this brings me to the main point of my essay, and to one of the most important and beautiful manifestations of the Moral Influence of Free Trade.

I have described the Moral Influence of Free Trade as consisting in *its tendency to promote pacific and friendly relations among the nations of the world, and to diffuse the light of civilization and true religion over the whole earth.* I proceed to consider the former of these effects.

Neither the Christian, nor the philanthropist, nor the philosopher can review the most striking events in the history of mankind through all ages, without feelings of shame and horror at the blood-stained scene. The annals of man are little else than a record of wars and conquests. It might almost be supposed that the whole race were descended from the first murderer. What spot is there of this fair world, which has not been steeped in the blood of its inhabitants? Is there a valley so beautiful, that strife has not polluted it? Is there a shore so happy, that war has not invaded it? Are there natural obstacles so great, that men have not surmounted them to imbrue their hands in the blood of their brethren? What desert so vast and sun-scorched, what mountain so steep and frozen, what sea so wide and tempestuous, that armies have not crossed them to deal destruction on the children of men? The Christian poet sighed for "a lodge in some vast wilderness," where alone he should be able to avoid the rumour

"Of wrong and outrage with which earth is fill'd."

Justly did he complain that

"Lands intersected by a narrow frith
Abhor each other: mountains interposed
Make enemies of nations, which had else
Like kindred drops been mingled into one."

Rooted antipathies, exerting themselves in devastation and slaughter, have even existed between nations who seemed to have been destined by nature to live under one government and in the closest bonds of union.* The possession of a few acres of wilderness has been contested with a fierceness that has torn continents, and drained

* The English and Scotch.

the blood and treasure of powerful kingdoms.* Colonies have been won at an expense, of which the whole value of their commerce would not pay the interest,—colonies, which have been so worse than worthless, that it would have been wise to give the amount of their purchase-money to avoid the burden of connexion with them.

A large proportion of the wars which have desolated the earth have arisen out of conflicting claims to distant portions of territory, which were of no value except for the purposes of commerce, or out of an avaricious desire on the part of governments to secure *exclusive privileges* in trade. I think I shall be able to show that the general establishment of Free Trade would have prevented many of the wars undertaken for the acquisition of colonies, and all those arising out of a claim to exclusive privileges; and would have so bound the nations of the world together by the ties of affection and mutual interest, as to have restrained monarchs from going to war to gratify their own ambition. If this be made to appear, I may safely assert that the universal establishment of Free Trade would be one of the greatest blessings that the philanthropist or the Christian could desire.

In proceeding to consider this point, let me ask—Does a survey of the natural world lead us to

* The Seven Years' War originated in a dispute between the French and English concerning the boundaries of Canada and the United Provinces of North America.

conclude, that the human species were intended by their Creator, or—which is the same thing—that it would conduce to their happiness, to live in numerous distinct communities, each isolated from the rest, unconnected with them by interest or sympathy, wrapping itself up in its own concerns, ignorant of all others, and averse to intercourse with them?—*or*, to live as federal portions of the great commonwealth of man, associated indeed under different governments, but united in sympathy and interest, exchanging the diversified products of their soil and industry, communicating and receiving all useful knowledge, each participating in the prosperity of the rest, each contributing according to its opportunities and advantages to the general stock of human science and human happiness, and thus all linked together by innumerable bonds in the harmonious society that becomes children of a common parent?

I answer that the state last described is that which was manifestly destined for us by our Maker, who has scattered the bounties of his hand variously, but wisely, over the whole surface of the earth, so as to tempt men to an interchange of benefits, and has given us for our strongest bond of union a universal law of love.

In looking at the different countries of the world, we shall find none that combine all the advantages which nature has provided for the comfort and welfare of men, and none that are wholly destitute of them.* One country enjoys a rich soil, fruitful in all agricultural produce; another possesses mines of metals and coal, which fit it for the production of manufactures. The different kinds of food and fruits are peculiar to different countries and climates. The materials out of which the various kinds of clothing are manufactured come from every quarter of the globe. The torrid zone supplies articles which comfort or delight the inhabitants of the frigid; and the latter in return furnishes materials which refresh the people of the tropics. Both contribute to the wants and luxuries of the inhabitants of the temperate zone, which is able amply to repay the obligation.

Let me take a single country, by way of giving reality and force to the illustration, and

* This fact is beautifully illustrated by Virgil—

"Hic segetes, illic veniunt feliciùs uvæ;
Arborei fetus alibi, atque injussa virescunt
Gramina. Nonne vides croceos ut Tmolus odores,
India mittit ebur, molles sua thura Sabæi,
At Chalybes nudi ferrum, virosaque Pontus
Castorea, Eliadum palmas Epirus equarum?
*Continuò has leges æternaque fœdera certis
Imposuit* NATURA *locis*."—*Georgics, Book* I.

"Here golden harvests wave, there vineyards glow,
Fruit bends the bough, or herbs unbidden grow—
Her saffron, Tmolus, Ind her ivory boasts,
Spice wings the gale round Saba's balmy coasts:
The naked Chalybes their iron yield,
The pow'rful Castor scents the Pontic field,
While fam'd Epirus rears th' equestrian breed,
Born for the palm that crowns th' Olympic steed.
In stated regions, from th' eternal Cause,
Such Nature's compact, and unbroken laws."—*Sotheby's Translation.*

show how an extensive commerce binds it in the ties of profitable connexion to all the principal countries of the earth,—how the wants and comforts of its own inhabitants are supplied by that commerce,—and how the country is thereby interested in the peace and prosperity of the whole world. No country will answer this purpose so well as England. And, in order to make the illustration more complete, let us begin at home, and see how the different counties and districts of England vary in their productions, and how the freest intercourse between them tends to the general prosperity.

Several of the low and flat counties of England, as Lincolnshire, Norfolk, and Cambridgeshire, have a soil well suited to the growth of corn: some parts are more favourable to wheat, others to oats, others to barley. Other districts, as Craven in Yorkshire, and Leicestershire, are calculated for grazing land, and they fatten the cattle bred upon the high lands of Scotland. Wool is raised in Lincolnshire, Leicestershire, Northumberland, Scotland, Yorkshire, the South Downs, and many other parts. Herefordshire, Worcestershire, and Devonshire are covered with orchards, and produce an abundance of apples and pears, from which cider and perry are made. Kent and Worcestershire are peculiarly favourable to the growth of hops. Hampshire and other counties produce fine timber for the use of the navy; and the hills of England and Scotland are clothed with forests of larch and fir. Several large districts possess valuable coal fields, as Northumberland, Durham, Yorkshire, Lancashire, Shropshire, and Staffordshire. Some are rich in iron ore, as Staffordshire, Warwickshire, Yorkshire, Furness in Lancashire, and South Wales. Cornwall abounds in mines of tin, copper, and other metals. Cumberland, Westmoreland, and Wales supply slate. Yorkshire, Somersetshire, the Isle of Portland, and Scotland furnish building stone. Salt is produced chiefly from the mines and springs of Cheshire; alum, from the Whitby and Cleveland mines; lime, from Derbyshire and many other counties. Some parts of the country are peculiarly fitted for manufactures, by possessing fuel, iron, numerous streams, and ready access to the sea; of which Yorkshire, Lancashire, and Lanarkshire are examples. Others are calculated by fine harbours and secure roads, to be the principal seats of foreign commerce and of the coasting trade;—as London, Liverpool, Hull, and Bristol. There are fisheries peculiar to the different coasts, as herrings to Yarmouth, pilchards to Cornwall, oysters to Essex and Kent, mackerel to the Thames, the Mersey, &c.: shell fish, I believe, are more abundant on the east coast; salmon, in the rivers of the west.

So great is the variety in the productions of one small island; and you must have observed, as

I proceeded, that no one district produces all, or nearly all, the articles which every district wants, and which are now universally diffused by our coasting and inland navigation and by roads. Suppose that the days of the Heptarchy were recalled, and that England was again divided into seven kingdoms, which were either frequently at war, or repelling mutual intercourse by commercial jealousies and lines of custom-houses,—how much poorer and more destitute would be the inhabitants of all!—of how much less happiness, and how much smaller advances in civilization, would they be capable! Is it difficult to apply the lesson afforded by the districts of England, to the countries of the world? Can the advantages be so striking on the small scale, and would they disappear on the large? Or is it not a desideratum worthy of the aspirations and prayers of every good man, that the peace, harmony, and prosperity which Englishmen enjoy from their internal union, should be extended by the same means to the whole brotherhood of man?

Let us turn our eyes abroad. We have seen that a great variety of productions necessary or useful to man are found within our own territory; but how many of the articles which we now deem necessaries are products of distant countries, and only to be brought within our reach by foreign commerce! There is scarcely a country on the face of the earth, which does not pour its treasures into our harbours, and which does not in turn receive the products of English industry. From the icy regions of Archangel, round the whole circuit of the old continent, to Behring's Straits, and thence, round the entire compass of the new continent, to the frozen seas of Greenland, our ships enter almost every gulf and every port in the pursuits of commerce. We bring tar and tallow from the White Sea, and timber from Norway: we penetrate the Baltic, and bring home the iron and timber of Sweden, the flax, furs, tar, and tallow of Russia, the fine wool of Saxony, and (sometimes) the corn of Poland. Holland yields us flax, cheese, spirits, madder, and various other productions; France affords wines, brandy, and articles of taste and fancy; Spain sends us wool, wines, and fruits; Portugal also furnishes the two last commodities. We make the sweep of the Mediterranean, and reap a luxuriant harvest of oil and wine: from Italy we obtain silk, oil, olives, marble, corals, pictures and statues; from Sicily, oranges and wine; currants, from the Ionian Islands; figs, silk, and cotton, from Smyrna; cotton and antiquities from Egypt. From the coast of Africa we fetch palm oil, gold dust, ivory, timber, and many of the curiosities of our menageries and museums. The Mauritius produces sugar. The Persian Gulf yields us silks, leather, and precious stones. India pours in her large tribute of raw silk, cotton, indigo, silk goods, gems, shells, rice, sugar and coffee.

China supplies every English lady with her tea; and the islands of Australasia render their rich and aromatic cargoes of gums and spices. The South Sea affords our whalers spermaceti and oil. Peru sends us the precious metals of gold and silver; Chili, the useful metal of copper; Buenos Ayres supplies us with hides from her well-stocked plains; Brazil, with dye-woods, ornamental woods, fruits, sugar, cotton, and gold. From the Gulf of Mexico we bring dye-woods, mahogany, indigo, cochineal, and the precious metals. Our colonies in the West Indies supply our vast consumption of sugar, coffee, cocoa, rum, and molasses. From the United States we derive the raw material of our most extensive manufacture, cotton wool, and also tobacco, rice, tar, turpentine, and ashes. Our Canadian colonies supply timber, staves, oil, and fish. From Hudson's Bay we receive the hunter's harvest of furs; and the icy seas of Greenland yield to our whalers their oil, whalebone, and seal-skin.

So large, constant, and certain is the supply of these numerous commodities, that in every huckster's shop are sold, and every kitchen consumes, the products of the furthest East as regularly as those which are raised at our doors. I once obtained refreshment in the cottage of a small farmer, in one of the deepest recesses of the mountains of Cumberland, and from what I saw there "I could not but reflect on the all-pervading power of commerce, which brought into those secluded valleys, and to the use of the ignorant peasant, the luxuries of the most distant climes: he comforts himself on his sheep-walk with a soothing quid from Virginia, and is refreshed after his day's labour with an infusion of the plants of China, sweetened by the sugar of the Indies. His rude pepper-box is filled with the produce of Java; the nutmeg of Borneo is a plaything for his children; and his careful spouse dresses their hurts with the spermaceti of the Antarctic Ocean."*

Addison, in one of the Numbers of the Spectator, in which he beautifully exhibits the advantages of commerce, takes an illustration from a different class of life: "The single dress of a woman of quality," he says, "is often the product of a hundred climates. The muff and the fan come together from different ends of the earth. The scarf is sent from the torrid zone, and the tippet from beneath the pole. The brocade petticoat rises out of the mines of Peru, and the diamond necklace out of the bowels of Indostan."

Thus is this island, of which it has been said that "it can make no further advances towards a plum than to a sloe, and carries an apple to no greater perfection than a crab," made the receptacle of the products and luxuries of the globe. And thus is it bound to the remotest nations by the ties

* Companion to the Lakes.

of self-interest. For not only is this commerce beneficial in ministering to our comfort and gratification; it employs and feeds our artizans, and is the spring of our manufacturing industry. No nation supplies us with its products, without receiving an equivalent. The manufactures of England penetrate into every quarter of the globe. The Negro of Guinea, the Esquimaux of Labrador, the wandering Tartar and Arab, the Mandarin of China, and the Nabob of Hindoostan, are all our customers. Leeds, Manchester, Birmingham, and Sheffield supply them with clothing, weapons, utensils, and numberless articles of use and ornament. Thus we indefinitely multiply our customers and increase our resources, and thus we become interested in the peace and prosperity of the whole world.

No nation could be blotted from the face of the earth, without England feeling the void. No war can rage in any quarter, of which England does not experience the effects, and which our government does not hasten to terminate by its mediation. Of this the late war between Brazil and Buenos Ayres is an example. We ourselves could not go to war without such inconvenience and loss to our merchants and manufacturers, as would make both the people and the government slow to take offence. No great public calamity could happen in any country with which our intercourse is considerable, but the chord of sympathy would vibrate to the heart of England. Our case is the reverse of Ishmael's: "our hand is *with* every man, and every man's hand is *with* us."

If there are any exceptions to this rule, they are precisely those countries from which we are held aloof by commercial restrictions either on their part or on ours. Were trade universally free, there would be no exceptions.

I would ask, what are the wars into which England is at this moment the most likely to be plunged? They are those which may arise out of commercial differences, either on our own behalf or on that of our colonies. But unless the colonial system were a restrictive system, or unless other nations attempted unjustly to injure our commerce, this danger would not exist. I do not inquire whether it would be politic for England to renounce her colonies, or wholly to liberate their trade from restrictions; I merely show the general principle, and that principle I maintain to be, that the restrictive and monopolizing system exposes a nation to frequent quarrels and contests, which would be avoided under a system of Free Trade.*

* Adam Smith has well expressed the sum of the evidence of history as to the effect of commercial jealousies in provoking international contests:—"Nations have been taught," says he, "that their interest consisted in beggaring all their neighbours. Each nation has been made to look with an invidious eye upon the prosperity of all the nations with which it trades, and to consider their gain as its own loss. Commerce, which ought naturally to be among nations, as among individuals, a bond of union and friendship, has become the most fertile source of discord and animosity. The capricious ambition of kings and ministers has not, during the present

It will be perceived that the operation of Free Trade is two-fold: it tends to the general harmony of nations both positively and negatively,—positively, by making it much to their interest to agree, and negatively, by lessening the occasions of difference.

I confess that in taking the case of England, I have taken the most favourable case that could be selected for my purpose. It is not to be supposed that many nations would have a commerce so universal, or could be bound to the rest of the world by ties so numerous, as ourselves. But the principle is the same, though not the degree. In proportion as the access to any country is free, its commerce is likely to be extensive; and in proportion as its commerce extends, its ties of friendship and interest with other countries are multiplied. Nor can we calculate the extent to which commerce might be carried, if all restrictions were annihilated. We know that in our own country every facility given to travelling and to carriage causes a great increase of traffic.* We know that wherever a port is declared free in any part of the world, trade accumulates in it in a remarkable manner.† And

and the preceding century, been more fatal to the repose of Europe, than the impertinent jealousy of merchants and manufacturers."—*Inquiry into the Nature and Causes of the Wealth of Nations; by Adam Smith, LL.D.* Book IV., chap. III.

* The formation of the Stockton and Darlington Railway has increased the number of travellers and the amount of business on that line more than tenfold.

† E. g. Leghorn, Genoa, Cadiz, Trieste, Singapore.

I have no doubt that the general establishment of Free Trade would increase a hundred or a thousand fold the commerce of the globe. In the same proportion would the motives to harmony and tranquillity be increased, and the occasions of war diminished.

I do not wish to conceal that a universal system of Free Trade would leave all countries open to competition with each other in manufactures and every kind of produce. That this might cause inconvenience to some, if adopted in an artificial state of society, I do not deny; for I repeat that I am not considering what should be done in an artificial state of things. But in a natural state the effect would only be just what takes place within the limits of a country like England, where the manufactures of different towns and counties compete with each other, but never cause hostility, and where they always adjust themselves without legislative interference. Under a system of Free Trade, that country which had the greatest advantages for trade, by the number and excellence of its productions, would be the greatest gainer. And it is for the interest of mankind that it should be so: the largest population ought to exist where there are the best means of maintaining them. It is an absurd and most pernicious error to suppose that one country is injured by the prosperity of another. The richer and more populous a country is, the better customer is it to surrounding countries: much of its abundance must overflow upon its neighbours. As the land is rendered more valuable near a populous city, so would every neighbouring country be enriched from its mere contiguity to an opulent nation.

I have thus answered the only objections that I can anticipate to my principle, that Free Trade has a tendency to promote pacific and friendly relations among the nations of the world. I proceed to the second class of effects which I ascribe to Free Trade, namely, *its tendency to diffuse the light of civilization and true religion over the whole earth.*

A moment's reflection will show to my hearers that I am entering on a large and fertile field, where interesting facts lie thickly strewn, and where reasonable speculations concerning matters of vast import present themselves. Yet I intend to be brief, principally because the facts are so well known, and the inferences so obvious, that it would be useless to do more than just to awaken the trains of thought in your minds.

Need I, in this commercial town,—need I, in the present day, when commerce has done so much for the world,—need I, before this Literary Society, to whom the history of ancient times is familiar,—need I point out the wide spreading and potent influence of a great commercial state on the rest of the world? If I allude to these facts, it is not to inform your minds, but only to bring the facts to your recollection, that you may perceive the force of my argument.

There is scarcely a nation of antiquity which did not owe its civilization to the influence of foreigners, who were generally brought to its shores either directly in the pursuit of commerce, or at least by means of vessels employed in trade. When Egypt and Phœnicia were highly civilized, Greece, Italy, and the whole of Europe were involved in the depth of barbarism. Yet from the two former countries went out Cecrops, Cadmus, and the principal lawgivers of the Greek republics. The trade of Tyre, Carthage, and Egypt was the chief means of civilizing the countries on the shores of the Mediterranean. The active intercourse amongst the Greeks of Greece Proper, Asia Minor, Magna Græcia, Sicily, and the Levant, wonderfully accelerated the march of civilization. Their lawgivers, philosophers, and literati were nearly all travellers, several of whom visited other countries for mercantile purposes, and several from a mere love of science and useful knowledge. I may mention, amongst the most distinguished of those who, after years spent in travelling, brought back the sciences, arts, and letters of Egypt and the East to their native countries, Solon, Pythagoras, Herodotus, Plato, and Xenophon.

The history of the world leads us to conclude that civilization is of extremely slow growth, except under the culture of intercourse with more refined nations. What nation can be mentioned, which advanced beyond barbarism by its inherent tendency to improvement? Where do we find the arts and sciences springing up as indigenous to the soil? The useful and fine arts, and most of the sciences, may be traced back from empire to empire, from shore to shore, till their origin is lost in remote antiquity. But we can no where find a community of barbarians forming for themselves a government and laws, establishing social order, resorting to agriculture, commerce, and manufactures, superadding letters and the fine arts to the useful arts, and thus proceeding in their upward progress to the elevation of a civilized state, without having received the seeds of improvement from a foreign land. On the contrary, we see savage nations continuing for centuries in their native forests, as barren and unchanged as the bogs and marshes around them, whose stagnancy chokes every tendency of nature to improvement, and makes them the scene of feculence, putrefaction, and disease. Nature seems to shun and abhor uniformity: trees and plants will not long flourish without a change of soil; animals degenerate where there is no mixture of breeds; and the human species deteriorates both corporeally and mentally, when any of its tribes shut themselves out from intercourse with the rest of the world, and continue from age to age amidst the same scenes, inheriting the same ideas and prejudices, and transmitting the same diseases, vices, and superstitions. On the other hand, an uncivilized people who are visited by foreigners in the way of commerce, and some of whom in turn visit distant countries, manifest the beneficial effects of this intercourse in many striking ways. Their intellects are excited and sharpened by dealings with men of different language and manners: their curiosity is aroused by every thing new brought under their eyes: they long for any objects of use, ornament, or luxury, which they do not themselves possess. In visiting other countries they observe usages different from their own, and are thereby induced to reflect on the reasonableness of each. They find a better system of government, better institutions, new and delightful amusements, a splendid architecture, elegant clothing, useful machines, the refinements of poetry and music, the speculations of philosophy, and perhaps a religion which puts to shame the grossness of their own. Thus a wholesome disturbance is given to their ideas; their dormant faculties are aroused to the contemplation of the novelties and wonders presented to them; the sloth of barbarism is shaken off; they desire to possess the things which they admire; they gladly exchange for them those things of which they have an abundance; they become ashamed of their past condition; and they start in that career of improvement, which may conduct them to the proudest heights of science, power, and glory.

Thus it was that Athens and the Greek republics,—thus that their flourishing colonies on the shores of Asia Minor, Africa, Italy, and Sicily, sprung up from the condition of lawless barbarians, to give models to all future ages in arts and literature.

We know too little of the ancient nations of the East, to speak with confidence of the sources of their wealth and refinement. But there is undoubted authority for asserting that their commerce must have been extensive from a very early period. Some of the spices of which the anointing oil was made according to the Mosaic ordinance, must have come from the islands of Australasia, through the commerce of the Arabs with the East, and were not, as has been supposed, the produce of Arabia.* Long before the Christian era an extensive commerce was carried on by the Arabs and Egyptians with India and China by sea, and by the Persians with the same countries by land. The spices, gums, silks, gold, precious stones, and other valuable commodities which constituted the luxuries of Rome, Tyre, and Carthage, were brought from India and China through the ports of the Red Sea and the Persian Gulf. The same commerce enriched the Arabs in the flour-

* History of Maritime and Inland Discovery—Dr. Lardner's Cabinet Cyclopædia, chap. ix.

ishing days of the Caliphs, constituted the commercial greatness of Alexandria through so many ages, stimulated the commerce of the Italian republics, and ultimately fired the enterprise which led the Spaniards to discover the New World and the Portuguese to find the new route to India.

The Roman Empire had its feeble origin in a band of foreign settlers; it derived its civilization from the foreigners whom it subdued; and the boundless wealth and luxury which characterized the period of its universal dominion were created by the joint contributions of all peoples and climes, which, being united under one sway by the prowess of the conquerors, poured their tribute and their commerce into the metropolis of the world. In the height of the Roman power, the commerce of the Mediterranean was immense, and an unrestrained intercourse existed among the countries of Europe, Asia, and Africa. It was by means of foreign arts and foreign intercourse, then, that so many barbarous nations were suddenly raised into civility and refinement, and the plains of Italy, Gaul, and Asia covered with those magnificent cities, which centuries of war and barbarism have not been able entirely to sweep from their surface.

I scarcely need remind you that the states in which the first dawnings of intellectual light appeared after the gloom of the Middle Ages, were precisely those which had engaged the most actively in foreign trade. Venice, Genoa, Pisa, Florence, and Amalfi restored the literature and arts of Italy and the world. Flanders and the Hanse Towns became their rivals equally in commerce and intellectual improvement. Holland followed in the same distinguished course. France and Spain had extensive trade in the Mediterranean. And the former also in the north of Europe. The countries which were last in the general march of improvement were those the farthest removed from commercial intercourse.

A desire to extend their commerce led to the bold efforts made by Spain and Portugal, at the close of the fifteenth century, to perfect the geography of the world. It was the golden vision of the trade of India that unfurled the sail and conducted the sublime enterprise of Columbus. The same object animated the efforts of Don Henry of Portugal, Vasco de Gama, and Sebastian Cabot in a different direction, and led to the discovery of the route to the East by the Cape of Good Hope, and of Brazil. The discoveries of the English navigators, from the time of Sir Walter Raleigh to that of Captain Cook, are to be ascribed more or less directly to the influence of trade; and those of the Dutch navigators may be attributed wholly to that cause. It is true that the sovereigns who sent out expeditions about the time of the discovery of America, were influenced by the ambition of obtaining colonies; but the chief value of these colonies must necessarily consist in their commerce, which was therefore the main spring of those great enterprises.

And here let me press upon you the consideration, that to the grasping spirit of monopoly which closed the vast colonies of Spain and Portugal against the commerce of any other countries, is owing much of the horrible carnage which attended the first conquest of America, and of the degradation and slow rate of improvement of that continent down to our own times. If the colonial system had not been one of monopoly, the discoverers of Mexico and Peru would have had little temptation to urge their murderous way to the entire conquest of those countries. They might have traded with the natives for the gold which inflamed their avarice. But a desire to secure the whole for themselves led them on to the extermination of peoples and dynasties—to those frightful atrocities which besmear the page of their history, and which seem to have been avenged by the subsequent decline and present degradation of the countries that did the wrong. It is true that America derived signal advantages from the introduction of the arts, manners, and usages of Europe, and from the admixture of European blood with that of the aboriginal inhabitants: but the rigid prohibitory system adopted by their governors rendered these advantages infinitely less than they might have been. It is impossible to calculate what might have been the present condition of Mexico, Colombia, Peru, Brazil, Chili, and Buenos Ayres—countries which combine so many advantages for agriculture and commerce, and which nature seems to have cast in the mould of mighty empires—if they had for the last three centuries been open to the commerce of the world, instead of being fettered by the gyves of a selfish, short-sighted, and despicable tyranny. But that they would have been far other than they now are—that they would have been much more populous and wealthy, their soil better cultivated, their noble harbours teeming with commerce, and the moral and political condition of their people incomparably higher—there cannot be a moment's doubt. What can be imagined more certain to repress any tendency they might have to improvement, than that their intercourse should be restricted to such a country as Spain, and that they should be shut out from all knowledge of the politics and literature of Europe, except what passed through the small sieve of monkish censorships and inquisitions? It seems more than probable that the commercial intercourse of these colonies with England during the Peninsular War, gave them that taste for liberty which afterwards led them to throw off the yoke of Spain. It is also to my purpose to mention that several of the men who took the most active part in effecting these revolutions, especially the great Liberator, Simon Bolivar, had travelled in England and

Europe, and there learned to detest the system of bondage under which the Spanish colonies suffered.

I have been led, by mentioning the discovery of America, to anticipate the order of time. Our own country, as being the greatest commercial state that ever had existence, demands our particular attention. I have already given some idea of the vast extent of English commerce. Exalted as Britain now is in civilization, wealth, and power, I may say she has nothing which she did not at first receive from her intercourse with other countries. The various manufactures in which she now outstrips the whole world, and which are a grand source of her riches, were brought to her from Flanders, Holland, France, and India. She gave birth to none of them: but when they were transplanted from their former seats either by the rude hand of war or persecution, or by gentler appliances, she received them into a kindly soil, and afforded them careful shelter. The industry and energy of her people,—the freedom and general stability of her government,—her excellent commercial situation,—her unequalled advantages for manufactures, in the abundance of fuel, metals, and streams,—her great maritime power, which was at once an effect and a cause of her extensive commerce,—all these have combined to nurse up her manufacturing and commercial greatness beyond any example of ancient or modern times.

I need not say that commerce has enriched and refined this country. Her progress in philosophy, letters, and the elegancies of civilized life has kept pace with the extension of her trade. This would alone furnish a presumption that commerce has been a chief cause of our advancement in civilization. The concurrence of the same cause and effect in all other distinguished commercial states converts the presumption into certainty. Trade creates riches; and riches afford both the leisure to cultivate intellectual pursuits, and the means of patronizing the fine arts. Trade has essentially improved the agriculture of England, and very greatly augmented her population. Itself deriving support and stability from a considerable extent of fertile soil, it has amply repaid the obligation, by providing a greater number of consumers for the produce of agriculture, and affording the means of carrying cultivation to an unequalled degree of perfection. A mere addition to the numbers of a people tends to forward every species of improvement that depends upon the physical and intellectual energies of man. It facilitates the division of labour, without which no art can be brought to perfection; it affords the various stimuli of example, competition, and emulation to the energies of individuals, and brings many objects within the reach of combined efforts which solitary exertion could never accomplish.

It does not come within the object of this paper to trace more minutely either the commercial history of England or the growth of its civilization. The connexion between those things is too evident, and too universally admitted, to need further proof. I have thus, in a very rapid survey, shown, that the nations most famous in ancient and modern times for wealth, power, and refinement, have all been indebted for the origin of their greatness to external causes—to the access of light and knowledge from *without;* and I have also shown that the advances they made were generally, if not always, proportioned to the activity and extent of their commerce. It has further appeared that nations who had thus derived the benefits which commerce is calculated to afford, have in their turn diffused the same benefits to others by the same kind of instrumentality. In this manner nearly the whole continent of America has been added to the civilized world. And I may add, that to England belongs the honour of having trained up the most flourishing colonies in the world. The United States, whose infancy was like the infancy of Hercules, and who now hold so important a rank among civilized nations, owe to England their parentage and much of what is excellent and great among them—their language, their literature, their laws, their representative system, their commercial character, and their religion. The mother-country lost those colonies by an act of short-sighted avarice; but it is to be remembered that they owed their superiority over the colonies of all other European nations to the greater liberality with which she had treated them both in their internal government and their foreign trade. The great American Republic, therefore, like the principal nations of the Old World, is the creature of commerce. Since it acquired independence, it has advanced even more rapidly than before in every thing that constitutes the greatness of a nation. Its commerce is now second only to that of England, and it extends to every country under heaven.

One general observation, of the greatest consequence, applies to the nations of whose commercial history I have given this rapid sketch—namely, that trade has ever been the most prosperous where it has been the most free. When repressed by restrictions, we have seen it avoid the most fertile and best situated countries, whilst it has established itself and prospered in the least favourable places where it enjoyed freedom. How small a stock of industry and enterprise has been sufficient to lay the foundations of flourishing states, with the aid of the single principle of free commerce! A port on a small barren island, where every vessel is welcomed, where every seller is at liberty to sell, and every buyer to buy, has more attractions than the harbours of the largest empires when set round with custom-houses and prohibitions. It was Free Trade that reared the splendours of Tyre upon a miserable islet,—that raised the glories of Palmyra in the midst of the sandy desert,—that built the marble palaces and churches of Venice on the shoals which scarcely rise above the surface of the Adriatic,—that fixed wealth and letters on the frowning rocks of Amalfi,—and that so over-filled the unwholesome marshes of Holland with riches and inhabitants, that the latter built their fine cities on piles, and encroached on the domain of the ocean. I admit that trade was not absolutely free in all those places; but it was much more free from shackles of every kind than in the surrounding countries; and in proportion to its freedom was generally its success.* May we not assert with entire confidence that if trade had been absolutely and universally free, many poor countries would have been made rich, and the rich countries would have increased in opulence?—that many barbarous nations would have

* Dr. Adam Smith says—"Every town and country, in proportion as they have opened their ports to all nations, instead of being ruined by this free trade, as the principles of the commercial system would lead us to expect, have been enriched by it. Though there are in Europe, indeed, a few towns which in some respects deserve the name of free ports, there is no country which does so. Holland, perhaps, approaches the nearest to this character of any, though still very remote from it; and Holland, it is acknowledged, not only derives its whole wealth, but a great part of its necessary subsistence, from foreign trade." *Wealth of Nations*, book iv. chap. iii.

been civilized, and the civilized nations would have made still further progress in refinement?—that many desolating wars would have been avoided, and that the world would not now have been so full of ignorance, and so divided by hatred and jealousy, as it actually is?

Thus much for the experience of past times. Let us apply the lessons it teaches us to the future. If commerce has been the principal means of civilizing nations in former ages, we must look to it as the most powerful agent in reclaiming the countries that yet lie in barbarism. And if it is most operative where it is most free, we may infer that its absolute freedom would be infinitely beneficial to the human race.

It is chilling to reflect how large a part of our species is at this moment lying in barbarism and superstition, how imperfectly other parts are civilized, and how the most prosperous and enlightened nations are divided by mutual jealousies. Ignorance and wickedness, which are never separated, reign despotically over by far the greatest portion of the globe. "The dark places of the earth are full of the habitations of cruelty." I fervently hope, and as confidently believe, that this will not always be the condition of our species. I trust the day-spring will yet arise upon many nations, who are now involved in the gloom of a mental and spiritual midnight.

It is my conviction that science and letters, the useful and the fine arts, will penetrate the remotest parts of the earth,—that truth will gain the ascendancy over error,—and that the Almighty Creator of the world will be more known, acknowledged, and obeyed by his creatures than he now is.

I think the symptoms of improvement are already apparent, and that there are strong grounds to expect its steady advance. The effects of the press, in extending and perpetuating knowledge, can scarcely be too highly estimated. Books are now circulated in every known language, and every vessel that sails from the civilized parts of the earth to the unenlightened might be made the bearer of these instruments of knowledge. The utility of a free and extensive commerce is then obvious, in conveying civilized men, and books, which are the repositories of knowledge, over the whole world. It is true that philanthropy and religion may do something—may do much, by expeditions undertaken from motives of duty and benevolence to the regions of superstition; but is it not obvious that commerce has been, is, and is likely to be, the most powerful *agent* of benevolence? How few, alas! would be the sails that traversed the ocean, if there were none but those which benevolence sent forth! Commerce, on the other hand, with as many wings and as many tongues as the poet has ascribed to

Fame, flies with unwearied activity over all lands—

——— Multiplici populos sermone replebat
Gaudens.

As she collects, she may also scatter. Though set in motion by the powerful spring of self-interest, commerce may be made the messenger of knowledge and of truth.

It is to commerce that we owe the various settlements of civilized men amongst nations comparatively barbarous. Establishments formed for the purposes of trade are *points d'appui* for those who invade the territories of ignorance. In this light we may consider the British settlements in India, Africa, and America.

I could not excuse myself if, in treating of the spread of civilization, and of the future benefits to be derived from commerce, I omitted to refer to the astonishing changes and improvements effected of late years in many of the islands of the South Sea, by means of Christian Missionaries. These events have been little noticed in the literary and scientific world, but I do not hesitate to say, that, as far as my knowlege of history extends, they are the most remarkable instances of the sudden civilization of barbarous nations recorded in the annals of mankind. There is the most unexceptionable evidence to prove that the inhabitants of several considerable islands, who, less than twenty years since, lived in the practice of the grossest and bloodiest superstitions, and of the worst vices and cruelties of savage life, have been entirely reclaimed from their abominations, have assumed the habits, dress, and usages of Europeans, and whilst they profess the form, also powerfully display the spirit, of Christianity. These facts do not rest on the authority of one individual, but of many—of persons whose characters and talents place them above suspicion; and they are not merely asserted in vague generalities, but proved by innumerable details which defy misrepresentation or doubt.* If one fact be more convincing than another, it is perhaps, not that they have abandoned their idols and their human sacrifices, but that the *men* have relinquished their habits of indolent, gross, and brutal sensuality, and no longer treat their women as worse than slaves, but now live each man with his own wife, in virtue and purity, and treating her with the honour and courtesy which Englishwomen are accustomed to receive.

In a paper read before the Society during the present Session, the learned author expressed his opinion that the Missionaries had done less to christianize than to civilize the nations whom they had reformed. The Missionaries themselves, however, are unanimously of opinion that they

* See Polynesian Researches, by the Rev. Wm. Ellis.

civilized only *by* christianizing.* They assert that no impression whatever was made on the habits or morals of the savages, until their minds were awakened to the great truths of religion. This was the spark which first illuminated their blind understandings, and enabled them to see not merely the true character of God, but the excellence of social order, and of the comforts and decencies of civilized life.

It is contrary to the Laws of this Society to discuss the subject of religion ; but I think it is not irregular to speak of religion as an agent in civilization, or to imply that men may be influenced by higher motives and springs of action than any connected with temporal interests. And I have been more desirous of expressing my opinion on this great phenomenon in the history of the world, because many who deem themselves philosophers have, in a spirit the most unphilosophical, slighted the evidence presented to them of facts for which on their own principles they could not account.

But how do these facts bear on my subject? In this way—I have attributed the very discovery of the islands of the Pacific Ocean to commerce ; and it is by the instruments of commerce, by merchant ships visiting those distant shores, that the Missionaries were taken out, and have since

* See Dr. Philip's Researches in South Africa, and the Rev. Wm. Ellis's Polynesian Researches.

been supplied with necessaries from Europe. I proceed to argue that the more extensive is the connexion between Europe and the islands of the Pacific, and the more active the intercourse of those islands with each other, the more rapidly will the light of knowledge and religion spread amongst them. I think it is obvious that if the Pacific Ocean were covered with ships, exchanging the products of its innumerable islands, their natural resources would soon be developed, and their communities of half-starved savages and cannibals would be raised to the condition of civilized states. Can there be a doubt that any restrictions placed on that intercourse would make their improvement more slow and uncertain? And who shall presume to say what may be the future destiny of that immense Archipelago, where there is space for unnumbered constellations of glorious states, each as extensive, refined, and illustrious as the republics of ancient Greece?

I have said that I do not apply my principles to any particular trade in an artificial state of society. But as the islands of Polynesia may be considered to be in a natural state, without commerce and of course without commercial restrictions, I should like to appeal to the common sense of any plain man, whether the principles of Free Trade, or systems of restrictions and prohibitions, would be most likely to promote the prosperity, peace, and intellectual improvement of those clusters of islands. Swift never composed a keener sarcasm on the folly of governments, than he might have done by applying the commercial regulations of the countries of the Old World to the embryo states of the South Sea. He might have shown them quarreling with their neighbours, with whom a close connexion would be very profitable, and forming alliances with islands thousands of miles distant, with whom intercourse was difficult and expensive. He might have exhibited them solemnly forbidding the importation of iron, because it would throw out of work some dozens of persons who wrought in bone;—refusing to receive tow or canvass for the manufacture of their ropes and sails, and preferring to make them of the fragile bark of their native trees, lest they should injure their agricultural interest;—choosing bad cocoa nut oil from a remote island, rather than good from a contiguous island;—singling out comparatively barren shores for colonies, and binding themselves to take their produce, though they paid for it twice as much of their own productions as was necessary;—and restricting all traffic in particular articles to the vessels or canoes of particular islands. An island with a fertile soil, and teeming with natural productions, might be shown neglecting these advantages, and compelling its inhabitants to become manufacturers, by excluding all foreign articles of manufacture. Another island, whose surface was sterile, but whose bowels were rich in the useful metals, might be exhibited retaliating this conduct, by neglecting manufactures, and raising on its own surface the food which it might have obtained at half the cost from its neighbour. The *Society* Islands might become *unsociable*; the *Friendly* Islands *quarrelsome*; and they might prefer forming political and commercial relations with the Sandwich Islands, several thousand miles off, to forming them among themselves. The government of Hawaii might take a particular liking to that of Tongataboo, separated as far from it as Europe is from America, whilst it had a mortal hatred for that of Oahu, almost within sight; and it might bind its subjects to trade with the former, whilst it erected a *chevaux de frise* of custom-houses against the productions of the latter. The introduction of the loom and the spade might be prohibited under the severest penalties, lest the people should construct their cloths and mattings at a more ruinously rapid speed than at present, or starve their population by cultivating the soil more easily. And thus they might be shown at every step contravening nature, checking the progress of art, indulging a short-sighted and pitiful jealousy, yet blessing their stars that they are plain practical men, and know nothing of political economy!

I have already attempted to show that the intellectual advancement of nations is generally in proportion to their growth in trade, wealth, and population. Any system, therefore, which would retard the latter, must equally impede the former. But if the intellectual improvement of nations now uncivilized should be impeded, their moral improvement would be affected in like manner. The maxim that "ignorance is the mother of devotion" is founded in craft and falsehood. The poetical notion that rustic ignorance is favourable to innocence and honesty, seems to me to be equally remote from the truth. The mind and heart of man are not naturally so prone to virtue, that unless vice is artificially implanted, the fruits of the life will be good. Many entertain just the opposite opinion. I may perhaps think with them; but as the express declaration of my views on this subject might be considered as entering on the forbidden theme of religion, I shall content myself with saying that I believe intellectual cultivation to be favourable both to religion and morals. Believing, also, that truth is omnipotent and will prevail, I apprehend that the cultivation of the human understanding, and the increase of knowledge, must be of essential advantage to the cause of truth throughout the world. I would court discussion and investigation on all subjects, and not less on morals and religion than on any other. "That the soul be without knowledge is not good." At all events, it will not be disputed that the moral principles which have been established in Christendom are superior to those which reign in Polynesia, and that the inhabitants of the latter could scarcely change for the worse.

I have now submitted to you the considerations which lead me to believe that the principles of Free Trade are highly favourable to the interests of mankind.

I have endeavoured to show, by way of introduction, that Free Trade is eminently conducive to the wealth and prosperity of nations, and that the objections made to it, by those who would shackle commerce in order to protect domestic industry, are founded in error. I have further shown, that the Moral Influence of Free Trade is excellent;—that it tends to unite the nations of the world in peaceful and friendly relations, by the powerful tie of self-interest;—that, if generally established, it would remove many of the occasions of war;—that commerce has been in all ages, and is likely to be, the chief instrument in civilizing mankind:—that it has ever been the most flourishing, and most beneficial in its effects, where it has been the most free;—that commercial monopolies and restrictions have been a fruitful source of war and colonial oppression;—and that Free Trade would have the effect of hastening the spread of civilization, and the moral and religious improvement of our species.

If in any of these views I am mistaken, I respectfully invite the correction of any Member of this Society.

If, on the other hand, my views are correct, my Paper may possibly remove some prejudices, and convince my hearers that Free Trade is not, as it has been characterized in sweeping language, a senseless and heartless theory, but is a just, reasonable, benevolent, and philanthropic principle; and that it beautifully illustrates on a large scale the saying of the poet—

"True self-love and social are the same."

There are two points, which have not been discussed in this Paper, from an apprehension that they might be thought to bear too closely on the practical measures now under public discussion, but on which the author may be permitted here to express an opinion. He believes, 1st, that taxation affords no ground for the imposing of duties on foreign commodities, by way of protection to the home producer, except where similar commodities produced at home are burdened with *special* taxes; and 2d, that the benefits of Free Trade do not wholly depend on the reciprocation of the system by other countries; but that Free Trade would be beneficial to a nation, even though all other nations persevered in a system of restrictions. The first of these positions is clearly established by Ricardo, in his pamphlet "On Protection to Agriculture;" and the second is proved elsewhere by the same distinguished economist, by Professor Macculloch, in the article "Political Economy," in the Supplement to the Encyclopædia Britannica, and by other writers.

Edward Baines Junior (1800–90)

Most of Baines's published works are on education. His works on free trade and related subjects include:

An address to the unemployed workmen of Yorkshire and Lancashire, on the present distress, and on machinery, London: Ridgway, 1826.

On the moral influence of free trade, and its effects on the prosperity of nations; a paper read before the Leeds philosophical and literary society, on the 19th February 1830, London: Ridgway, 1830.

History of the cotton manufacture in Great Britain; with a notice of its early history in the East, and in all the quarters of the globe, London: H. Fisher, R. Fisher, and P. Jackson, 1835.

Mr. Owen's establishment, at New Lanark, a failure!! As proved by Edward Baines, and other gentlemen, deputed with him by the parishioners of Leeds, to visit and inspect that establishment, and report thereon, Leeds: Leeds District Board of the Association of all Classes of all Nations, 1838.

The corn law. National distress proved by increased exports, combined with diminished production, London: J. B. Nicholls & Son, [1840?].

Reasons in favour of free trade in corn, and against a fixed duty. In three letters to the Right Honourable Lord John Russell, Leeds: E. Baines and sons, 1843.

Five letters to the Right Honourable the Earl of Harewood . . . for keeping up the price of bread and the rent of the land, London: Simpkin, Marshall, & Co., 1844.

REASONS IN FAVOUR OF

FREE TRADE IN CORN,

AND AGAINST A

FIXED DUTY.

IN

THREE LETTERS

TO THE RIGHT HONOURABLE

LORD JOHN RUSSELL,

BY EDWARD BAINES, JUN.

(From the Leeds Mercury.)

LETTER I.

OBJECTIONS TO A FIXED DUTY.

MY LORD,—In the recent debate on LORD HOWICK's motion, the real and great dispute between the Opposition and the Government was this, namely, whether the principles of Free Trade, which last year dictated the relaxation of the Tariff, ought not now to be applied to two of the most important articles of consumption, *Corn* and *Sugar*. Your Lordship and the Opposition maintained that they ought: the supporters of Ministers said they ought not: and Ministers themselves shuffled, saying neither one thing nor the other, or rather perhaps saying one thing and doing another.

IT was on all hands agreed that the distress of the country was extreme. LORD HOWICK and your Lordship insisted that relief should be given; and the remedies you pleaded for on behalf of the people were *More Trade* and *Cheaper Food*. The State Doctor had exhausted his remedies last year, with the exception of a contingent dose from Brazil,—having consented that the English shall have cheaper Sugar, and shall preserve one of the best markets for their goods, if the Brazilians will be good Christians and abolish the Slave Trade!

WERE I to indulge party spirit, I might point out the inconsistencies and false arguments of some of the Ministerial speakers, the bad feeling of others, and the practical evils that flow from the policy of that side of the House.

BUT, being much more anxious for the triumph of a great principle than for the triumph of party, I prefer inviting, with unfeigned respect and deference, your Lordship's attention to the serious anomalies which exist in the position of your own party on the great question of the day, the Repeal of the Corn Laws. I do it with the conviction that your Lordship has no motive whatever, in your conduct as a statesman, but a conscientious sense of duty and regard for the public good; but with an equally clear conviction, that in one respect you occupy a false position, and that that position is prejudicial to a great cause.

YOUR Lordship is, or at least was, the advocate of a Fixed Duty on Foreign Corn. This was not indeed avowed in your speech of last Friday (Feb. 17:) on the contrary, some things were said, which might induce the belief that you think the palliative measures recommended in 1841 too feeble for 1843, and the policy which might have been satisfactory in the former year not calculated for the more advanced state of the public mind in the latter. But as you have not avowed a change of opinion, and as, though open to conviction, you do not change your opinions lightly, I apprehend you must still be ranked with the friends of a Fixed Duty. At all events, this is the case with many of your party; and it is the object of the present letter to show that of which I am firmly convinced, namely, that this position is untenable, and is productive of various and great evils. Your Lordship will not refuse to listen to argument, and to give it the weight which it may deserve.

WE may regard all who voted for LORD HOWICK's motion as opposed to the present Corn Law and to the Sliding Scale. But they are not equally agreed on the measure that should be adopted if SIR ROBT. PEEL's Corn Law were abrogated. They belong to two very distinct classes, namely, those who support a *Fixed Duty*, and those who advocate a *Free Trade in Corn*.

IT is proper to observe that both these classes profess to believe in the perfect soundness of the principles of Free Trade; and that SIR ROBT. PEEL, MR. GLADSTONE, and even SIR JAS. GRAHAM, declare those principles to be indisputable, and to be the dictates of "common sense." It would therefore be a waste of time to enter into any argument in defence of Free Trade doctrines: we may assume them as granted, and may argue from them: but it may be permitted to inquire whether a Fixed Duty on Foreign Corn is consistent with those doctrines. I maintain that it is not.

THE advocates of a Fixed Duty are not at one with themselves. So far from it, they rest their advocacy of that measure on distinct and irreconcileable grounds. One class support a Fixed Duty on the ground of *Protection to Agriculture:* another class, to which belong EARL FITZWILLIAM and LORD PALMERSTON, support it on the ground of *Revenue* alone, altogether repudiating Protection. And your Lordship, equally denying the right to Protection, supports a Fixed Duty solely on the ground of the *special Taxes* which you suppose to press upon the land-owners ;—adding, however, that you wish the protection which agriculture has so long enjoyed to be withdrawn *gradually*, and not at once.

WITHOUT examining at present these various grounds, but simply declaring my belief that none of them will justify a Fixed Duty, I would draw attention to the *practical measure* which they all concur to support, namely, A RESTRICTION ON THE SUPPLY OF THE PEOPLE'S FOOD,—*a diminution in its quantity*, and *an enhancement of its price*. Now these are precisely the objects sought by the ultra partizans or Monopoly ; and therefore the advocacy of a Fixed Duty, however small, has the unfortunate effect of throwing your Lordship and other friends of Free Trade principles into an alliance with the enemies of those principles, to oppose that which ought to lie at the foundation of a sound commercial policy, namely, *perfect Freedom in the Supply of Food*. There is a difference in *degree* ; and it would be very unjust to overlook either that difference, or the fact that you and your supporters denounce the many evils of the *Sliding Scale*, which is the most preposterous invention to disturb trade and to provoke the commercial hostility of other countries that is to be found in the history of legislation. I should be sorry indeed to impute to your Lordship any portion of the blame of such a measure. But nevertheless the broad fact remains, that the friends of a Fixed Duty *are not practically Free Traders*,—that they hold aloof from them,—that they cannot boldly and fully argue on Free Trade principles,—nay, that they recommend a measure which would necessarily have the effect of *stinting the quantity and raising the price of Food.*

THE following OBJECTIONS lie against *the advocacy of a Fixed Duty :—*

1ST. That *it countenances the doctrine of "Protection."* Though your Lordship and a few others advocate it on other grounds, there lurks at the bottom of its advocacy on the part of the immense majority of its supporters a reluctance to abandon Protection. Sir ROBERT PEEL also continually uses it against you as a *tu quoque* argument, whilst he adduces your authority against the Free Traders to convict them of being visionaries. Now it would be well for those who still cling to the "protection" involved in a "moderate fixed duty" to make up their own minds on the point whether *Plenty*, which necessarily implies *Cheapness of Food*, is a *good* or an *evil*. Till this point is settled, they can reason to no purpose. If *Plenty* be an *evil*, then Protection is doubtless justifiable: but then another consequence follows, namely, that that Protection cannot be too complete. If *Plenty* be an *evil*, then not only a Fixed Duty, but a Sliding Scale, and not only Protection, but Prohibition, will be justified. But if, on the other hand, *Plenty* should be decided to be a *good*, then all restriction, whatever its name, kind, or degree, must be condemned. No one doubts that high prices are good for the seller, at least temporarily: but we have to consider the buyer, as well as the seller: we have to look to the *general* and *permanent* interests of the *Nation*. In point of principle there is no medium between absolute Prohibition and absolute Freedom; and the man who shrinks from the latter may easily in argument be driven to the former. Therefore the advocates of a Fixed Duty, by stopping short of Free Trade, give up the only tenable ground, and place themselves on the *inclined plane*, on the *sliding scale*, of Protection.

2D. The advocacy of a Fixed Duty *keeps the opponents of the present Corn Laws disunited*. Of course they sustain all the enfeebling influence of disunion. Jealous of each other, and often opposing each other, they do not set shoulder to shoulder in a phalanx against the common enemy. Only half united now, and looking forward to a future split if the present Ministers should be driven from power, they want the spirit which can alone support them in an arduous struggle and lead them to victory.

3D. THE advocacy of a Fixed Duty *takes away the moral influence that would result from proclaiming a grand, plain, and intelligible principle, clearly involving substantial benefit to the People*. A Fixed Duty, though supported by many respectable land-owners and merchants, could never become popular; and if not popular, it could not enable its advocates to overturn the more prohibitory Corn Law which now exists.

4TH. THE advocacy of a Fixed Duty *prevents the establishment of Free Trade as the governing principle of our commercial legislation*. It supports all other Protections and Monopolies, colonial, commercial, and manufacturing, as well as agricultural. It does this both by preventing the establishment of the true principle of Free Trade in men's minds, and by affording a practical justification for all minor violations of the principle. This was seen last Session, when every class whose interests were endangered by the removal of protections objected to the New Tariff on this reasonable ground, that the great monopoly of all was left untouched,—that Food, the raw material of labour, was much dearer in this than in all other countries,—and that it was therefore unjust to expose the Labour of England to the competition of Labour which is more cheaply fed. How one monopoly may be defended by another monopoly is seen in the entirely artificial system of France. Nor can the protecting system ever be broken down, so as to give Industry and Capital a fair field and no favour, till that which forms the substratum of the whole, namely, the restriction on the supply of Food, is removed. The Corn Law may therefore be regarded as aiming at the very root of Free Trade; and there can be no safety for the latter but in aiming at the root of the Corn Law. But this cannot be done by the advocates of a Fixed Duty.

5TH. A Fixed Duty, if carried, *would sanction the protecting Duties enacted by all other countries, and would prevent the universal triumph of the just and beneficent principle of Free Trade.* It would thus do universal mischief. It would everywhere uphold false principles, and rivet the shackles imposed by short-sighted selfishness on Industry. And wherever it had this effect, it would inflict a practical injury on the trade of England. As no country in the world is so much interested in the general establishment of Free Trade, so there is no country whose example would have the same influence with that of England in promoting the adoption of the principle by other Governments. By upholding the system of protection, therefore, even by a Fixed Duty, however moderate, we are injuring ourselves both at home and abroad, and are by our example injuring the people of all other countries. We are marring the moral influence of England, which ought to be used for the advancement of truth and reason throughout the world.

6TH. A Fixed Duty *would impose a heavy tax on our own people, not for the benefit of the Government, but of a single class.* The revenue would indeed gain by the produce of the duty on the corn imported; but it would gain nothing by raising the price of the home-grown corn. Now it is self-evident that a fixed duty would *raise the price of all the corn grown at home*, which must always form nine-tenths and perhaps nineteen-twentieths of the consumption of the people. Therefore it would only benefit the revenue to the extent of one-tenth or one-twentieth of what it took from the people. All the rest would go as "protection" to the land-owner.

7TH. A Fixed Duty would therefore *be a burden and a fetter on our manufacturers and merchants in their competition with foreigners, and would be a premium to their rivals.* Every shilling, perhaps I might say every penny, added to the price of Food, may lose us the sale of some fabric in one or in many foreign markets. Every shilling, and even every penny, added to the price of food, is necessarily a disadvantage imposed on the Labour and the Capital of Englishmen. We have rivals, some of whom are older manufacturers than ourselves,—some of whom excel us in one department or another of manufacturing skill,—and some of whom have superior natural advantages, in the possession of the raw material, or in other respects. Why should we play into their hands, by artificially raising the price of food to our own people?

8TH. A Fixed Duty *would be a just and constant ground of popular discontent.* It would be assailed at every period of distress,—would be a source of weakness to any Government,—and would afford a plausible pretext, if not a substantial ground of objection, to the enemies of the Constitution.

9TH. A Fixed Duty *could not be maintained in a period of scarcity.* This argument has been so forcibly pressed upon you by Sir ROBERT PEEL, that you have felt yourself constrained to admit that the duty must vanish, or become nominal, at a certain point of price.

10TH. A Fixed Duty *would not base the prosperity of Agriculture on its only sure and permanent foundation.* It would still leave room for changes of the law, for the diminution or removal of protection, and therefore would expose the land-owner and farmer to uncertainty, and possibly to loss consequent upon leases or agreements made under a temporary system. The farmer will never be secure till every prop of protection is knocked away, and he stands upon the solid earth. He would then know what rent he could afford. He would then make his calculations safely. He would then invest capital without fear of being deserted by a treacherous law. He would then know what kind of land was worth cultivation. Relying upon his own energy, skill, science, and thrift, with that *natural* protection which vicinity to the best markets in the world gives him, and of which he could never be deprived, he would have as good a prospect as any other capitalist or workman of realizing a fair return and steady prosperity. But these advantages he could never possess under a so-called Fixed Duty.

SUCH, my Lord, are the reasons which present themselves to me against the advocacy of a Fixed Duty on Corn, and which press with great weight on my mind. There are, however, some reasons in its favour which have prevailed with able men, though they seem to me altogether insufficient. To state and examine them now would unduly lengthen this letter; but I purpose doing so next week.

I have the honour to be,
My Lord,
Your Lordship's obedient humble servant,

EDWARD BAINES, JUN.

Leeds Mercury-Office,
February 24th, 1843.

LETTER II.

REPLY TO THE ADVOCATES OF A FIXED DUTY.

MY LORD,—In the Letter which I last week addressed to your Lordship, I stated the principal reasons which have convinced me that *perfect Freedom* of the Corn Trade was immensely preferable to a *Fixed Duty*,—that the former was consistent, and the latter inconsistent, with those principles of Free Trade which are now received as incontrovertible by all men whose opinions are worth notice,—and that the practical effects of a Fixed Duty, both direct and indirect, on the interests of England and those of the civilized world, would be highly unfavourable.

MY object, in the present Letter, is to reply to the arguments urged in defence of a Fixed Duty.

AND first, my Lord, I beg leave to vindicate your Lordship against the strictures of those thorough partizans of a Fixed Duty, who blame you for admitting that, when Corn rises to a very high price, the Duty could not and ought not to be maintained.. You have admitted that when Wheat is above 70s. a quarter, the Duty must vanish or become merely nominal. This is thought by some of your friends to be an error; and they believe, as was contended by MR. JOHN GELLIBRAND HUBBARD, in his "*Vindication of a Fixed Duty on Corn*," published at the beginning of last year, that when Corn is dear, *the Duty does not add to the price*, but simply deducts from the profit that would otherwise be gained by the importer.

MR. J. G. HUBBARD, your Lordship is aware, is not a Free Trader, but a Protectionist: his pamphlet, though containing some good points, takes a narrow view of the question, is defective in its principles, and fallacious in some of its main arguments. We may say of the pamphlet, as of a lady's letter, that the Postscript is its most important part—for the answer to MR. CHRISTOPHER is good. MR. HUBBARD contends that the Duty on Corn (which he would have 10s. a quarter) ought to be maintained even if the price in England had risen to 90s. a quarter! Arguing on that supposition, he says—

> "I venture to assert that the advantages derived from the reduction of the duty by the *consumer* would be so small as to be *imperceptible*; and that the *gain* would go to the *corn-holder* upon the wheat already here (that is, in bond), and to the *foreigner* upon that subsequently purchased."

Now this I hold to be a great and glaring error. MR. HUBBARD sees that the remission of the duty would be "a gain" to the *corn-holder* here and abroad; but he most strangely overlooks the fact, that that very "gain," that increased profit, would be the strongest inducement to the corn-merchants here and in every part of the world to bring *fresh supplies* of corn to the English market, in order still further to increase their "gain;" and that those additional supplies would *keep down the price*, and *thus* benefit "the consumer."

To a certain small extent MR. HUBBARD is right. He is right in denying—what has been maintained by some—that the price of home-grown corn would *in all cases* be raised *exactly* to the amount of the duty on Foreign Corn. When the price is *moderate*, indeed, the effect of a duty on foreign corn would be to raise the price of all the home-grown corn to the amount of the duty, or *thereabouts*. It would do this by raising to a given amount, namely, the amount of the duty, the price at which foreign corn could be imported to sell here with a profit: and by *as much as* the price of *foreign* corn was thereby *raised*, by *so much* would the price of *home-grown* corn be *kept up*. But when the price is *high*, the amount of the duty would no longer constitute the exact *measure* of the enhancement of price caused by that duty. When wheat is above a certain price, say 70s. a quarter—however much or however little it may be above it—the English market would probably draw off all the wheat that there might be in the warehouses of *Dantzic* and the other *Baltic ports.* But, inasmuch as the gain of the importer would be much greater without the duty than with it, his motive for obtaining *fresh supplies* for the English market would be much stronger without the duty than with it. Therefore, we are not only to look, as MR. HUBBARD appears to do, at the effect produced in such a port as Dantzic, or in any small number of ports, but at the effect produced over *the whole corn-producing world.*

THE grand question, in considering every thing relating to corn, is, *what* QUANTITY *would be brought to market.* For *quantity* governs *price*, and price decides the degree of comfort or suffering of the people.

Now it is clear that the greater the charges upon the import of foreign corn (including duty among those charges), the smaller would be the quantity of corn brought to market in England ; and, *vice versâ*, the smaller those charges, the greater would be the quantity brought to market. Under a certain duty it might be possible to import corn with a profit from Hamburg, and not from Dantzic,—or from Dantzic, and not from Odessa,—or from Odessa, and not from the Mississippi. Whatever adds to the charges on import, necessarily *circumscribes the field of supply.* Whatever circumscribes the field of supply, *diminishes the quantity of corn brought to market.* And whatever diminishes the quantity brought to market, *raises the price.*

THE greater the profit of the importer, and *the more intense is the attraction* of corn to the English market. An attraction of a certain force might draw all the corn from Dantzic, Odessa, or New York ; but a more intense attraction might empty the granaries in the *heart* of Russia, Austria, or the United States. Now not merely a duty of 10s., but a duty even of 1s., would diminish the intensity of the attraction. Therefore a Fixed Duty would inevitably have the effect of diminishing the quantity of corn in our market, and consequently of raising the price.

IT follows, then, that a Fixed Duty could not with justice or prudence be maintained when Corn had risen to the *scarcity price.* To attempt it would endanger a rebellion.

THUS I vindicate your Lordship, for the concession you felt yourself compelled to make.

BUT here I turn upon you, my Lord, and, having found your vulnerable heel, I shall send a shaft into it. If you would abandon your Fixed Duty at 70s., why not at 69s.? Why not at 68s.? Why not at 60s.? Why not at 50s.? *Where* do you draw the line? By what *principle* do you draw it *any where*? If the difference between 75s. and 70s. might save thousands from perishing, the difference between 60s. and 55s. might save scores from perishing. If 5s. in the upper part of the scale of price would avert famine, 5s. in the lower part of the scale might save some considerable branch of manufacturing industry from being destroyed by foreign competition. With 1,400,000 paupers in England and Wales, we surely cannot afford to add one unnecessary penny to the price of the loaf. With a still larger number of men, women, and children always on the verge of want, can we without criminality add *any thing*, by legislation, to the stress upon the bow which is already strained almost to breaking? There is not one point in the scale, at which you could maintain your position unquestioned, till you had got to the point which *Nature* herself has fixed, namely, *the lowest possible at which Food can be had.*

But see, my Lord, the position in which you are placed in another respect. Constrained by humanity and prudence—I may say, by necessity—you abandon the Fixed Duty at a certain point of price, say 70s. But, thus doing, you give up one of the chief advantages of the Fixed Duty, and incur one of the great evils of the Sliding Scale. For whenever the price rose above 60s., so as to afford the least chance of its reaching 70s., all the corn merchants at home and abroad would combine to force up the prices: they would keep back their corn from the market for months: they would "work the averages:" as the price approached the point at which duty vanished, all the fever and speculation that attend the Sliding Scale would be seen again: the *lottery* would be re-opened. If the price were to reach 70s., the whole accumulated mass of corn would pour upon the market in a flood; and down would go the price 10s. or 12s. a quarter, *just before* our farmers could bring their corn to market, and probably *just before* the arrival of corn from distant countries where it had been purchased at a high price by the unlucky speculators. Again should we see a *drain of gold*,—again, *enormous freights* given to *foreign* vessels,—again, the *foreign* corn-holder running away with nearly all the benefit of the advanced price! If, on the other hand, the speculators failed in raising the price to 70s., and a favourable harvest should occur, then we should see the corn-merchants ruined by hundreds, as we did last year! In short, we should have nearly all the evils of a *Sliding Scale*, under the name—the *misnomer*—of a *Fixed* Duty!

Thus, then, my Lord, you are in a dilemma. Shunning Scylla, you are drawn into Charybdis. I see no escape but by avoiding the straits altogether. Free Trade would give you sea-room.

I come now to examine the argument in favour of a moderate Fixed Duty for Revenue.

Such a duty is recommended by no less an authority than Earl Fitzwilliam,—a man of chivalrous integrity, disinterestedness, and patriotism, of penetrating and enlarged mind, and who, in his unflinching attachment to Free Trade, disregarded all the prejudices of his manufacturing constituents against the export of wool, and not less disregarded the prejudices of his own order in favour of the Corn Laws;—a man, moreover, so superior to selfishness and weakness that he is proof even against flattery. If I could be deterred from advocating what I believe to be the truth, by the authority of men whom I most entirely respect, it would be when called upon to differ from Earl Fitzwilliam and yourself.

In the present case, however, it is some relief to me that your Lordship and Earl Fitzwilliam, though both advocating a Fixed Duty, do it on quite different grounds. The latter Nobleman, in his letter to my father at the Leeds Anti-Corn Law Soirée, insists in the strongest terms on "adopting the principle of Free Trade throughout:" "all "reservations must be cast away," said he, "and the "principle acted upon without exception." His Lordship added—

"You are probably aware that I consider Corn *as fit as any other article of import* to contribute to *the national revenue*, by a *uniform* duty levied for that purpose; but this is perfectly consistent (and is so considered by foreign countries) with the most complete freedom of trade. Such a duty is no more in contravention of Free Trade, than the tolls or rates paid by navigators or passengers to the Aire and Calder Navigation, or to the North Midland Railway. It is, in truth, a payment of precisely the same character, viz. for the maintenance of the establishment, and for the interest of the debt of the community."

It must be admitted that the principle of Free Trade is not *intentionally* violated by a duty imposed solely for the purpose of *revenue;* though it is difficult to admit that Free Trade is not really violated, when we find that the far greater number of those who advocate the measure do it avowedly for the purpose of "*protection*," and expressly disclaiming the motive of revenue.

But admitting a Fixed Duty on Corn to be not inconsistent with Free Trade, and taking up the question as one of *Taxation* merely, I must dissent from the doctrine that "Corn is *as fit as any other article of import* to contribute to "the national revenue, by a uniform duty levied for that "purpose."

And, first, I observe that a duty on imported corn, though it might be "*uniform*" in the sense intended by Lord Fitzwilliam, that is, as a *Fixed* Duty, is in another sense *not* "uniform," because it is levied on imported corn alone, and not on corn grown at home. In the later and worse days of Holland there was a really "uniform" corn duty, which was *levied at the mill* on *all* corn or flour alike. Now, if we are to consider the question simply as one of *revenue*, the Dutch plan was far better than a moderate Fixed Duty on corn imported. For suppose that the Duty were 5s. a quarter on Wheat, and that on the average 2,000,000 quarters were imported, the produce of the duty would be only £500,000 a year: but suppose that the same duty of 5s. were levied upon the whole of the wheat grown in England, which is thought to be about 16,000,000 quarters, its produce would be £4,000,000; or, adding the 16,000,000 qrs. of English wheat to the 2,000,000 qrs. of Foreign, making a total of 18,000,000 qrs., the produce of a duty of 5s. a qr. on the whole would be £4,500,000. Therefore the Dutch plan of an *excise* duty would be nine times as productive *to the revenue* as a *customs* duty of the same amount on foreign corn imported. If, then, it be merely a question of *revenue*, the tax would be a very bad one.

Does any one doubt that the effect of a duty on Foreign corn is to raise the price of *English* corn? If there be such a person, I would ask him—*for what object is the duty advocated, if not because of its manifest effect in keeping up the price of corn?* And if this be its effect, as the common sense of all men declares that it is, it keeps up the price not merely of the small quantity imported, but of the large quantity grown at home. Yet the Government levies its duty only on the small quantity imported. Therefore the enhanced price of the home-grown corn goes, not into the public treasury, but into the pockets of the land-owners. The consumer *pays it*,—the Government *does not receive it*,—it goes wholly to the *landlord*.

Then it is obvious that whilst a Fixed Duty of 5s. on imported wheat would only produce £500,000 to the revenue, *it would take £4,500,000 out of the pockets of the consumer.* This, then, would be a gross violation of one of Adam Smith's well-known and admitted axioms on the subject of taxation, viz. that—

"Every tax ought to be so contrived as both to take out and to keep out of the pockets of the people *as little as possible over and above what it brings into the public treasury of the state.*"

Can any thing be a grosser violation of this axiom, than to take £4,500,000 from the people, in order to bring £500,000 into the treasury?

In case the price of corn were so low in England that foreign corn could not be imported at all, of course *this source of revenue would wholly fail.* Therefore on this ground the duty is objectionable.

Next, I must dissent from the doctrine that "Corn is "as fit as any other article of import to contribute to the "national revenue," on this ground, namely, that a tax on the *prime necessary of life* is *more burdensome* to the people, and especially to the *poor*, than taxes on articles of less absolute necessity. Surely *Corn* cannot be "*as fit* to con- "tribute to the national revenue" as tobacco, or spirits, or wine, or even as sugar, tea, coffee, and fruits. These are luxuries and comforts, which men may dispense with, and not suffer in health or strength. But Bread is the very staff of life; and there can be no greater calamity either to individuals or nations than to have that staff broken.

It is universally admitted that some taxes are more mischievous than others, by pressing more directly on the *springs of industry*, and thereby stopping at their source the streams of national income and prosperity. Such are the taxes on *the raw materials of manufactures*, which all Governments admit to be bad, and avoid them as far as possible. Sir R. Peel avowedly based his New Tariff on that principle. Now Corn is really and truly a *raw material.* It is, as Mr. Ewart once said, the *raw material* of MAN. And being such, a tax upon it presses most directly not only on the *springs of industry*, but also on the *springs of life.*

It may be argued that a tax on Bread raises wages, and, therefore, does not really fall upon the labourer, but upon the consumers of the commodities which he produces. It is true that a tax on Bread raises wages in those departments of industry which can afford it, and where the supply of labour is not too large; but in our principal manufactures there is a controlling power, namely, *foreign competition*, which *limits* the possible advance of wages; and there is also another limit, in the limited *power of consumption* both at home and abroad. If, however, a tax on Bread makes wages artificially high, it thereby makes goods artificially dear; and this artificial dearness of goods impairs, and may even destroy, foreign trade; and thus it *re-acts upon wages, pulls them down*, and *deprives workmen altogether of their employment.*

WHETHER, therefore, the high price of Bread raises wages or it does not,—whether it tells upon the labourer directly or indirectly,—it is *sure to reach him at last.*

THE effect of foreign competition, too, is incomparably more extensive than is generally supposed. For it acts not only upon the price of the English manufactures sold abroad, but *equally upon the price of all the manufactures sold at home.* There cannot be two prices for the same article in the same market,—one price for the article to be sold at home, and another price for the same article to be sent abroad. Why should the London warehouseman give more to the Manchester manufacturer for cottons to be sold in London, than an American merchant gives to the same manufacturer for similar cottons to be sent to New York? It is obvious that he would not; and we know in point of fact that *he does not.* If, therefore, any cause, such as the competition of foreign manufacturers, should bring down the price at *New York*, it would *inevitably bring down the price to the same extent at Manchester and in London.* There is no possible escape from this effect. We must either *abandon our foreign trade*, or we must *sell at the same price as our foreign competitors sell at in foreign markets.* But we can no more abandon our foreign trade than we can abandon trade altogether. Our exports of manufactures to foreign parts amount to nearly FIFTY MILLIONS *sterling a year*: in the Cotton trade, a greater quantity of our fabrics is exported than is consumed at home: in the woollen, the linen, the silk, the hardware, the cutlery, and the earthenware trades, our exports are immense.

THIS being the case, I entreat your Lordship to observe the extremely important consequences that follow. In every branch of manufactures in which we sell to foreign countries, and in which we have to encounter competition, the *foreign price governs the home price.* The foreign price is itself governed by *the cost of producing manufactures* in the country where they can be produced *the cheapest.* If any foreign country should produce a fabric cheaper than England, it will inevitably *pull down the*

English price to the level of *its own price*. This price, thus controlled, governs both the *profits of the capitalist* and the *wages of the workman*. Nor is this all. If profits and wages are reduced in one or in a few great branches of industry, the tendency is to reduce them *in all other branches of industry*, aye, and not merely manufacturing but agricultural too. The only check upon this operation is to be found in *abandoning the trade* in which profits and wages have been so reduced. But, I repeat, we *cannot* abandon the *great* branches of our foreign trade and of our foreign manufacture. We are committed to a competition with the manufacturing world—committed irrevocably; and, but for the iniquitous Corn Laws, we can carry on that competition and triumph. There is nothing to fear for the manufactures of England, if our own Government will give them *Fair Play*. But are not the whole capital and industry of England exposed to fearful peril, so long as we MUST compete with foreign industry, and so long as that foreign industry *is fed at a rate so much cheaper than English industry?*

IT follows from these considerations, that a *tax* which presses on the *chief necessaries* of life is extremely objectionable on every ground, but most of all for its effects upon *the working class*, who must always be the greatest sufferers either from *decaying Trade* or from *dear Food*.

To escape from all the perplexities in which the labourer may find himself involved by discussions about wages and prices, let him look at this simple FACT, which it is impossible to misunderstand, namely, that the universally admitted effect of a duty on Foreign Corn *is to diminish the* QUANTITY *of Corn* EATEN *in this country*. That is intelligible. And it is decisive.

I had hoped, my Lord, in this letter to reply to all the main arguments urged in support of a Fixed Duty. But having left to the last your own grounds, namely, the argument derived from the special taxes which the land bears, and also the desirableness of the change being gradual, I find it impossible to consider them now without unduly extending this letter. I must therefore, though reluctantly, trespass upon your Lordship with a third and concluding Letter next week.

I have the honour to be,

My Lord,

Your Lordship's most obedient humble Servant,

EDWARD BAINES, JUN.

Leeds Mercury Office, March 3, 1843.

LETTER III.

REPLY TO THE PLEA OF "SPECIAL TAXES."

My Lord,—In moving an amendment on Sir Robert Peel's new Corn Bill, on the 14th of February, 1842, you distinctly admitted that "the general principle with respect to corn is one of *not legislating at all* on the subject," but leaving the trade perfectly free. You added, however,—

"The *only exceptions* to this rule would be, that if the agricultural interest bore any *special Taxes* pressing *peculiarly* on them, protection to that amount would be just; and it might also be right, if large capitals had been invested under a false system of legislation, to make the return to a right system *gradual* rather than sudden."

Before examining particularly the taxes which are alleged to press specially upon the agricultural interest, I beg to offer the following considerations, which apply to the whole subject of taxes on the land:—

1st. That there is *no class* in the state who *might* be so justly and properly called upon to bear a *peculiar* tax as the *owners of land.* I give at once a reason and an authority for this position, in the following passage from Adam Smith:—

"Both ground rents and the ordinary rent of land are a species of revenue which the owner, in many cases, enjoys *without any care or attention of his own.* Though a part of this revenue should be taken from him in order to defray the expenses of the state, *no discouragement will thereby be given to any species of industry.* The annual produce of the land and labour of the society, the real wealth and revenue of the great body of the people, might be the same after such a tax as before. *Ground rents, and the ordinary rent of land, are therefore perhaps the species of revenue which can best bear to have a peculiar tax imposed upon them.*"*

2d. That this doctrine is acted upon by nearly all the other governments in the world, to such an extent that *a far larger proportion* of the taxation raised by those governments comes directly from the land than in England. When, therefore, the English and the foreign landowner are competitors in the supply of the English market, the disadvantage arising out of taxation is on the side of the *foreigner*, not of our own land-owner. The following table, constructed from facts stated by the well-informed Secretary of the Board of Trade, Mr. Macgregor, in his pamphlet "*The Preference Interests, or the miscalled Protective Duties, shown to be Public Oppression,*" and confirmed in his

* Wealth of Nations, book v. chap. ii.

other works, will strikingly exhibit the contrast between the burdens borne by land at home and abroad :—

	Public Revenue.	Amount of Revenue derived from *taxes on land.*
In Prussia .... *thalers*	51,740,000	26,630,000
In Austria .... *florins*	164,000,000	87,000,000
In France............... *francs*	1,018,750,000	579,069,030
In England .... £	52,226,959	1,531,915

"In the other German States (says Mr. Macgregor) and in Belgium and Holland the proportion from land-taxes contributed to the Revenue is generally as great or greater than in Prussia." (p. 18.)

"The landed interests of France, Flanders, Holland, all Germany, and all Italy, pay *at least* one-half of the national taxation by *a direct tax upon land.*" (p. 17.)

The "special taxes" on land are therefore immensely heavier in other countries than in England ; and consequently the English land-owner has a great advantage, so far as government taxes are concerned, in his competition with the foreign land-owner.

3d. That in England *a far larger proportion* of the public revenue was raised from the land *in ancient times* than at the present day. Compared with other interests, therefore, the land-owners in modern times have been doubly gainers,—for their proportion of taxation has been diminished, whilst their rentals have very greatly increased.

4th. That *fixed* and *ancient taxes,* such as *tithes,* fall upon the landlord's *rent,* not upon the price of corn : and that having thus fallen immemorially, *the tax cannot be said to bear upon the present owners of the land at all.* A certain portion of the produce of the land has been long since by law appropriated to the use of the church : none of the present owners ever enjoyed that portion of their estates,—nor their fathers, nor their grandfathers, nor their ancestors, as far back as they can trace them : it was never theirs : for many centuries it has belonged to another class : the land-owners are permitted by law to hold for ever the whole soil of the kingdom, notwithstanding the increase of population to be fed upon that soil, but it is subject to the condition of paying the tithe. All who have bought lands, bought them subject to that condition, and *paid less for them* in proportion to the fixed charges attached to them.—The same principle applies to the *Land Tax,* which has existed for the benefit of the Government, in its present form, for a century and a half ; and prior to that, taxes far more onerous were raised from the land. The land-tax falls on the *rent*, and its effect has long since been *exhausted*; so that no land-owner and no farmer in the kingdom now feels it at all. Again I quote the authority of ADAM SMITH :—

"TAXES upon the produce of the land are in reality *taxes upon the rent*; and though they may be originally advanced by the farmer, are finally paid by the landlord. When a certain portion of the produce is to be paid away for a tax, the farmer computes, as well as he can, what the value of this portion is, one year with another, likely to amount to, and he makes a proportionable abatement in the rent which he agrees to pay to the landlord. There is no farmer who does not compute beforehand what the church-tythe, which is a land-tax of this kind, is one year with another likely to amount to."*

5TH. THAT the agricultural interest have some peculiar *exemptions* from taxation ;—such as exemption from the probate duty and legacy duty on the descent of landed property, from the duty on windows in farm houses, from the duty on husbandry horses, sheep dogs, &c.

6TH. THAT if it could be established—which I believe it cannot—that the agricultural interest bear more than their fair proportion of the public burdens, it would be for the advantage of the nation to *reduce their taxation* to its just amount, rather than to reimburse them by a tax on the importation of necessary food ; because the latter is open to the enormous objections of pressing chiefly on labour, of restricting trade, discouraging our own manufactures, and countenancing the false and pernicious doctrine of "protection."

7TH. THAT *the rental of land has been immensely increased*, owing to the increase of trade and population, and with little exertion on the part of the landowners themselves ; and that under these circumstances it is at once *unjust* in that class to uphold artificial rents by arbitrary restrictions on the supply of the people's food, *impolitic* thus to impair the real foundations of their own prosperity, and *paltry* to allege taxes which even on their own showing are of insignificant amount, and which are no more than their just share, as a ground for taxing the people's bread. In 1692, the valued land-rental of England and Wales (exclusive of houses and buildings, and other hereditaments), according to the valuation for the land-tax, was £6,500,000. In 1771, it was estimated by ARTHUR YOUNG at £16,000,000. And in 1815, it was ascertained by the Property Tax returns

* Wealth of Nations, book v. chap. ii.

to be £31,330,462, exclusive of houses, mines, minerals, fisheries, &c. Mr. M'CULLOCH* estimated it, in 1838, at £29,500,000. Therefore the land-rental of England and Wales would appear to have been *nearly five times* as great in 1838 as in 1692: allowing for an unduly low return in 1692, we may say that the land-rental has been *quadrupled* since that time. The land-rental of Scotland, at the Union in 1706 (including mines, &c.) was less than £400,000. It is stated by Mr. M'CULLOCH to have been from £1,000,000 to £1,200,000 in 1770. And by the Property Tax returns it appears to have been £4,851,404 in 1810.† Here, therefore, the rental increased *twelve-fold*. The gross land-rental of Ireland was computed by MR. BROWN, in 1727, at £2,824,000; by ARTHUR YOUNG, in 1778, at £6,000,000; and it appears from the elaborate estimate laid by MR. GRIFFITH before the Tithe Committee of the House of Lords in 1832 to be now £12,715,478.‡ Here, therefore, the rental increased *four and a half fold*.

PUT Great Britain and Ireland together:—

LAND RENTAL OF THE UNITED KINGDOM.

	At the beginning of the 18th Century.	At present.
	£.	£.
England and Wales	6,500,000	29,500,000
Scotland	400,000	4,851,404
Ireland	2,824,000	12,715,478
Total of the United Kingdom	£9,724,000	£47,066,882

WE see, then, that the annual rental of the landowners of the United Kingdom, for land alone, exclusive of houses, buildings, mines, &c., increased about *five-fold* in less than a century and a half: it increased by about £37,000,000 sterling per annum: it did this from no exertion of the landowners, but as the result of the industry and skill of others—of the increase of trade, manufactures, and population: and yet we now find these landowners haggling and huckstering about a compensation for their share of the taxes—a share which is not one penny more than they ought to pay!

AND now, my Lord, let us glance at the several taxes which have been alleged to press *peculiarly* on the agricultural interest. (It is superfluous to say that the *general*

* Statistical Account of the British Empire, vol. i., p. 535.
† Ibid, vol. i., p. 544-5. ‡ vol. i., p. 546-7.

taxation of the country, whatever its amount, affords no ground for "protection" to the agricultural interest).

THE "special taxes" are said to be the Land Tax, the Malt and Hop Duties, Highway Rates, County Rates, Poor Rates, and Tithes.

1ST. THE LAND TAX.—The amount of the Land Tax in 1839 was £1,174,100; but, as a considerable part of the tax has been redeemed, let us call it the same as in that portion of the reign of William III. when it was at its *maximum*, and when it raised £1,800,000. Now so far from the Land Tax affording any ground for "protection," it only suggests to us how cunningly the landowners have "protected" themselves, by causing the tax to be levied at the same *valuation* from 1696 to the present time, though the real *value* or *rental* of the land has been *quadrupled* since that time! During the reign of William III., the average annual produce of the public revenue was £3,895,205; and the average annual produce of the land-tax was £1,420,300:* and now, when the public revenue exceeds £52,000,000, the land-tax only yields £1,800,000! At the former period the land tax constituted *thirty-six* per cent. of the whole revenue; and at the latter period only *three and a half* per cent.!!! A pretty ground of *complaint* for the *landlords!* Would it not be better to *let this rest?*

2D. THE MALT AND HOP DUTIES.—These fall wholly on the *consumer*.

3D. HIGHWAY RATES.—The highways (not being turnpike-roads) are made and kept up mainly for the advantage of the owners and occupiers of the soil: they are indispensable to the cultivation of the estates, and to the conveyance of the produce to market: they are chiefly under the management of the landed proprietors, and are always constructed with a special regard to their taste, comfort, and interest: they have unquestionably raised the value of the land far beyond the charge which they impose upon it. *Each parish* makes and repairs *its own* highways. As to the *turnpike-roads*, the inhabitants of towns use them indeed, but *they pay for the use by tolls*. If, beyond this, the country gives any accommodation to the towns in point of roads, the towns amply repay the accommodation by providing market-places, public conveyances, canals, and railways.

---

* See Sir John Sinclair's "Hist. of the Public Revenue of the British Empire," part III. chap. I. At 4s. in the £, at which rate it was ultimately made permanent, the land-tax raised £1,300,000 on land *alone*, and £1,800,000 *in the whole*, including land, houses, buildings, other hereditaments, and personal estates.

4TH. THE POOR'S RATES AND COUNTY RATES.—The amount of money levied by assessment for Poor's Rates and County Rates together in 1840-1 was £6,351,828; of which the County Rate was £1,026,035, and the Poor's Rate £5,325,793. Now as the Poor's Rate is raised in each parish, agricultural and manufacturing, according to the particular wants of that parish, of course the *agricultural interest* raise what is necessary to *support* THEIR OWN *poor*, and no more. Is it contended that the manufacturing and trading part of the nation should contribute to support the poor in the rural parishes? If not, what ground is there for a duty on foreign corn to countervail the Poor's rate? I am not aware of any return showing the proportions of the Poor's rate and County rate paid by the land, dwelling-houses, mills, &c., later than that for 1832-3, when the rates were one-fourth higher than at present. In that year the total amount raised by assessment in England and Wales was £8,606,501, of which £5,434,890 was raised from land, and £3,171,611 from dwelling-houses, mills, factories, manorial profits, navigation,* &c. It is probable that the reform in the administration of the poor has relieved the land to a greater extent than the town population: but supposing the proportions contributed were the same in 1840-1 as in 1832-3, it would show that of a total of £6,351,000, the sum of £4,010,000 is raised from land, and £2,341,000 from houses, mills, &c. The difference between these sums is £1,669,000. Now whether we consider the numbers of the rural and town populations respectively, or the annual income of those classes as indicated by the Property Tax returns, or the simple fact that the parishes raise the sums requisite for the support of their own poor, I see nothing here to justify the opinion that the land bears an undue share of the rates; and still less any thing, either in the respective proportions or in the total amount borne by the land, to justify a tax on the food of the whole people by way of countervailing it.

5TH. TITHES.—The considerations mentioned in the earlier part of this letter, under the fourth head, seem to me absolutely to negative all claim which the agricultural interest may set up on the score of Tithes. The Tithes fall upon rent; and as they have existed immemorially, they cannot be considered as a deduction from the income which the land-owners or their ancestors ever enjoyed. Tithes were of course paid during the first 70 years of the last century, when agriculture had not any effective protection,

* Papers published by the Board of Trade, vol. iii. p. 34.

and could not have it, for this plain reason, that England then regularly *exported* corn. There was indeed an absurd and improper bounty of 5s. per quarter on the export of wheat: but this would do no more than cover the expenses of conveying the grain to foreign markets, so that the price of corn must have been nearly the same in this country as abroad: and if so, agriculture had not any material "protection." Now if Tithes were paid by the land-owners for centuries, have they any shadow of a claim to put them off on the rest of the people at the present duty?

Mr. RICARDO contended, in opposition to ADAM SMITH, that tithes do not fall upon rent, but raise the price of agricultural produce; and Mr. McCULLOCH contends that the tithes "fall in about equal proportions on the land-" lords and the public."* Both conclude that there should be some countervailing duty on foreign corn imported. But I humbly conceive that those able writers are mistaken. We may safely assume that at the period when English corn competed with foreign corn in foreign markets, the tithe fell upon rent, and did not raise the price of the article. For if it had raised the price, the grower would not have been able to export corn, (as he did for a long series of years), and to sell it at the price obtaining in foreign markets. Now all the change that has taken place since that time has been in favour of the landlord, whose rental has been enormously increased by the advance in the price of corn and the improvements in husbandry. And such a change--so entirely favourable to the landlord—cannot have given him a right to transfer the payment of the tithe from himself to the consumer. Or, if the artificial prices which have existed for the last fifty years have *virtually* enabled him to do this, it is neither more nor less than *a part of that extraordinary increase of rent* which his *monopoly* of the market (enforced by the legislation of his own class) has enabled him to obtain. But surely the fact of his having had an unjust monopoly is not to be a reason for the perpetuation of that monopoly and its fruits. Extortion is surely not thus to become its own law and its own defence. It is possible that the high and artificial prices may have brought into corn cultivation some lands which with a free Corn trade could not remain under the plough. It is possible that, on *that part* of his property, the land-owner might sustain a loss of rent, if the Corn Laws were removed. But is the nation, through all future time, to pay the land-owners for

* Encyclop. Brit., article, "Taxation."

the loss of a monopoly which they themselves enacted, and which they never ought to have enjoyed? Are we thus to *reward them for their own wrong*, and *to perpetuate that wrong*? Are we to guarantee them against the consequences of their own bad speculations? Would not this be the most preposterous violation of common sense, as well as justice? If, however, the nation ought not to pay the landlords in perpetuity the *rents* which they have for a time enjoyed, neither ought it to compensate them for the *tithe* which they have for a time contrived to transfer from themselves to the consumer.

It is almost superfluous to observe that the Tithe Commutation Act of 1836 has removed the grand objection which so long lay against tithes, from the vexatious and irritating manner in which they were imposed and collected. Alluding to the discouragement which this gave to improvement, and the annoyance in the collection, Mr. Mc. Culloch says—"The truth is, that tithe is decidedly more injurious from its indirect operation, and more unpopular from the mode in which it is assessed, than from the magnitude of the burden which it really lays on the public." "Were it not for the mode in which it is imposed, *it would not be sensibly felt* either by the landlords or the public."*

I have thus, my Lord, stated my reasons for believing that there are no special taxes pressing peculiarly on the agricultural interest, that can entitle them to tax the people's Food. *The land bears no more than its share of the public burdens:* if it did, however, according to Adam Smith, there would be no injustice in it: if it did, it would still bear less than the land bears in other countries: if it did, the enormous increase in the value of land would make the disproportion light and easy to be borne. But, in fact, the proportion of the public burdens sustained by land has been *exceedingly diminished* within the last century and a half. And I may venture to say that *there is not now in any country of the world, and that there never was in any former age, a body of land-owners so favoured by circumstances, so enriched by the industry of others, independent of any exertion or merit of their own, and so secure against the possibility of any material reduction of their income, as the land-owners of England.*

Their dangers are these—that they may kill (by starvation) the goose which lays the golden eggs; and that they may provoke the indignation of an over-crowded and underfed people to that point when property becomes a source, not of security, but of peril.

* Encyclop. Brit., article "Taxation."

I can only offer a few words on your Lordship's wish that the repeal of the Corn Laws should be "*gradual.*" I admit the desirableness of avoiding a shock or a panic. But, if the repeal were not immediate, what is the alternative? Either that we must endure the evil for ever, or that agriculture will be exposed to a *transition* prolonged through several years. I venture to say that such a lingering transition would be the most miserable and intolerable state in which any interest could be placed. It would paralyse all energy and enterprise, and would create universal discontent. But, above all, it would injure the tenant, by giving his landlord an excuse for delaying to reduce his rent, and thus gradually wasting away his capital.

THERE is, then, I humbly conceive, no wise, right, and enlarged policy for a statesman who admits the soundness of Free Trade principles, but in carrying those principles consistently into practice. I am certain that your Lordship, if convinced that this would be the best for your suffering country, would magnanimously act on the conviction. You would give the weight of your honoured name to the cause of justice. You would plant your standard on the rock of Freedom, and would proclaim that for this great and industrious people, pressing against the sides of their narrow territory, there can be *no safety* for the present, and no hope of future advancement, but in letting commerce flow upon its shores as freely as the waves of the ocean. You would declare that THE FIRST WANT OF ENGLAND IS AN UNRESTRICTED SUPPLY OF FOOD.

YOU would bid the *land-owners* be thankful for advantages never equalled, and which they can only lose if the industry of the country should decay: you would bid them rely on national prosperity, and not on monopoly. You would tell the *farmers*, that they have no interest but in keeping up the general rate of profit on capital, by which general rate their own must inevitably be governed. You would leave *industry* of every kind to exert itself in the field which was found to yield the largest return. Thus you would promote the highest prosperity of the country, and make England an example to the world of *industrial*, as she now is of *political Freedom*.

I have the honour to be, my Lord,

Your Lordship's most obedient humble Servant,

EDWARD BAINES, JUN.

Leeds Mercury Office, March 10th, 1843.

RECIPROCITY.

BY

A MANUFACTURER.

LEEDS: BAINES & NEWSOME;

AND SOLD IN LONDON BY

SIMPKIN, MARSHALL, & CO., STATIONERS' HALL COURT;

AND

SMITH, ELDER, & CO., CORNHILL.

PREFACE.

"FREE Trade is an excellent thing in the abstract;—very desirable if it could be placed upon an equitable system of reciprocity."

Such is the substance of remarks which I have frequently heard from merchants or manufacturers of high standing, practical in their views of any other subject but that of Free Trade. The application of this question they stave off until certain very improbable or impossible conditions can be fulfilled, viz., that Foreign Powers should receive our manufactures on favourable conditions, whilst we accept only their raw produce.

In most cases affecting their own interests, these practical men are shrewd enough ; but their expectations of the benefits to be reaped from commercial treaties are vague and ill defined, whilst they blindly surrender into the variable policy of party administrations, a full control over duties which have a most injurious effect upon their trade. A want of self reliance and a craving from Government for measures of relief beyond the power of the legislature to afford, are the prevalent errors of tradesmen at home and abroad. Hence foreign administrations are pestered by conflicting claims for protection from rival manufactures, more especially from the cheap productions of Great Britain;—hence our own landowners cling with desperate pertinacity to their protecting Corn Laws;—and hence our manufacturers loudly call on our Foreign Secretary to attempt vain negotiations, for the purpose of moderating the hostility of foreign tariffs.

The object of this pamphlet is to give a practical aim to our pressure upon Government, to point out what we may expect, and to restrict our efforts to such measures as we may hope eventually to carry. Foreign tariffs are beyond our power to regulate; but our own, which oppresses us still more heavily, is within our reach. A combined movement, on the part of the commercial interest, may readily carry such alterations in our prohibitory and protective tariffs, as are essential to the expansion of our commerce.

Gaining a lesson from the past revulsions of trade, the time is arrived when the manufacturer should learn what security he has for the extent and continuance of his business, or how far he is justified on the faith of *our* existing tariff, in fixing his capital in mills or machinery. It is hard that he should suffer from foreign prohibitive tariffs, but the evil is aggravated by the vacillating attempts of our own Government to negotiate more favourable treaties.

Foreign prohibitions are best met by the enterprise of our own merchants.

In the ensuing pages I have fully discussed the indefinite notions of reciprocity which are gaining ground with the public, and I have branched off to certain popular objections against Free Trade, which, trite as they are to the political economist, still retain their secret hold in the breasts of many tradesmen. As a manufacturer myself, I have honestly and sincerely endeavoured to dispel the false alarm which has been so industriously circulated, of the danger to our manufacturing superiority from the spread of manufactures abroad. I apprehend no danger, but a positive benefit. If even the alarm were well founded, why not meet it like men?

If, unfortunately, some unintentional error be discovered in this short work, my apology must be, that it has been written in the intervals of a weighty business, with but few leisure hours at my disposal. It was commenced before the clear-headed author of "Corn and Currency" had taken the field in the *Economist*, and to his vigorous advocacy I leave the support of a cause to which I lend a more willing than able assistance.

My object is to convince—not to shine. If I succeed in furnishing some who are not deeply read in the science of political economy, especially my brother manufacturers, whose avocations engross their attention, with more correct notions of Free Trade and Reciprocity,—if I aid in dispelling the doubts and fears arising from the spread of manufactures abroad,—if I induce my commercial readers to ask from Government such measures only as are practicable, and to rely mainly upon their own energies for the opening of foreign markets, I shall rest satisfied that I have not written in vain.

A MANUFACTURER.

CHAPTER I.

WHAT IS THE ORDINARY MEANING OF RECIPROCITY—PROBABILITY OF OBTAINING RECIPROCAL TARIFFS — MODERN ATTEMPTS — ABSURDITY — COLONEL TORRENS'S ARGUMENT—HOW CAN WE MEET HOSTILE TARIFFS?—INDEPENDENT COURSE OF ACTION FOR THIS COUNTRY TO PURSUE.

THERE is a vague idea, exceedingly prevalent amongst commercial men, that all foreign treaties should stipulate for reciprocal advantages:—that, in fact, they should be made a matter of bargain; *our* object being to secure an unlimited market for our manufactures, at the lowest possible rate of duty, and receive back merely the raw materials of manufacture or agricultural produce.

This notion of reciprocity is borrowed from the existing navigation treaties, which have been concluded with nearly all the foreign powers since 1815. Herein the shipping interest alone has been consulted; but our mercantile navy, as the source whence our men-of-war draw their experienced hands, has ever been deemed by our monarchs of paramount importance. The powerful combination of shipowners needs to be reminded, that they are merely *carriers*, and that their prosperity is dependant upon the home manufacturer and foreign producer.

The history of our navigation laws is instructive. In 1651 we attempted, by our famous navigation act, to drive off the seas the Dutch vessels, our only rivals. All their vessels were excluded from our ports. The Republican

Parliament overlooked one necessary result, that hereby they shut out a considerable portion of Dutch and German produce ;—a strange way of increasing our commerce, by lessening our imports ! According to M'Culloch, the act failed in its operation. " It is not to our navigation law, or " the restrictive regulations of other foreign powers, but to " the abuse of the funding system, and the excess of taxation, " that the decline of the commercial greatness and maritime " power of Holland was really owing."

The folly of injuring our manufacturing interest for the sake of the shipowners, and the recoil upon the latter, were not fully exemplified until the Americans retorted this very act upon us, almost in the identical words, immediately after they had succeeded in establishing their independence. At first we attempted to retaliate, but " at length it became obvious to every one that we had engaged in an unequal struggle, and that the real effect of our policy was to give a bounty on the importations of manufactured goods of other countries into the United States, and thus gradually exclude both our manufactures and ships from the ports of the Republic."* The result of this conviction was the establishment of a treaty between Great Britain and the United States, in 1815, and the first introduction of the principle of reciprocity in our commercial treaties, as set forth in the fourth section of the act 6 Geo. IV., c 1, " That his Majesty " may, by an order in council, admit the ships of foreign " states into our ports, on payment of the like duties that are " charged on British vessels, provided that British ships are " admitted into the ports of such foreign states, on payment " of the like duties that are charged on their vessels."

Other Powers were not slow to adopt the same mode of bringing us to terms. Prussia took similar measures against us in 1822 ; and in 1824 Mr. Huskisson found it imperative to make a similar concession. Denmark, Sweden, France, Austria, Russia, and other Powers, have subsequently brought us to the same terms.

* M'Culloch's Dictionary of Commerce.

Mutual benefits have resulted from this extension of our navigation act. Our previous attempts at monopoly and overreaching had militated against us, and placed Great Britain in a most humiliating and dangerous position. Our system of exclusion had induced other Powers to apply the same means, and then it was discovered that we had more to lose than to gain by the system. Most unwillingly was our Government forced to submit to fair dealing; nay, to beg for it.

A growing conviction is springing up, that this system of reciprocity has fallen short of its most important end. Of what use to gain an entrance for our vessels into foreign ports, if their cargoes be excluded? Why not apply to our manufactures the same freedom of ingress which is granted to our shipping? Why not negotiate with foreign powers to take our goods at the same duties as those we levy upon their produce, and *vice versa*?

These questions suggest themselves to all who are desirous of accomplishing so great a desideratum as that of a reciprocal system of Free Trade. So far from depreciating this object, I would uphold it as the greatest boon to commerce. Whether or not it may be safe to depend upon the legislature or the executive, for the accomplishment of this purpose, requires from every practical man a searching investigation.

The first difficulty arises out of the very words of the navigation act we have previously alluded to. Each separate treaty contains a provision, that there is to be "no priority or preference," but that the vessels and cargo of the contracting Power are to be admitted "on the terms of the most favoured nations." If, then, we negotiate a reduction in our duties upon the imports of any separate Power, in order to induce such Power to receive our goods on favourable terms, we directly admit, by our previous treaties, other nations, growing the same products, to a participation in the benefits of our concession. A nominal distinction may be made in our tariff betwixt the products of various countries, thus:—Portuguese wines might possibly be classed at higher duties than French or Rhenish wines. Such an attempt I hold to be a virtual infraction of the navigation act, and in other cases it would not apply. If, for instance, we attempted to negotiate with Prussia for the free introduction of our manufactures into the territories of the Zoll Verein, and offered in return to modify our duties upon *their* corn or timber, we are bound to admit, at the same duty, Russian or American corn. With Brazils the case is different. She offers us tropical produce, interfered with only by our own colonies. Hence a marked and exclusive distinction is readily made in our tariff.

A still greater obstacle to the formation of reciprocal duties, has been the want of sincerity, and the spirit of monopoly or exclusion which have characterized the pretended efforts of governments in behalf of commerce; above all, a growing jealousy of our manufacturing power, which is rife amongst our neighbours, coupled with the false inference that this power is or has been propped up by our system of protection.

As the preliminaries to a reciprocal treaty of commerce, an uniform *ad valorem* rate of duty, and the abolition of all differential duties, are requisite. Any import calculated by weight, would fall heavily upon a bulky class of commodities, such as are consumed by the lower orders, or used in various processes of manufacture. Instance our trade with the States of the German League, and suppose for a moment that we opened a reciprocal tariff with them, founded on their own principles. Our imports from thence, being chiefly wool, corn, and produce, would be taxed much more heavily than our exports, which consist chiefly of light manufactured goods and yarn. Again, suppose we retained in our tariff the present distinction betwixt the rates applied to raw materials and those levied on articles of greater value, whereon more labour had been bestowed.—we should lightly tax Prussian imports; but if Prussia were to adopt the same principles, (which, to carry out the system of reciprocity, she necessarily must,) our manufactured produce would in return be taxed much more heavily. It is evident, therefore, that no commercial treaty based upon an equitable adjustment of mutual reciprocity, could be drawn up, unless founded upon an uniform *ad valorem* rate of duty. If our Government had been willing to accede to these terms, there would have been little difficulty at one period in establishing a system of reciprocal tariffs co-extensive with our navigation treaties. Suppose we had offered to Prussia an admission of her exports on payment of 10 per cent. duty, to press equally on every article without distinction, on condition that she admitted our produce on the same terms, there is little doubt that she would have accepted our offer. We must, then, have given up our antiquated notions of protection; the argument of vested interests, meaning, in other words, *powerful interests*, must have been relinquished; the differential duties in favour of our colonies would have been abandoned, or placed under new regulations; and we should have been prepared to extend the system to all other countries that chose to accept it. Other difficulties might be started. The various necessities of foreign powers prompt them to levy different scales of taxation on imports or exports for the purpose of revenue. When the national treasury becomes exhausted, a common resource has been to advance the duties, —certainly not always with a corresponding advantage; yet if this resource were taken away by the fixedness of the duty, and the necessity of forming another treaty before an alteration could be effected, other measures of finance must be adopted. When we have to consider not only our own complicated interests, but those of negotiating Powers,—whilst on the one hand we view our first statesmen continually evading the application of views of commercial policy which they acknowledge to be just, and, on the other hand, observe the jealous rivalry of other Powers, and their all-absorbing desire to copy our manufactures,—we are led to despair of ever seeing such a principle of reciprocity carried out.

What shall we say to the miserable attempts at negotiating commercial treaties, which have lately exercised the diplomatic skill of our Secretary for Foreign Affairs, and his corps of ambassadors, consuls, attachés, &c. Nothing can exceed their ludicrousness, but the humiliation they bring upon this country. Our very anxiety to negotiate treaties and obtain modifications of foreign tariffs, causes jealous suspicions in the breast of the Government we want to deal with, that we are a set of sharpers, trying to overreach and arrogate to ourselves some peculiar advantages. The contracting party is led to infer, that by taking our manufactured goods, he confers a benefit only half requited by our churlish acceptance of his raw produce. Look at our present position with commercial nations. We have earnestly and deprecatingly begged of Prussia not to raise her duties upon certain descriptions of our goods, and to give the most favourable interpretation to the new tariff of the Zoll Verein. Repulsed in this quarter, we make an application to our favourite child, Portugal, whom we have nourished with our treasure, and protected with our blood,—for whom we have vitiated our palate, and cherished an exclusive taste for the medicated port and sherry, to the neglect of the more genuine wines of France or the Rhine. We allude to our ancient treaties of alliance, the Methuen treaty of commerce, and argue that we have a claim upon her for a market for our woollens in return for our imports of her wines. After months spent in making offers and refusing absurd proposals, whilst the hopes and fears of merchants and manufacturers are kept in a state of feverish suspense, all negotiations are abruptly broken off, in order to create a semi-monopoly for some half-dozen rude Portuguese fabrics, wherein a member of the Government is interested. In reference to these protracted negotiations, the Lisbon correspondent of *The Times* newspaper well remarks :—

"The untoward delays which have marked the progress of these negotiations, have done more to discredit diplomacy than any event of modern times. The preference obviously given to individual considerations over the momentous pressure of national interests,—to the desire of displaying mere personal dexterity, finesse, and cunning of fence,—to the determination (no matter what thousands may suffer) to outwit antagonists, or come off at least with the reputation of having effected that pettiest of triumphs, and still worse, the unblushing coolness with which weeks and months have been suffered to elapse, for the mere chance of tiring out the patience of rival negotiators, or wresting some advantage from their fears, or deriving some possible benefit from the unopened chapter of accidents,—must have pointedly directed men's attention to the question, how far they are benefitted by the existing forms of international dealing. The world has outlived the babyhood of ceremonial and the pupilage of sounding names. It is things, not mere logomachy, that can satisfy the aspirations and the wants of the community; and it is not difficult to predict, that before many years shall have elapsed, all questions of tariff regulation, and shipping and commercial interest, will be decided without reference to so-called Excellencies, who are excellent only for producing complication, embarrassment, and delay, by the simple machinery of a mixed commission of merchants."

The same correspondent remarks further on the 27th of March "The present conduct of the negotiators on the "part of Portugal is downright insulting. They trifle with "us as if we were children."

Not yet discouraged, but manfully bearing up against disappointment, our Foreign Secretary next paid his respects to the proud offset from the house of Braganza—to Brazils. The first point at issue was the termination of the existing treaty;—the Brazilian Government maintaining that it expired in November, 1842, whilst Great Britain contended that it remained in force until November, 1844. Eventually Brazils conceded the point somewhat grudgingly, as if anxious to escape from an arrangement which she considered injurious to her interests, and refused to enter into farther stipulations until the expiration of the treaty. The communications of their minister, Senor Continho, contains a few remarks derogatory to the good faith of our Government, and furnishes another illustration of the rebuffs we experience in our begging petitions for commercial treaties.

"However much the imperial government may respect the opinion of that of her Britannic Majesty, they cannot be brought to a conviction that their own is erroneous, and consider they have the same right to insist on the conditions of the treaty alluded to being deemed mutually obligatory on Brazils and Great Britain, only to November, 1842, the term when they believe it ought to expire. But, notwithstanding, as the two governments have not been able, to the present moment, to agree as to the due interpretation of the contested clause, and as the term designated is fast approaching, the government of his Majesty the Emperor, anxious always to make manifest its moderation and good faith, at the same time protesting against the construction put upon the said article by the government of her Majesty the Queen, have consented to issue the necessary orders to the respective public officers concerned, for the stipulation of the said treaty to be continued in full force and vigour, as hitherto, until November, 1844, provided the two governments should not in the meantime come to a mutual understanding as to the precise period of its termination; the imperial government being fully confident, that that of her Britannic Majesty will be finally convinced, that the construction given by them to the article in question is the most conformable to reason, and to the spirit and letter thereof. And inasmuch as these disputations are a sufficient proof of the necessity of maturely weighing and duly considering any engagements of this nature, between two sovereigns who deem it their duty to consult the interests of the people over whom they preside, his Majesty, the Emperor, considers it incumbent on him *to defer, until the period at which the said treaty shall terminate, his determination whether in his wisdom he shall consider it proper and convenient to enter into any new engagement*, and will then take into consideration the different items contained in the outline submitted by Mr. Hamilton to the consideration of the imperial government."

Public opinion in Brazils runs counter to the formation of another treaty with Great Britain, on the terms of the existing tariff. An opposition journal at Rio observes:—

"It is feared that the machinations of England will too soon follow this up with a lasting convention, which will establish in favour of her commerce a monopoly that will be useful neither to the Brazilian treasury, nor to the actual circumstances of the country, and that cannot fail to excite serious clamours and vehement protests on the part of those Governments which have not concluded treaties with Brazil."

There is manifestly a fear of being taken in—an alarm on the part of the Brazilians lest England should overreach them in commercial diplomacy. They seem to be thoroughly acquainted with our internal struggles to expand trade and throw off protection; they take a comprehensive view of our commercial position, and keep a watchful eye upon the relative state of parties in this country. Witness the shrewd remarks of one of their senators, Senor H. Rezende—

"It was his conviction, and he should maintain it until he was convinced to the contrary, that the English nation, by which he did not mean either the Government or the aristocracy, but the people, lost more by the existing treaties than the people of Brazil, and that the commerce of England was more injured by them than the commerce of Brazil. This opinion was at present gaining ground in England, and on this account the English Cabinet was strongly urged to do justice with respect to the productions of Brazil. What, in fact, had been the conduct of England with regard to colonial produce? It received the cotton of Brazil because the West Indian colonies produce no cotton. It received their coffee, by way of the Cape of Good Hope, because the West Indian colonies did not produce as much coffee as was wanted; but it refused to receive their sugar, because the West Indies produced that article. All the world knew that the English population was sacrificed to the interests of the English landowners and of the proprietors of the West Indian estates. All the world knew that the consumption of Brazilian sugar was prohibited in England, but that it was refined there and sent to the West Indies, in order that the planters of Jamaica and the other islands might be able to buy it at a very low price there, and in that way be able to send all their produce to England, to be sold at monopoly prices to the English people. All the world knew that the interests of the English people were thus sacrificed; but they had long been accustomed to submit to monopolies of all descriptions. Now, however, that the English population was becoming familiar with the discussion of such questions—now that they saw the flagrant injustice of sacrificing the working and labouring population to the proprietors—now that they saw that they were not allowed to taste the cheap sugars of Brazil, but were restricted to the dear ones of the Antilles, whilst the West Indians were allowed to purchase Brazilian sugars at a low price—from this time it would be impossible for the English Cabinet to maintain the interests of the aristocracy against those of the nation."

Such being the tone of public feeling in Rio with respect to commercial relations with England, it is not surprising that Mr. Ellis, who was sent over to negotiate a further treaty, altogether failed in the object of his mission.

These failures in our attempts to enlarge our intercourse with other nations by means of treaties, are only what might be expected from former experience. For more than two centuries the Government of this country has attempted to prop its trade by securing to itself peculiar advantages through such means; and what is our present position? There is not existing a treaty which may be called reciprocal, as admitting the goods of this country on favourable terms; unless that with Brazils, which is about to expire, be excepted. On the contrary, we find that foreign tariffs are gradually increasing their *protection* against British goods.

What then! are we to buoy ourselves up with the vain hope, that the same repeated attempts may yet melt the stony hearts of foreign powers? It is high time the delusion should be exposed. Unless we resort to different means, we seem as far from the attainment of our object as ever.

Now, it becomes important to ascertain what means we have at our disposal to induce other countries to trade with us. The ancient mode of coercing nations into customers by war has been found expensive, and is out of fashion; unless with an empire like that of China, semi-barbarous, which places itself out of the code of civilized warfare. The only inducement remaining is that of interest, either by favourable offers, or by threats of retaliation. We find, however, that when we attempt to persuade contracting powers, such as Brazils, Portugal, &c., that it is for their benefit to take our goods, they are apt to constitute themselves the judges of their own interests, and tell us to mind our own business. And if we retaliate prohibition by prohibition, the result is that we diminish our exports and imports,—thereby injuring ourselves more than the parties whom we wish to bring to terms.

Probably the British Government might have succeeded, immediately after the war, in obtaining modifications of foreign tariffs, on condition that concessions were mutual, and protection abandoned by both parties. At present our chance has gone by. The world at large attributes the wealth and power of England to her manufactures, and are attempting to follow her example. Regardless of the natural superiority which Great Britain possesses, in her insular position and her vast coal beds,—the growth of centuries, now the source of power,—foreigners imagine that they have only to acquire our machinery, to spy out our improvements, and to foster their own infant manufactures by legislative protection, in order to supply themselves with woven fabrics, if not to rival us in neutral markets. This mania for manufacturing pervades North Europe, France, Spain, and Portugal, and the United States. But their hot-bed manufactures could not possibly compete with ours on equal terms, excepting certain branches which afford peculiar local advantages. It is vain to expect that these kingdoms will expose their infant, pet fabrics, to our full-grown competition on equal terms;—but a treaty of reciprocity with a manufacturing country like ours could not exist on other terms—hence it is idle to think of negotiating with any would-be manufacturing nation. When all are wishing to sell the same description of goods, and none want to buy, what possibility is there of coming to an agreement?

Great Britain, to consult her proper dignity, should at once assume an independent position, and cease from that posture of commercial begging into which she has lately sunk. Nay, she is compelled to do so, for she finds herself unable to influence materially the tariffs of those nations she is most ambitious to deal with. It remains, therefore, for her to consider what is the course to pursue under the discouraging aspect of foreign rivalry, foreign protection, and foreign prohibition!

M'Culloch, speaking of the object of commercial treaties, (see his Dictionary,) remarks—

"Instead of confining them to their legitimate and proper purposes—the security of merchants and navigators, and the facility of commercial transactions—they have been employed as engines for promoting the commerce of one country at the expense of another. Hence these compacts are full of regulations as to the duties to be charged on certain articles, and the privileges to be enjoyed by certain ships, according as they were produced by, or belonged to, certain countries. It was in the adjustment and regulation of those duties that the skill of the negotiator was put to the test. It was expected that he should be thoroughly acquainted with the state of every branch of industry both in his own country and the country with which he was negotiating; and he was to endeavour so to adjust the tariff of duties, that those branches in which his own country was deficient might be benefitted, and those in which the other was superior might be depressed! The idea of conducting a negotiation of this sort on a fair principle of reciprocity is of late origin. Success in circumventing, in over-reaching, or in extorting from fear or ignorance, some oppressive, but at the same time worthless, privilege, was long esteemed the only proof of superior talent in negotiators."

Query—Have not the late negotiators for treaties with Portugal and Brazils been acting up to these instructions?

M'Culloch further adduces a fundamental principle, as laid down by Sir Henry Parnell, that "generally speaking, "all *treaties which determine what the duties on exportation "or importation shall be, or stipulate for preferences, are "radically objectionable.* Nations ought to regulate their "tariffs in whatever mode they judge best for the promotion "of their own interests, without being shackled by engage-"ments with others."

Fortified by these authorities, I might proceed to argue upon the *policy* of Great Britain framing her tariff so as best to promote the interests of her own subjects, perfectly regardless of the hostility of foreign tariffs; but, I repeat, it is no longer a question of policy;—it is a matter of *necessity*. Our Government has utterly failed in every attempt to modify foreign tariffs; nay, the converse result has followed. The question, then, as to what other countries may do, cannot affect our decision: we must presuppose a commercial hostility to this country, and ascertain how far their restrictive tariffs can affect our commerce, and what is our best mode of meeting them.

The present Government has, in a great measure, recognised the necessity or policy of an independent course of action in the late important alterations in our tariff. The principles which Sir Robert Peel laid down as the basis of these alterations were not rendered conditional as applicable to reciprocating countries only, but as a general line of policy for this country to pursue.

The rules are these:—

1. The removal of prohibitions, and diminution of duties virtually prohibitory.

2. The reduction of duties on raw materials generally to 5 per cent. as their maximum.

3. On semi-manufactured articles to 10 or 12 per cent.

4. On fully manufactured articles to 20 per cent.

5. The introduction of additional remissions of duty in favour of the productions of our colonies.

6. The abolition of export duties on our manufactures.

By a strange inconsistency, Sir Robert resisted the application of these rules to certain articles of the greatest consumption,—corn, sugar, wines. The exceptions were made on the two latter articles, on the ground of certain negotiations then going forwards with Portugal and Brazils. It was contended, that if these reductions were delayed, certain valuable commercial equivalents might be obtained from the contracting parties, in return for the proposed concessions. The foolishness of these exceptions has been proved by the result, and the wisdom of a general rule of financial policy confirmed. Our proposals have been rejected, and Government is reduced to the alternative of granting as a boon that which it made a matter of bargain, or continuing a heavy tax upon articles of great consumption, with a positive loss to the revenue, and a serious injury to the expansion of our crippled commerce.

Before proceeding further with our inquiry, it may not be amiss to ascertain the existing condition of our trade with these non-reciprocal, protective, manufacturing countries. Paradoxical as it may seem, our exports to them amount in round numbers to £20,000,000 declared value, or two-fifths of the whole of our exports. We find, then, that the protective system of other countries does not exclude our goods; and that the sanction of a commercial treaty is by no means essential to the formation of a valuable intercourse with other countries. Governments would fain attribute to themselves the credit of opening and securing foreign markets; merchants, however, stand on no ceremony; they wait not long for legislative interference, but force, by their own enterprise, an outlet for the products of national industry.

It may be deemed conclusive that foreign powers are unable fully to protect themselves, as they call it, against our cheap goods. The bare extent of our exports to those countries, where the system of protection is carried out to the fullest extent, shows its futility. Great Britain, with the most efficient preventive service in the world, has failed in the attempt, and other Governments meet with no better success.

The war against hostile tariffs cannot be carried on by our Government: it may safely be entrusted to the skill and activity of the private trader. The premium paid to the smugglers for the introduction of contraband articles, is the true measure of the extent to which protection can be carried, and of the barriers which Governments can interpose in the way of trade.

But, derogatory as it most assuredly would be to the honour of the British Ministry to aid and abet British subjects in breaking the tariff regulations of friendly nations, it forms no part of the duty of our legislature to enforce upon this country the observance of foreign prohibitions or commercial regulations. Surely we are not called upon to aid France or Germany in excluding our own manufactures! This suicidal policy has met with favour from a false philanthropy, as applied to the opium trade with China; but this is an exception. Revenue officers in general, however watchful and severe they may be in punishing offences against the laws they are appointed to enforce, have no objection to infringements upon their neighbours. The introduction of contraband goods from France is connived at by the French authorities, and *vice versa*. Yet to retaliate prohibition by prohibition—to meet excessive import duties by the same—is a portion of this very self-destructive policy. It is the only mode of enforcing the exclusive system of rival nations. Notwithstanding the prohibitive duties upon the introduction of English manufactures into France, our exports for 1841 were nearly three millions; but if both parties adopted a system of mutual prohibition, and were able to enforce it, all interchange would cease. Merchants may contend against foreign prohibitions, but when the difficulties are aggravated by the obstacles interposed in the shape of duty upon their returns, the barrier to intercourse becomes insurmountable.

We hear great outcry against this "one-sided system of trade," as it is called, from parties whose opinion is entitled to great weight. For instance, Colonel Torrens, in a letter addressed to R. Cobden, Esq., M.P., and inserted in the *Sun* newspaper of May 14, concedes—

"That it is by the amount of our imports, and not by that of our exports, that the wealth of the country is increased; that if we take care of the imports, the exports will take care of themselves; that America will not give us her corn for nothing; that she will demand payment in goods or in money; that if her tariff should render it impracticable for us to pay in goods, we should send goods to other markets in order to enable us to pay in money; and that as surely as we purchase foreign produce to an increased amount, we must, either by a direct or by a circuitous trade, sell British goods to an equally increased amount, in order to pay for it." "These positions," says the Colonel, "are self-evident truths, yet have no bearing upon the question whether the prosperity of the country would be promoted by admitting American produce free of duty, whilst America refuses to relax her tariff. The real question at issue is, whether the increased amount of our exports would be effected, without such a reduction in value of British goods as would cause a decline both in profit and wages."

How the value of goods could be reduced, when, as the Colonel confesses, there must be increased exports to pay for the increased imports, or in other words, an increased demand, is not clearly explained! If the relative price of an article depend upon the ratio betwixt supply and demand, when you increase the demand you must also increase the relative price.

But the Colonel further argues—

"Explain to me the terms upon which, while America retains her tariff, England could pay to that country an additional £4,000,000 per annum for imported corn? Would you effect this payment by exporting to the United States increased quantities of the staples of Yorkshire and Lancashire? If you did you would have to encounter "ad valorem" duties of from 30 to 40 per cent., and would be compelled, in order to compete with the similar fabrics of America, to sell your goods at prices lower by 30 and 40 per cent. than those which the American manufacturer might realize. Now, American labour is as efficacious as English labour, and therefore when you sold the produce of English labour at prices reduced by 30 and 40 per cent. below the prices of the produce of American labour, you would be compelled to reduce the wages of the English operative from 30 to 40 per cent. below the wages of the American operative. A considerable decline of wages, and an insuperable obstacle to an advance of wages, would be the inevitable results of paying, during the continuance of the American tariff, for large importations of American corn, by a direct exportation of British goods to the American market."

If this argument be valid, we must, *at present*, sell the goods we export to America at 30 to 40 per cent. loss, or otherwise reduce the wages to that amount below American wages: and if our import duties on American produce were levied to the same per centage, (on cotton, as on tobacco and corn,) the English labourer would first have to sell his labour at 30 to 40 per cent. less than the American, and with his diminished earnings, would have to pay 30 to 40 per cent. more than the American labourer for articles of consumption. A converse conclusion may fairly be drawn, viz., that the English labourer, being *now* compelled to compete with the American and continental labourer at a disadvantage of 30 to 40 per cent., should not have the additional burden of a higher price to pay for subsistence. As to the £4,000,000 additional imports, it is clear that they must be paid; and if our English merchant have a difficulty in meeting his engagements, or the American seller find his payments made very tardily, the adjustment may safely be left to the parties interested, without the clumsy interference of any legislative enactment. The Americans would eventually trust us no more than we could pay for, and the English merchant would in future avoid placing himself in a situation of difficulty. Hitherto the state of affairs has been the reverse. The English merchant and manufacturer have poured into the States their surplus goods, and the depressed condition of the home trade has unnaturally forced our exports through this tempting outlet. But our own tariff has stepped in and prevented the returns of a most important part of American produce,—I mean articles of subsistence. Britain being the wealthier country, has, like a rich banker, been tempted to lend her money out at interest. America gave us her cotton and tobacco against our millions sterling of exported goods, state stocks, bank shares, &c.; she further offered us her corn, which we were so foolish as not to accept,—hence the loss has fallen upon our own shoulders, and hence the paralysis of our manufacturing industry, with a decline in wages. Colonel Torrens's caution amounts to this, that we should not buy of a poorer nation more than we can repay—a nation, moreover, which owes us a heavy balance of an old account. Surely a needless caution, and a very questionable evil! But how are we to pay for the £4,000,000 increased imports, which create such alarm in the Colonel's breast? It must be in manufactured produce, colonial or foreign produce, or gold? If paid for in produce, there must be a greater demand, and consequently a tendency to advance the price, as also those portions of it which may be resolved into labour and profit. If in gold, the value of the precious metals would be slightly raised at home; and when higher than the continental price, an influx would inevitably occur, (as it always has done on similar occasions,) and the balance after all be paid in produce. All this might be done without any material alteration in the standard of value, or a revulsion of prices. Our expanive system of paper money is ever ready to supply a deficient currency, whilst under proper regulations the abuse is prevented.

The Colonel's concluding argument is this:—

"Were you to increase the demand for foreign production by repealing our import duties, while the retention of hostile tariffs prevented a corresponding increase in the foreign demand for British goods, you would reduce the value of the produce of British labour in relation to the produce of foreign labour; or in other words, you would raise the value of foreign commodities as compared with domestic commodities. Now gold is a foreign commodity, and consequently you would raise the value of gold in relation to British labour and its products."

To this it may be replied, that the repeal of our import duties, pending the retention of foreign hostile tariffs, can at all events have no effect in diminishing our exports. Supposing, then, that with stationary exports, our imports increase, the increased quantity of our imports is equivalent only to the same amount of returns, and consequently the proportionate value of foreign produce in the home market will be diminished, according to the increase in quantity, (although it may be raised abroad,) whilst domestic produce will maintain its price, inasmuch as the demand will be stationary. Meanwhile the very efforts of our merchants to make returns to foreign exporters, and the self-interest of those exporters, will mutually aid each other in breaking through the hostile tariffs. In proportion to this success will follow an increased consumption of British manufactures, and an advance in price. In this war against hostile tariffs the British merchant has peculiar advantages. Foreign produce consists chiefly of articles of bulk, raw produce, cotton and corn, which are exceedingly difficult to be smuggled into Britain. But if the barriers against importation be thrown down, there is little difficulty in effecting payment by the introduction of our light, condensed, valuable manufactures. The ultimate loss to the revenues of foreign powers will prevent the permanent imposition of excessively high protective duties against British manufactures.

Before we adopt a retaliatory tariff, or attempt to meet high duties by maintaining them ourselves, it may be well to ascertain who are the parties upon whom the burden falls. Now, if we could retort commercial hostility, by raising the import duties on the produce of the offending nations, and thus repay the manufacturers for the injury done to them by closed markets, there would be a method in our revenge, and a probability of reducing them to terms. But the consumer pays for taxation upon articles of consumption, and it would be a strange way of punishing others to impoverish themselves. Simple as this proposition is, and apparently self-evident, yet several well-informed politicians have denied the truth of it—perhaps none more strenuously than Lord Monteagle. To prove it more forcibly, let us trace the operations of import duties upon price, and suppose that in consequence of the rejection of our offers by the Brazilian Government, an additional duty of 6d. per lb. was levied on their coffee. Who would pay the duty? Why, most certainly the British merchant who took the coffee out of bond for home consumption; the Brazilian exporter would *receive* returns for his produce, and not have to *pay* to us. The British merchant would resell his coffee to the wholesale grocer, with duty added; the next purchaser would be the retail grocer; and ultimately the consumer would have to pay;—upon him, as the last purchaser, the duty must eventually fall. So with all import duties.

True it is, that the foreign grower and exporter would suffer *indirectly* from the diminished consumption attendant upon a higher price, just as we suffer by hostile tariffs; but this is very different from maintaining that foreigners pay our import duties on their produce, or that we have to pay foreign taxes upon our goods.

Be it fully understood then, that in maintaining our high tariff, either as a protection or retaliation against the exclusiveness of other Powers, we tax ourselves without inflicting a corresponding burden upon our opponents, and the punishment falls principally upon ourselves. Moreover, the revenue reaps no adequate benefit from a high duty,—in most cases a positive loss from a falling off in consumption. Thus, in adopting a retaliatory tariff, our folly would be more manifest than the gratification of our revenge;—blinded by an ill-regulated desire to injure our rivals, we should rivet upon *ourselves* the fetters which we were trying to impose upon *their* commerce.

In the article in the first No. of the *Foreign and Colonial Quarterly Review*, generally attributed to the late Vice-President of the Board of Trade, there is an amusing illustration of the recoil of a system of protection upon its originators, as lately exemplified in France. The talented author remarks:—

"In doubling the duties on linen yarns, it was necessary to make an equivalent augmentation in the duties on cloths, or the manufacturer who purchased his yarns at an artificially enhanced price, would have been open to competition on unequal terms with those who could obtain their materials free from the burden of any such charge. The duties on linen cloth were raised accordingly. This measure fell heavily upon the importations from North Germany. The Zoll Verein exhibited no reluctance to enter upon reprisals. The Congress of Stutgard forthwith raised to double their former amount the duties upon certain articles, chiefly imported from France, including quincaillerie, bijouterie, and the other articles of Parisian industry,—gloves, cognac, and paper hangings.

"The Parisian manufacturers, good innocent folks, forsooth, are up in arms: they complain grievously, and, if they were not sympathisers with the ordonnance of June, justly, of the stroke thus aimed at their tasteful industry: their disputations besiege the very same doors of the Minister at which the flax spinners, a few months ago, knocked so imperiously for a purpose the contradictory of theirs: their complaints jar in horrible dissonance with the exultations of those who preceded them; and France, before the eyes of the world, bears witness against herself in the matter of customs' warfare."

The difficulty of negotiating favourable commercial treaties with independent nations, has directed public attention to our colonies, as being under our own exclusive control. But here another obstacle stares us in the face. Whatever advantages we claim for the introduction of our manufactures into the colonies, are claimed by them in like manner for the introduction of their produce into the mother country. Hence the long list of differential duties, incumbering our tariff, and rendering its provisions oppressive to all parties concerned. The colonies are frequently obliged to purchase in our distant market, at a dear rate, articles which they might obtain at a less price from a neighbouring country; and foreign commodities are brought to us by an expensive circuitous voyage, in order to obtain the benefit of an entry as colonial produce at our custom-house: thus protector and protected have each to suffer a useless, wasteful expenditure. But the subject is so important that we devote a separate chapter to it.

CHAPTER II.

COMPARATIVE MERITS OF COLONIAL AND GENERAL FOREIGN TRADE—FOLLY OF DEPENDING UPON COLONIES, HOWEVER FLOURISHING AND WEALTH-BRINGING—ILLUSTRATED BY REFERENCE TO SPAIN—NO SECURITY FOR THE PERMANENCY OF OUR COLONIAL DEPENDENCIES—THE UNITED STATES OF MORE VALUE TO US SINCE THEY ATTAINED THEIR INDEPENDENCE—EXTENSIVE COLONIES A SOURCE OF WEAKNESS.

IT is quite the fashion to magnify the value and importance of our colonies. Many of those alarmists, who frighten the manufacturers at the progress of machinery on the continent, comfort them with a recommendation to depend upon our vast colonies for a market—"A market," say they, "which is sure "and steadfast, inferior only to the home trade. Our vast "dominions in the East, if properly treated, may take one-half "of our manufactured exports. Look to the returns! you will "find our exports to the East Indies increasing every year, "whilst to the continent there is a gradual declension. You "may look forward to a period when the Europeans will fabri-"cate their own goods entirely, and you will inevitably be shut "out of their markets. The only prospect of good trade "dawns upon us from our colonies."

Suppose it granted that this mighty change in the channel of our trade must inevitably occur—that our colonial exports increase beyond the most sanguine anticipations, and instead of comprising little more than one-fourth, they should constitute one-half, or three-fourths,—what are we to gain by the change? What possible difference can it make to the humble wearer of printed calico, whether the raw cotton of which the fabric is composed be imported from the United States, from Brazils, or from Bengal? The only inquiry of the purchaser is, "pray, which is the cheapest, or the best?" Shall we dwell very uncomfortably in houses roofed with Baltic timber, instead of Canadian? All we ask is, "Is the roof safe, is the timber sound?" We naturally prefer that which affords the more durability and strength at the same price, and do not voluntarily endanger the safety of our houses, in order to uphold our colonies. Some few ladies, who are cruizing for an Indian nabob, may dilate upon the praises of Assam tea, "How much they prefer it to souchong or hyson!" but the thrifty housewives of England will in general care little about the name, if the herb possess the flavour they prefer.

Many of our agriculturists have a peculiar pleasure in living upon the produce of their own farms. It is their pride to say, "This mutton is of my own feeding—the beef is from stock which I have raised." But this pride would not extend to the farmers' guests, in case the mutton were rank and ill-flavoured, or the beef tough. Our Government seems to have a considerable share of the farmers' pride. It has secured a fine timber country in Canada, taken possession of large sugar estates in the West Indies, and is using every effort to provide us with cotton and tea of our own growth in the East Indies. It has furnished us with extensive sheep-walks in Australia, and a prospect of cultivating our own flax in New Zealand. Moreover, we establish our own hotels on the high road of nations. When John Bull takes a trip to the Mediterranean, he puts up at the sign of the Union Jack, in Gibraltar, Malta, or the Ionian Isles. When he makes a voyage to his East Indian possessions, he casts anchor at the Cape of Good Hope, refreshes at the Mauritius, calls at Ceylon, and eventually makes Calcutta his head-quarters.

John Bull's pride of ownership is gratified by the extent and magnificence of his territories. He forgets the yearly cost, or argues that it is not a mere question of cost. "He derives so many indirect benefits from his colonies." The healthy nurseries of Australia, New Zealand, or the Canadas, afford a wide outlet for his surplus population, or convenient settlements for his needy offspring. They supply places for the younger scions of nobility, estates for the gentry, and a wide profitable field for the labour of the poor.

Doubtless our intimate connection with these vast continents,—whose climate, soil, and productions approximate so closely to those of Europe, where Englishmen thrive and luxuriate like indigenous plants, gradually replacing the aborigines with a new, healthy, vigorous, energetic race,—whither our countrymen are transplanted without the necessity of changing their mother tongue, or subjecting themselves to a new form of government—where security of property is guaranteed, and the chances of life are not endangered,—is productive of real solid advantages, not to be estimated from a table of our exports and imports. The torrid clime of India, where so many of our countrymen have found an early grave, and our race in vain attempts to strike root, holds out no such claims to our regards.

It is not the mere fact of those countries being our colonies which constitutes their acceptance in our eyes. It is the intrinsic adaptation of the soil and climate to our constitution and wants, and the temptations to settlement which the scanty possession of a few miserable hunting tribes offers to our crowded population—these are the attractions for our hordes of emigrants, which no change of government can repel.

I know not whether we are to class as emigrants those crowds of our wealthy gentry who flock to classic Italy, fill the German watering-places, and settle in great numbers in the towns of Brussels, Paris, Boulogne, &c., giving to several the character of a mixed population. In Brussels alone there are upwards of 10,000 resident English. But, exclusive of these *settlers* in Europe, the emigration returns ending January, 1842, are—

United States	45,017
North American Colonies	38,164
Australian Colonies	32,625
West Indies and Cape of Good Hope	2,634
Central America and Texas	152
Total	118,592

Hence the emigration to the United States is the greatest in amount, and it would appear that two-fifths of our emigrants prefer an independent government. It is not necessary, then, for the purposes of emigration, that the destined tracts should be subject to the mother country. On the contrary, we may infer from these returns, that their eligibilty is increased by their independence.

We are too prone to regard the colonies as a mere appendage of the British crown, intended to increase our revenues and resources. Whenever we have attempted this mistake, the colonists are ever the foremost to convince us of our error. The connection on our part is that of a parent watching over its child, nurturing and protecting its infancy, strengthening its riper years, and gradually instilling the spirit of self-government. When it arrives at the age and strength of manhood, our wisest policy would be to give it independence, but not before it has the energy to maintain that independence.

Our Government has discovered the impolicy of making use of our colonies as penal settlements, and has given a new version to the sentence of transportation. What, then, becomes of the peculiar advantages derived from our colonies, in contradistinction to our intercourse with independent nations? Could they be proved, who can guarantee the permanency of our colonies? We have already been separated by force of arms from the most important of them—the United States, after a long, unsuccessful, and humiliating effort to regain our sovereignty. Within a few years we have witnessed the sudden attempt of Canada to assert her independence; and to her internal divisions alone can be attributed her want of success. The storm has been allayed; but any imprudent act of legislature might rouse the latent passion, and sever the connection for ever. The acts of the House of Assembly in Jamaica have shown a spirit of defiance to the mother country, of which the ultimate aim cannot be mistaken. Possibly some fear of the emancipated slaves may have infused a greater share of moderation in their councils, and occasioned the desire of protection from Great Britain in case of need. Our invincibility in the East, upon which is based the vast superstructure of our dominions in that quarter of the globe, has been shaken. The rest of our colonies hang upon the thread of our naval superiority, which the American wars have taught us not to consider infallible. Are we, then, to trust our vast foreign trade, with the mighty attendant interests of "ships and commerce," upon so frail a tenure as the continuance of our colonies? It would be a risk—a miscalculation of chances, unworthy of a gambler!

Spain offers us an instructive example of the fugitive vanity of colonial possessions. The discovery of America aroused in her the ambition of conquering a hemisphere. With a miser's grasp she laid hold of the boundless riches of her new-born empire. Gold was then considered as the only wealth; and by the utmost exactions of a greedy despotism, she wrung from the toil of her Indian subjects the hardly-earned produce of the South American gold mines. By the most severe and prohibitive laws, she endeavoured to retain this wealth within her own dominions. Her commerce with the rest of Europe was neglected. All her attention, all her hopes were absorbed by her colonies. Spaniards lost their industry and enterprise. They revelled in their easily acquired riches. Yet, in spite of every precaution, their gold oozed out, to purchase from the rest of Europe articles which they had ceased to manufacture for themselves. Spain gradually sank in the scale of nations. By contact with an easy, indolent race, her subjects lost their energy and high state of cultivation. Eventually, the despised and oppressed colonists, roused by unjust exactions, levied solely for the benefit of the mother country, raised the standard of revolt, and boldly shook off an unworthy allegiance. Even the poor Indians, who so long were trampled underfoot, have turned short upon their scorners, and achieved their independence.

Commerce with a co-equal, powerful, civilized nation, raises a manly, healthy spirit of competition: all our energies are called into play. But over a feeble Hindoo, or effeminate Chinese, poor must be the triumph of our machine-aided skill. When our ability to cope with the nations of civilized Europe or the United States ceases, from that moment will date the retrogression—the decay of our commercial greatness! We have hitherto maintained our commercial superiority, solely by our supereminence in national industry and skill.

Suppose we take another view of the question, and institute a comparison betwixt the pecuniary value of our exports to the colonies and to the world at large. The proportion of our colonial trade in 1840 was about fifteen and a half millions out of fifty-one and a half; and in 1841, thirteen and a half out of a total nearly similar. But there are some heavy drawbacks. According to a Parliamentary return, the net expenditure incurred by Great Britain, on account of her several military, maritime stations, colonies, and plantations, during 1833 and 1834, was £2,364,309. This may be considered an average, and a very moderate one. Most assuredly the year 1841 would present no diminution: on the contrary, if the expenses of the war in Affghanistan were added, the amount would be considerably increased. Again, we have to estimate the loss to the revenue from differential duties. According to M'Culloch, the loss upon timber alone, by the old tariff, would be £1,500,000. Perhaps, by the new tariff, it would not exceed £1,000,000. Then upon sugar, the differential duties are still greater. In fact, the duty on foreign sugar is prohibitory. Add to the loss upon sugar, that upon other articles of the tariff, we shall be considerably under the mark in calling the amount at £2,000,000. But there is a farther loss to the consumer, which does not benefit the revenue, and might be justly included in our estimate. The profit and loss account would then stand as follows:—

COLONIES' PROFIT AND LOSS ACCOUNT.

DR.		£	*Per contra—CR.*	£	£
To annual average of Expenses incurred in maintenance and defence......		2,364,309	By annual exports...........	13,500,000	
To annual loss to revenue from differential duties...		3,000,000	Deduct cost of raw materials..	3,000,000	
To interest on outlay—	£		Labour and Profit...........		10,500,000
Slave Manumission	20,000,000				
Outlay in Sierra Leone	3,000,000				
Original cost of conquering the colonies, or wresting them from other countries, under-estimated	22,000,000				
	£50,000,000				
Annual interest, at 3 per ct.		1,500,000			
To Balance		3,635,691			
		£10,500,000			£10,500,000

It is more than probable that the loss to the consumers in the mother country and her colonies, occasioned by these differential duties—and a loss which is no gain to the revenue—will more than cover the balance of £3,635,691. Should this hasty sketch at all approximate to the real state of the case, it may tend to remove all visionary notions of the pecuniary profit we derive from our colonial trade. In fact, it is a question whether the total value of our colonial exports is not swallowed up by the annual cost, (including loss to the revenue and consumers, and interest on the extraordinary sums granted directly or indirectly on account of our colonies.) In the case of the United States, we derived no advantage from them until they acquired their independence. Lord Sheffield, as quoted by M'Culloch, says:—

"By the war of 1739, which may truly be called an American contest, we incurred a debt of upwards of £31,000,000: by the war of 1755 we incurred a farther debt of £71,500,000: and by the war of revolt we have added to both these sums nearly £100,000,000 more! And thus we have expended a far larger sum in defending and retaining our colonies, than the value of all the merchandise we have ever sent them. So egregious has our impolicy been in rearing colonists for the sake of their custom."

Query, are we not still pursuing the same impolicy?

The very magnitude of our colonies proves a source of weakness. During the alarm of a foreign invasion from Napoleon, when the circuit of our coast bristled with forts, we found no small difficulty in presenting the show of defence on every vulnerable point. But now we have spread out our branches, and the plucking of the farthermost twig inflicts a wound. We have the straggling frontiers of Canada, the numberless circles of our West Indian archipelago, the interminable coast of our Australian continent, with the accompanying islands, the vast limits of our East Indian territory, besides our innumerable military stations, all these we have to defend, and at every pore we may imbibe *war!* A threatened irruption on the farthermost boundary of our Eastern territory by a mountain horde, sets in motion all our complicated military organization, and ends in a sacrifice of 20,000 lives, at the cost of several millions sterling, under the plea of preserving our position and increasing our strength!

It is often argued that the large naval and military establishments, entailed upon us by our colonies, are a great cause of our national strength. If so, the United States must be weak, for they have no standing army; France must have enfeebled herself by disbanding 100,000 soldiers; and Algiers prove a national benefit. When a government annually exhausts her treasury by the pomp and parade of war, she is manifestly less prepared for the extraordinary efforts which a real emergency requires. Her strength lies in the character of her people, in their numbers, their industry, their hardihood, and their intelligence—not in the number of her soldiers. The United States have the smallest standing army, in proportion to their population, of any civilized nation; yet they are the last we should wish to engage in war.

Sufficient has already been advanced to prove the impolicy of directing attention to our colonies, as the best market for the produce of the mother country, to the neglect of nearer and better customers. The unprofitableness, and indeed the *danger* of such a course, are equally conclusive. Do away with all differential duties—throw upon our colonies every fair and reasonable charge for their own protection—leave commerce to find her own channels—and the relative advantage of the colonial trade will soon show itself. Such a policy would relieve both parties of a very heavy indirect taxation; and the colonists themselves would eventually find it the greatest boon we could confer upon them.

If we may venture to draw an inference from the United States, our commerce would receive a fresh impulse from the independence of our colonies. At the commencement of the revolutionary war in 1776, our exports to the North American colonies were £1,300,000; but after the acknowledgment of the independence of the United States, our merchants expected that the whole of the American trade would be taken up by the other nations of Europe, more especially by the French, who had been the allies of the States. It was predicted that all the advantages we had derived from our late colonies would henceforth be lost to us. Yet what was the result? Why, in 1784, the official value of our exports to the newly recognised States had increased to £3,600,000. Subsequently the declared value in one year (1836) reached the enormous amount of £12,425,605 of British and Irish produce and manufactures. The history of our commerce with the United States leaves us no cause to regret their independence. In every respect we have been considerable gainers by the change.

Whilst we are propping up our colonial interests by differential duties, (more especially on the article of sugar,) Jamaica, the most important of our West Indian possessions, is returning the compliment, by raising her scale of duties on home produce. Such is the gratitude we meet with for our spendthrift philanthropy, in paying an extravagant price for the manumission of their slaves, and our grant to them of a monopoly of the home market for sugar.

The following communication was made to Government by the Cork Committee of Merchants, March 17th, 1843 :—

" STATEMENT.

" A new schedule of inland duties has lately passed the Legislature of Jamaica, for the purpose of raising a revenue for that colony, and now waits the sanction of the home Government.

" Finding that these proposed duties are very considerably increased, and unequally proportioned, the Committee of Merchants of Cork have directed the attention of the Secretary to the Colonies, Lord Stanley, to the subject, as one which would be seriously disadvantageous to Irish commerce and agriculture, and demanding the most decided interference on his part.

" The proposed new scale is to this effect :—

" On beef 20s. a barrel, equal to from 30 to 75 per cent., according to quality.

" Pork 20s. per barrel, equal to 45 per cent.

" Butter 4s. per 64 lbs. equal to 8½ per cent.

" Bacon 8s. per cwt., equal to 20 per cent.

" Candles 1s. 6d. on 56 lbs., equal to 7 per cent.

" Lard 3s. on 70 lbs., equal to 12½ per cent.

" Porter £3 3s. per ton, equal to 25 per cent.

" Soap 2s. per 56 lbs., equal to 25 per cent.

" Its rates on English manufactured goods, when contrasted with the preceding, are very unequal. On glass, silks, cotton, hardware, manufactured paper, &c., the duty proposed is no more than four per cent. on the value.

" The imports of Irish produce into the island of Jamaica for the year 1840, which may be considered a fair criterion on antecedent years, and before the introduction of foreign provisions into the West Indies, were

" 1,200 barrels of pork.
" 12,700 firkins of butter.
" 7,400 firkins of lard.
" 15,000 boxes of candles.
" 37,000 boxes of soap.

" Besides beef, porter, hams, and other articles.

" Irish imports into the other islands are also very considerable ; and though the new Jamaica tariff is of very deep importance, as has been shown, yet it is very possible that the other colonies may follow the example, unless the Irish interests unite without delay to check the present, as well as any other similar proceedings.

" The different duties in favour of articles the produce of the United Kingdom and its possessions, shall, in no case, be lower in the colonies than they are at home."

This statement requires no comment : but what becomes of the peculiar advantages, the special security, of our colonial trade, if, for the sake of revenue, the colonial legislatures are permitted to raise their duties at the very time we are reducing ours, and allowing increased privileges to their produce?

Porter's last volume of "The Progress of the Nation," article "Colonies," chap. i., contains some valuable remarks upon the colonies and our colonial system. He contends that

"If properly managed, they might be productive of great benefit to the mother country; but, under the influence of perverse causes, are sources of weakness rather than strength to the parent state. The principal cause of this fact is not difficult to point out. Until a recent period, the trade with our dependencies has been converted into a close monopoly in favour of England; and although various relaxations have been made in this selfish system, it is still sought to retain a great share of the supposed advantages of monopoly by means of differential duties chargeable in the colonies against the production and manufactures of foreign countries. In order to reconcile our colonists 'to this monopoly,' the legislature of England has sought to give them compensation, at the expense of other countries, by means of differential duties, that admitted the productions of our colonies at lower rates than the same productions brought from other countries. Every real benefit thus obtained from the colonies must be at the expense of the people at home; first, because of the high price which we pay for colonial articles, and without which higher price there could manifestly be no advantage to the colonist; and farther, because of the retaliatory measures which the system is sure to give rise to in other countries whose produce is thus placed at a disadvantage in our markets, and which measures of retaliation are levelled, not at the trade of our colonies, which, indeed, they cannot reach, but against that of the mother country.

"The amount of injury sustained from this last named cause cannot well be made the subject of calculation; but some idea may be formed of the ruinous effect of differential duties upon the expenditure of this nation, by showing the result produced in one year by the prohibitory duty upon a single article of colonial production—sugar. It is shown that we paid, for the quantity of sugar used in 1840, more than £5,000,000 beyond what would have been paid for the same quantity, irrespective of duties, by any other people of Europe. The total value of our manufactures exported in that year to our sugar colonies was under £4,000,000; so that the nation would have gained a million of money in that one year, by following the true principle of buying in the cheapest market, even though we had made the sugar growers a present of all the goods they took from us. It must be idle to suppose that colonies depend for their existence and progress upon such preferences. Unless prevented through the interference of legislative restrictions, they will certainly be able to apply their industry in some profitable channel. The very fact of their existence indicates that the inhabitants of colonies are in possession of advantages, whether of soil or climate, greater than are afforded by the country whence they have emigrated; and it must be reckoned amongst the evils inflicted by differential or *protective* duties, that they divert capital and industry from more profitable into less profitable, and sometimes even into hurtful branches of employment.

"Enough has been said to show that it is not by means of commercial restrictions and monopolies that colonies can be made valuable. Emancipate your colonies from all the shackles with which your shopkeeping spirit has loaded them; let them be free to adopt such commercial regulations as each may find best suited to its circumstances, and you may then safely proceed to emancipate yourselves from the countervailing shackles you have imposed upon your own commerce. Thenceforward your trade with your foreign possessions will be truly profitable to this nation. The settlers with whom it is carried on will have taken with them, or will have inherited from their fathers, a taste for the manufactures of the old country, and as they will for the most part be unable themselves to produce those manufactures, they will have every inducement to buy them from their countrymen, rather than resort to foreign markets for a supply. That England, which boasts of its power of competing successfully with the whole world in so many branches of manufacture should think it necessary to force her goods by fiscal regulations upon people who have already the strongest inducement to trade with her, seems an absurdity that one is at a loss to imagine how it could ever have been conceived. Such a course of legislation is not simply useless, it is positively mischievous, by interfering with the natural rights of the colonists, and inducing the feeling that there can be a diversity of interest between themselves and the parent country."

What conclusion is to be drawn from these arguments? Are we to emancipate our colonies? Not until they are desirous of emancipating themselves; since having undertaken their guardianship, we are morally bound to continue it until that period when they shall have gained constitutional strength to govern and protect themselves.

The immediate and only inference I have in view is the necessity of *an abolition of all differential duties;* a necessity which is equally forced upon us, whether we regard our own interests or those of our dependencies.

The absurdity of withdrawing our attention from our neighbouring customers in Europe and the United States, to the distant markets of our colonies, has already been proved, and an attempt made to show by precedent the danger of such a course.

It remains only to answer the question, whether by abolishing the differential duty on Brazilian coffee and sugar, we should not be encouraging slave produce, and endangering the success of our great measure for the freedom of slaves? But that measure was conclusive! Surely it was never contemplated, that in addition to the premium of £20,000,000, this heavily taxed country should be further subject to a yearly charge made by the planters in the shape of protection to their sugars! No such stipulation was ever made, and there is not the slightest pretence for asking it! Whilst we are striking the fetters from off the cramped limbs of the poor negro, shall we transfer the irons to that commerce which nature intended to be free as the occan? The freedom we ask *from*—the freedom we would grant *to* the colonies, to the *whole world*—is, "to sell in the dearest and buy in the cheapest markets."

CHAPTER III.

REMARKS ON THE COMMERCIAL POLICY OF MODERN EUROPE—ON THE BALANCE OF TRADE—THE SELF-REGULATING POWER OF COMMERCE, AND THE IMPOSSIBILITY OF CONFINING ITS ADVANTAGES TO ONE PARTY—EVILS OF PROTECTION.

IF we search into the history and character of the various commercial regulations instituted by the great Powers of the civilised world, we shall find them generally distinguished by this prevailing principle—the imposition of a heavy tax upon all imports of foreign produce, and a desire to exclude all articles which may directly or indirectly compete with native industry. Lord Howick, in the able speech he delivered on Ricardo's motion upon commercial negotiations, remarks—

"The whole policy rested on the assumption, that there was a great superiority of importance in the export trade over that of importation. Now it was impossible to look at the subject without perceiving that the whole fabric was based on delusion. It was the remains of the old received doctrine, that to *derive benefit from trade, they should export more than they imported, and obtain payment for the balance in the precious metals. Now the great advantage of trade consisted not in what was sent out, but what was received*—in the addition which trade made to those commodities which conduced to the well being of the people—in the increase of the necessaries, the comforts, and luxuries of life—in placing them at the disposal of the people. The export trade was valuable no doubt, but only as a means to an end, only as a means to import articles for the supply of our wants, real or artificial."

The direct tendency of this policy on the part of various Governments is to hurry on their subjects to bankruptcy; to tempt them by every legislative encouragement to send out the products of their industry, and then to stand betwixt the merchant and foreign customer, excluding the only payment which the latter has to offer. If the desideratum be an illimitable market, whence there shall be no return, yet a market sufficiently extensive to take off all surplus produce, the ocean offers a ready resource. The luckless underwriter knows to his cost that the murky deep renders little back.

But it may be remarked, that the most prohibitively jealous nation has no objection to receiving payment in *specie*; it is only payment in *kind* against which custom-house barriers are raised.

Now specie is useful only as a means of exchange, and if it were possible for this country to receive £50,000,000 per annum in gold, it would be useless to us until exchanged for articles of consumption. Why not receive at once their articles of consumption, and spare ourselves the trouble of hoarding up the precious metal with a miser's joy, which, of necessity, we must afterwards exchange for such articles of produce as were first offered us? We shall treat of this specie-fallacy more fully in the ensuing chapter.

Turkey presents a singular exception in her commercial code to the prevalent policy. Her tariff is based on the opposite notion, namely, that a country is enriched by what she receives, and impoverished by what she exports. Hence her exports are fettered by prohibitions and heavy duties, while she unreservedly admits the products of other countries. In our superior wisdom, we are apt to view such policy with compassionate self-complacency, and congratulate ourselves upon our own more enlightened views. Probably a little further examination may prove their error to be less than ours. The only test of the realised value of our exports is that which we receive in return for them; and if Turkey could succeed in her aim—to give as little as possible and receive as much as possible—she would evidently profit more by her system than we by ours. In order to balance the profit and loss of a foreign trade, an estimate must be drawn of the value of all that is received into, and all that is sent out of, the country. The profit will be the excess of the value of imports over the exports, and vice versa.

There is a class of discriminating duties in contradistinction to prohibitive or protecting duties. Sir Robert Peel, in his prepared rules, makes three distinctions of duty, viz., 5 per cent. on raw materials, 10 per cent. on semi-manufactured articles, and 20 per cent. on those fully manufactured. In so far as the minimum scale of 5 per cent. applies to raw materials, such as cotton wool, sheep's wool, flax, hemp, and silk, (which constitute a nucleus of labour, and are afterwards re-exported,) the arrangement is wisely ordered. If it be hence inferred that there is an abstract gain in exporting fully manufactured articles, and a disadvantage to the nation receiving them, in contradistinction to raw materials, the inference is strained, and cannot be borne out by facts.

Suppose England imports from Germany agricultural produce to the amount of £1,000,000 sterling, and pays for it in manufactured goods, on which side would preponderate the advantage? If, as some state, the benefits would accrue to the party which accumulated the most labour on its productions, England would be the favoured party. But the raw produce is worth its equivalent only, and if it fetch the same amount of goods, say £1,000,000 sterling, Germany would reap equal profits from the transaction. Moreover, the labourers of the two countries would derive a mutual and equal proportion of wages, provided the rates of taxation were equal. If taxation were heavier in Great Britain, her subjects would derive less benefit from exporting highly manufactured articles than Germany from the export of raw produce. In like manner it would be difficult to persuade the United States, or the Canadas, that in exchanging the indigenous growth of their native forests, or the ready produce of a willing soil, for British manufactures, they had the worst of the bargain. Our own agriculturists are in a similar position, and would be equally hard of belief. The mere growth of raw produce is dependent upon the bounty of Heaven and the fertility of the soil; but the preparation of the earth and the transportation of its produce, require a large share of human labour. Hence it will be found under ordinary circumstances, that, in the interchange betwixt manufacturers and agriculturists, equivalents of labour are given and received.

We may then spare ourselves a further discussion upon the differential character, per se, of the value of raw produce and manufactures as articles of export; proceeding to establish the principle, that the realized value of our exports is limited by the amount of our imports; and, vice versa, that the value of our imports is limited by that of our exports. This proposition is self-evident. The market price of an article is not that which the producer or the owner chooses to put upon it, but that which he can obtain in exchange; so the value of our exports is not that which the exporter affixes, but that which he receives. Now, it is to the interest of both exporter and importer that what we receive should be as large in amount as possible, compared with what we send out. Any obstructions, in the shape of high or prohibitory duties upon imports, must consequently operate most injuriously upon our foreign trade, and indirectly upon the home trade, by the double loss of diminished employment of labour, and diminished supply of articles of consumption.

At the first glance it might appear that the profit or loss of our foreign trade in general, or with any particular country, might readily be ascertained from our tables of imports and exports; but unfortunately we have no return of the export or import of the precious metals, and our tables of imports are based upon the uncertain standard of official value.

The great fluctuations in our exports tend to illustrate our previous argument. For instance, our exports to the United States in the year 1836 were £12,425,605 declared value, whilst in 1837 they dwindled town to £4,695,225. What is the inference from this sudden change? The reduction of our exports in 1837 arose from no falling off in our industrial power. We had the same mills, the same machinery, the same skill and industry, with a greater population, and a proportionate increase in our powers of labour. Making due allowance for a fall in prices attendant upon a monetary crisis, it must be evident that the main cause of this reduction was owing to inadequate returns, or disproportionate imports. Our merchants and manufacturers had sent out goods to an enormous extent, for which they could not obtain payment. Now, this insolvency on the part of the Americans did not arise from their want of means, but from the exclusive system of our own tariff, which almost forbade the payment of their debt in any other medium than that of cotton or gold. Their varied produce was abundant, but our imports of cotton alone were inadequate to meet the demands of the British creditor, and the attempt to pay us the balance in specie proved ruinous alike to debtor and creditor.

It is not attempted to deny that a wild, reckless spirit of speculation, tempted the Americans to run heedlessly into a debt which they had not existing means to discharge. The same feverish spirit led on the British capitalist to make rash advances, and to forget his habitual caution. We contend, however, that these evils might have been promptly remedied by the well-directed industry of the Americans, and by the fair development of their extraordinary energies in the discharge of their acknowledged debt, if our own tariff had not intervened. The United States gave us their cotton; they also offered us subsequently another staple article of produce, their corn—(the offering of free labour in contradistinction to that of slaves)—presenting the means of subsistence, of which our superabundant population stand much in need; but our own absurd laws prevented the willing creditor from accepting the honest offer, and the balance became a dead loss to this country.

The balance of trade, according to M'Culloch, "is the "term commonly used to express the difference between the "value of the exports from, and imports into, a country.

" The balance is said to be favourable when the value of the " exports exceeds that of the imports, and unfavourable " when the value of the imports exceeds that of exports." This notion is founded on the supposition that the balance was to be paid for in specie, which, as an article of currency, and as the medium in which taxes are usually paid, has a fictitious value in the eyes of Governments. M'Culloch proceeds to remark, that " so far from an excess of imports " over exports being any criterion of an advantageous com- " merce, it is directly the reverse ; and the truth is, not- " withstanding all that has been said and written to the " contrary, that unless the value of the imports exceeded that " of exports, foreign trade could not be carried on." The balance of trade, as we take it, must mean the profit or loss of trade ; and the greater our imports, in proportion to our exports, the more profit we receive—the more favourable the balance of trade. If our Government be really desirous of obtaining for British subjects a favourable balance, greater facilities should be afforded to importation.

There is a principle of self-adjustment in commerce, which it is dangerous for any legislature to meddle with. The balance is so nice and delicate, that any forcible regulation is sure to disturb it. With equal propriety might Government interfere in every relation of buyer or seller. Merchants manage their own affairs best, and all they ask from political Powers is, full liberty to pursue their avocations in peace.

Notwithstanding the continued efforts of grasping nations to monopolize the benefits of commerce by *protection*, and draw it into an artificial channel, all attempts have proved unavailing. The inducements to trade must be mutually tempting, or will prove vain. Laws and regulations may contract the range, but can never succeed in bestowing the profits on one party only. Commerce is founded on barter, and no person can be induced to exchange that which he has, for that which is offered in exchange, unless he prefer the latter. Commercial nations stand in the mutual relation of buyer and seller to each other, and each must see an advantage in dealing, or intercourse would cease. To speak of one-sided trade, therefore, is a contradiction and an absurdity. The thing cannot permanently exist. As previously exemplified in the case of our trade with the United States, Great Britain may foolishly send out more goods than can be paid for, (owing to our unwise tariff) but her merchants are shrewd enough not to continue a losing game, and our trade naturally sinks to its proper limits of a mutual profit. In trade, a man cannot benefit himself without to a certain extent benefiting others; and it is a singular illustration of the wisdom of Divine Government, that in civilized life, the best mode of supplying our own wants, is to minister to those of our neighbours. All classes aid, willingly or unwillingly, in supplying the wants of the people; whether in spending the wealth amassed by a previous generation, or in adding to the accumulations of productive industry. Here is manifest the true spirit of reciprocity, which constitutes a portion of our nature, and, like the physical growth of the human frame, requires only full scope to develop itself. The tender mercies of protecting legislatures are like the reclining boards, tight laces, &c., applied to the person in early life. They stunt the growth, and deform the shape of that body which they are intended to strengthen. Whenever a Sovereign or a minister takes a pet manufacture under his especial care, he is sure to stifle it in his embrace. Look at the silk manufacture! Until Huskisson took off its swaddling clothes, and exposed it to the healthy breeze of competition, it never flourished in this country.

The cotton manufacture fortunately escaped the fostering care of Government; and thanks to individual enterprise and the astounding development of machinery, it has attained a pre-eminence over all other branches. The woollen manufactures, on the contrary, have since the thirteenth century been the special object of many statutes in their behalf.

M'Culloch remarks in his Dictionary, "It may be doubted, "however, whether the woollen manufacture has derived any "real advantage from the numberless statutes passed in the

" view of contributing to its advancement. The benefit " derived from the prohibition of the exportation of long wool " was more apparent than real, inasmuch as it occasioned a " diminished growth of wool, at the same time that it was " impossible to prevent its clandestine exportation." It has been proved that the manufacture made more rapid progress during the reign of Elizabeth, when wool might be freely carried out of the kingdom, than it ever did during any equal period subsequent to the restriction and exportation.

In spite of the care and attention which favourable Sovereigns have bestowed upon our woollen manufacture, the total value is not two-thirds that of cotton.

In 1833.—Total value of Cotton Manufactures	.....	£34,000,000
" " " Woollen "	.....	21,000,000

Well may the manufacturers say—" Preserve us from our friends, we will take care of our enemies."

CHAPTER IV.

FALLACY OF THE ARGUMENT THAT FOREIGNERS WILL TAKE OUR GOLD IN RETURN FOR THEIR EXPORTS TO US—WHAT IS IT THAT REGULATES OUR SUPPLY OF THE PRECIOUS METALS?—GOLD IS NOT WEALTH, BUT THE REPRESENTATIVE OF WEALTH—ILLUSTRATION—FOREIGN MANUFACTURES WILL NOT INJURE THIS COUNTRY—PROOF—ILLUSTRATION.

ACCORDING to an estimate made by Mr. Horsley Palmer, the quantity of gold coin in circulation in the United Kingdom on the 15th February, 1833, was £30,000,000. What proportion, then, of our imports, which may be taken at £50,000,000, can we possibly pay for in specie? If we send abroad the whole of our gold coinage, it will not suffice to pay for nine months' imports. It is clearly impossible, therefore, that we can pay for a large proportion of our imports in gold.

But why are we more afraid of gold being exported than any other foreign production? Are we never alarmed at the idea of tea, coffee, sugar, cotton, &c., leaving this country? It is contended that our supply of these articles will not fail, so long as we have the means of paying for them, and the same argument will apply to the precious metals. To offer gold for gold would be an absurdity, unless in a different state of manufacture. The owners of the South American gold mines would not exchange their produce for bullion, or for our sovereigns; but would be tempted by our manufactures. All the gold now in our possession we have paid for by our produce, and we could purchase more, if we required it, by the same means. Gold is not wealth, but merely its representative. Robinson Crusoe found no use for his Spanish doubloons; he placed a value solely on those articles which assisted him in providing for his wants. We call ourselves the wealthiest people on the face of the globe; if so, we can bid higher and have a greater command over the precious metals than any other nation. We have, then, no occasion to fear that our stock of gold should be materially lessened by exportation, since we can at all times purchase back again as much as we require.

Specie is useful only as a medium of exchange. In this country it serves as a basis to a more expansive system of paper currency; and we require only a certain proportion, sufficient to sustain any sudden revulsion of credit in the ordinary paper money. If we possess more than is requisite to serve this purpose, the hoard of the Bank of England is increased, but the country reaps no benefit from its bloated stock of bullion.

The price of gold, like that of all other commodities, is governed by the proportion betwixt supply and demand. If the supply be large, the price falls; and no prohibition can prevent its flowing to those markets where it will fetch a greater quantity of commodities. If, on the contrary, the supply be diminished or the demand increase, and we have the means of purchasing, so surely as water rises by the action of the pump, will gold flow into our markets.

The amount of gold coin in circulation in Great Britain has, with certain oscillations, remained nearly stationary. Our succession of bad harvests caused a drain to the continent, to provide for sudden inlets of corn; but the tide is now reversed, and flows back again to this country. If it be granted that the average of our gold currency remains nearly stationary, it is manifest that our exports have been paid for by our own produce, and not by the precious metals.

There is an admirable inconsistency—a wilful blindness—about these monopolists of gold, which leads one to suspect that their arguments against "foreigners draining us of gold" are held for a sinister purpose, and not from an honest conviction of the evils of such a tendency in foreign trade. Do the same parties ever raise their voice against sending out gold to our colonies to pay the troops? Have they started the same objection against the Canadian insurrection, the Affghan irruption, or the Chinese war? At one moment they would hoard up coin with a niggard's hand; and anon they would squander it in the pomp and tinsel of war. If there be an evil in the so-called "drain of gold," it will apply with infinitely more force against the direct remittances of specie to our colonies or military stations, than to the possibility of paying in gold the balance of foreign trade, which is essentially a system of barter. But, even in the former case, the precious metals find their way back again to this country; and, ultimately, we pay for our expensive wars, colonial establishments, &c., by the produce of our own industry.

There is another objection urged against the soundness of our foreign trade, which tends to unnerve the arm of the British manufacturer,—to deaden his hope of reviving prosperity, and to fill him with the most serious alarm as to the future condition of the rising manufacturing population. If there be truth in the predictions of these croaking prophets, the towns of Manchester, Birmingham, Glasgow, &c., which have risen as it were by the hand of a magician, will sink with the same rapidity. Through what convulsive struggles must a starving population pass, ere so dreadful a result can be accomplished! The gloomy prophecy is this:—" That " the manufacturing greatness of England will depart from " her; that other nations are rivalling her in productive skill, " and will probably surpass her; that they are supplying " their own population from their own looms, and will shortly " cease to purchase goods from England; that the arrogant " claim of this country to manufacture for the world must be

" given up ; that we are gradually losing our markets, whilst " our productive powers increase ; and, ultimately, the only " markets we can retain will be the home and colonial."

Grant that foreigners are manufacturing for themselves, I deny the conclusion that they will cease to take our goods. If it be true that our commerce is limited by the extent of our imports, it is evident that the greater the productive skill of other countries, the larger will be the amount and variety of their products and our consequent intercourse. A merchant or manufacturer generally looks sharply after the credit of his customers. He rejoices when they thrive, for he can trust them to a larger amount, and cultivates their business still more assiduously. A poor customer he is afraid to trust. England, then, should rather rejoice at, than view with gloomy jealousy, the manufacturing skill of her rivals. As a nation grows in wealth, her taste for luxuries increases; the fund for the support of labour is enlarged; and her interchange of merchandise with other countries becomes more frequent. In proportion, then, as manufactures add to the wealth of our so-called rivals, in like manner will their ability to purchase from us be increased. The foundation of the error in the estimate of the effects of foreign manufactures, is traceable to the supposition that our taste for clothing, our appetite for wearing apparel, is a certain fixed want, capable neither of much increase nor diminution. But, in fact, this appetite grows with what it feeds upon. Civilization tends to increase our artificial wants, and upon none has it had a more remarkable effect than upon that of dress. The supply of bodily nourishment varies little in the savage or civilized man—in the prince or the peasant. The materials may differ, yet the quantity will be nearly equal. Our consumption of clothing is limited only by our means of purchase, or our tastes. Notwithstanding the vast increase in our powers of production, the demand has more than kept pace with it. If people had not worn more clothing, after the introduction of the spinning jenny and the power-loom, the markets would have been stocked immediately, and very little machinery would have been made,

—merely sufficient to displace the previously existing manual labour. Machinery has had the tendency to increase the demand for its products in a ratio greater than its supply. (If this be conceded, what becomes of the notion of over-production? So long as we obtain adequate returns for our manufactures, we are never producing too much. Any stoppage, any prohibition, of our returns, whether in the shape of duties on imports, or a bad harvest, will cause the phenomenon called "over-production.")

To relinquish theory for facts, let us see how our trade has been affected by the progress of manufactures on the continent. Saxony, Rhenish Prussia, and Belgium, are, with the exception of France, most advanced in manufacturing industry; yet, while in 1831 our exports of British and Irish produce and manufactures to Prussia, Germany, Holland, and Belgium, were under 6 millions, in 1842 they had increased to upwards of 10½ millions. Our exports to France also have increased from £475,884, declared value, in 1830, to £2,902,000 in 1842. The United States of late years have extended their manufactures, yet our exports, which in 1830 were £6,132,346, in 1842 were £7,098,642. In 1836, they reached upwards of 12 millions. Meanwhile our commerce with Brazil, a non-manufacturing country, has remained nearly stationary. In 1830, the exports of British and Irish produce and manufactures to Brazil were £2,452,103, and in 1842 they were only £2,556,554. During this interval they varied only in the slightest possible degree.

A further illustration is offered by the history of our silk trade with France. In 1826, the prohibition upon the importation of foreign silks was removed. Immediately the French shipped large quantities of their beautiful tasty fabrics to this country. Our home manufacturers expected nothing less than utter ruin in this disadvantageous competition with their neighbours. Their artisans were cramped by a long continuance of protection. Moreover, the French are much nearer the supply of the raw material, and have the first choice. What was the result? Our silk manufacturers, thrown upon their own resources, displayed the native energy of the British character. In 1823, our exports of silk manufactures were only £351,407;—in 1842, £788,894,—more than double. France has taught us the advantages of competition. The most remarkable feature of the case is, that a large proportion of our silk exports is sent to our rival, France. Thus have we received a salutary lesson on the benefits of competition, in a branch of manufacture which of all others is peculiarly hedged in with difficulties to this country. Why, then, are we alarmed, hesitating, and fearful at the progress of continental industry in the cotton or woollen fabrics? Herein we display a pusillanimity, a selfishness unworthy of the British name. "Hath our arm lost its strength, or our right hand its cunning?" 'Tis true we can no longer buoy up a false prosperity at the expense of the rest of the world; but we are able to carry on an honourable competition, in the arts of peace, by ministering to each other's wants. England may now base her prosperity upon that of her neighbours, and maintain her front position, by persevering in that course of national industry and integrity, which has mainly contributed to place her first amongst the nations of the earth.

CHAPTER V.

Customs viewed as a source of revenue—comparison of direct and indirect taxation—upon the effect which import duties have upon commerce.

Fiscal regulations are generally considered as peculiarly the province of the statesman; and the advocates of free trade have very carefully steered clear of the subject. They have wisely directed their exertions to pull down the so-called system of protection; and have not interfered with duties imposed for the sake of revenue. Without quarrelling with the amount of taxation, or attempting to lessen the revenue, it shall be my endeavour, in the present chapter, to show that the burden is not so placed as to be borne most advantageously. Common experience testifies how much greater weight an individual may carry when the load is skilfully poised, so as to leave the limbs unfettered, and give the muscular powers full play.

It is a question worthy of more ample discussion than it has yet met with, whether or no the whole principle of customs, as a tax levied for the sake of revenue, is not unsound. One great motive which has driven taxation into this channel, is the aversion which people generally entertain to the sight of a tax-gatherer. Consequently the Government, disguising the nauseous draught as an apothecary sweetens his bitter drugs, conceals, as much as possible, the operation of taxes from its subjects, and exposes their deformity only to the shipper. Hence indirect taxation is preferred, both by Government and the people.

Regardless of prejudices for or against any particular mode of taxation, and destitute of sympathy with that nervous feeling by which a man wilfully blinds himself to the items of his expenditure—that feeling which too often prevents the future bankrupt from properly investigating his affairs—let us start with the maxim, that the system of taxation which, in proportion to the revenue collected, imposes the least possible burden upon the people, is to be preferred.

One advantage of direct taxation is, that each individual knows exactly what proportion he has to bear. Without such a knowledge, taxation is generally slipped off the shoulders of the wealthy and powerful, to be saddled (without any regard to proportionate means), upon the backs of the poorest and most numerous class. Another advantage rests in the efficient check to extravagant expenditure on the part of Government, which arises out of the jealous suspicion with which every taxpayer observes how his own contribution is wasted. Again, the expense of collecting direct taxes is much less per cent than customs, enhanced by the cumbrous machinery of our preventive service. The mere expense of collecting customs is trifling, but is quadrupled by the means employed to prevent frauds. Look at our revenue cutters! our coast-guard encircling the whole island! and yet, in despite of all and every caution of the most efficient preventive service in the world, frauds upon the revenue, to the manifest injury of the fair trader, are daily, hourly occurring.

If it be conceded that direct taxation presses more equitably upon the people, affords a more efficient check against extravagant expenditure, and costs less in collection than customs, or indirect taxation, it is manifest that according to the maxim with which we started, the former is preferable.

But only half our case is stated. Independent of the extra cost of the collection of customs, occasioned by our preventive service, there is a still further loss to the community. Taxes levied upon imports increase the price of the commodities imported. In at least an equal proportion to the advance in price, do they lessen the consumption. But if consumption diminish, our imports diminish; and in like degree our exports to pay for those imports. The reduction in our exports must be followed by an attendant falling off in the demand for labour, which, by a further reaction, tends still more to diminish consumption.

To illustrate our argument, we will take as an example the duty upon coffee. "Of or from foreign countries" it is now 8d. per lb., and from British possessions 4d. The importer of foreign coffee must, of necessity, add 8d. to the original cost of the article, which the consumer will have to pay: a charge for profit upon the 8d. per lb., not less than upon the original cost, must also be added. This will make a further addition of about 1d. per lb. to the consumer. But 9d. per lb. added to the original cost necessarily diminishes consumption. Remove the duty, and the consumption would increase. Suppose the present price to the consumer to be 2s. per lb., and the duty one-third, or 8d. per lb., the first effect of the removal of duty would be to reduce the price in like proportion. Granting the means of the consumer to be the same in both cases, he could afford to purchase one-third more of coffee than before. Other persons, who could not hitherto purchase the article, may now become consumers. The consumption, according to past experience, would increase more than the proportionate fall in price: witness the following table:—

	Quantity entered for Home Consumption.	Duties on British Plantation.		Revenue.
	lbs.	s.	d.	£.
1807	1,170,164	1	8	161,245
1809	9,251,847	0	7	245,856
1819	7,429,352	1	0	292,154
1825	10,766,112	0	6	307,204
1841	28,370,857	0	6	887,747

The reduction of duty in 1809 to 7d., or about one-third of what was levied in 1807, occasioned an increase in consumption of eight-fold the previous amount; whereas in the simple proportion of the fall in duty, it should have been only threefold.

Now, in 1842, the quantity of coffee cleared for home consumption was 28,583,931 lbs. Supposing the consumption to increase in simple proportion to the fall in price, the additional quantity consumed would be 9,000,000 lbs., or about 80,000 cwt., which, at an average of 50s. per cwt. for foreign, free of duty, would amount to an increase of £200,000 in our imports, and a consequent demand for exports to the same extent. But of this £200,000 additional exports, the greater portion would be spent in labour, which would improve the condition of the labourer, and enable him to consume still more of coffee or other commodities, creating thereby a still further demand for imports, to meet this increased consumption. This two-fold action might probably raise our increased imports to £250,000.

Now, a considerable portion of the industry of the nation has, until lately, been forcibly kept idle, in consequence of a want of demand for labour. So far, then, as these increased exports to meet the increased imports would involve the employment of labour previously unproductive and dependent upon our poor laws for support, the nation would gain doubly —first, by a relief in the poor rates, and secondly, by the produce of industry which previously had no employment. State the matter thus:—

	£	
Increased exports to meet probable increased imports attendant upon a removal of the import duty on Coffee	250,000	
Less cost of raw materials	50,000	
Wages and Profit		200,000
Probable saving in relief to the poor		10,000
1d. per lb. on the previous consumption of 28,583,931 lbs. now charged as profit on the duty		100,000
		£310,000

Now, the net revenue derived from coffee in 1841, was £887,747 ; so that, to raise this sum, the country sustains a loss of £310,000, besides principal and cost of collection.

In the relation betwixt low prices and consumption there is a principle—an axiom—not generally understood. Consumption increases in *geometrical ratio* with the fall in price, the means of the consumer remaining the same. But when reduction in price springs from abundance, it often indicates increased means in the consumer, and tends still further to enhance consumption. The fall of price in cotton goods since the introduction of machinery, will scarcely reach 15 to 1. In Baines's History of the Cotton Manufacture, it is stated that in the year 1786, yarn 100 sold for 38s.; in 1832, the same counts sold for 2s. 11d., being a reduction of about 13 to 1. In 1814, a piece of calico sold for 24s. 7d.; whilst in 1833, the same quality sold for 6s. 2d. being a reduction of 4 to 1. Probably, then, the extreme of the reduction in price will be as 15 to 1; but meanwhile, we find that production has increased beyond all comparison with the fall in price. In the above-named work it is stated:—

> "Machines have been invented which enable one man to produce as much yarn as 250 or 300 men could have produced in 1760,—which enable one man and one boy to print as many goods as a hundred men and a hundred boys could have printed formerly; and the effect has been, that now the manufacture supports fifteen hundred thousand persons, or thirty-seven times as many as at the former period."

Now, if we estimate the increase in the powers of production of one man, aided by machinery, as compared with hand-labour, at an average of 200 to 1, and multiply by the increase in the number of persons employed, 37 to 1, we arrive at the amazing result of 7,400 to 1. In other words, there is 7,400 times the quantity of yarn or cloth manufactured from cotton which was manufactured in 1760, whilst the price is only 15 times as cheap. Meanwhile the quantity of cotton wool imported has increased from 3,870,392 lbs. in 1764, to 303,656,837, in 1833, or only about 80 to 1. The discrepancy may partly be accounted for by the increased fineness and lightness of the yarns and cloth now manufactured, as compared with those of 1760. The increase of population in England and Wales, as stated in Porter's Progress of the Nation, "From 1770 to 1800, is "computed to have amounted to 1,959,590, or $27\frac{1}{10}$ per cent.; "while the increase in the same space of time between 1801 "to 1831, as found by enumeration, reached to 5,024,000 "souls, or $56\frac{3}{4}$ per cent."

If, then, we state the increase in population from 1760, in round numbers, as having doubled itself, or increased as 2 to 1, this will not suffice to account for the wonderful increase in the consumption of cotton goods. Multiplying the fall in price of 15 to 1, by the increase in population of 2 to 1, gives 30 to 1 as the extent to which consumption could have increased in simple arithmetical proportion, whilst the actual consumption of raw cotton has increased as 80 to 1, and production as 7,400 to 1.

We might multiply examples as to the increased consumption of various luxuries, some of which are become necessaries of civilised life, brought about by a fall in the price of the article, and an improvement in the means of the consumer. Suffice it to mention such articles as tea, coffee, tobacco, candles, &c. The art of printing has multiplied books to a still greater degree than it has reduced their price.

The last instance on record is that of railway travelling. If we give credit to the returns of railway traffic, passengers, &c., half our population and the moveables travel by steam. Yet the reduction in fares, as compared with the old coach travelling, is by no means commensurate with the increase in passengers. As a further confirmation of our position, the third class passengers make better returns than the second, and the second than the first.

To revert to our argument—it is clear that the abolition or reduction of customs and duties must be accompanied by a diminution of price,—hence increased consumption attended with increased imports,—but any excess of imports will require a corresponding excess of exports to pay for the same, —hence increased demand for labour, and improvement in the condition of the labourer, to be followed by a further consumption. Upon our customs the country sustains, besides the amount of revenue collected,—firstly, a most expensive mode of collection, including our preventive service,—secondly, a loss of imports,—thirdly, a loss of exports, and the labour heaped upon them. If the examples we have adduced confirm our proposition, that consumption increases in geometrical ratio with a fall in price, it follows, that for every shilling Government imposes as a tax on imports, the country loses 2s; for every 2s. it loses 4s.; for every 4s., 16s.; and so on in like proportion. Herein are not included charges for levying the tax.

Unpopular as the Income or Property Tax may be with the middle classes, yet, if measures of Free Trade are to be carried out to the fullest extent, it will be difficult to find any other mode of taxation to supply the deficiency which will arise from any extensive reduction in import duties. True, it is, that the abolition of all protecting duties, and the adjustment of the tariff to that nice point, of *the greatest possible consumption with the greatest possible revenue*, might have superseded the necessity of an income tax. If it had come under a different aspect,—not as an addition to our already excessive burden of taxation, but as a substitute for duties upon the *necessaries* of life, upon articles of the greatest consumption,—it might have been welcomed as a boon. The produce of the property tax is not one-third of the customs; and if it had to be increased, so as to compensate for the absolute abolition of the latter, the outcry against it would be so universal and influential, as to prevent any minister, however bold, from making such a proposition. But, without any addition to the rate chargeable upon the present tax-payers, the produce might be amazingly increased by including other classes who now escape its operation. By the old mode of indirect taxation, the operatives, who are the bulk of the consumers, pay two-thirds of the taxation of the country, and in a proportion the very reverse of their means. From the income tax this class, and those considerably above it, whose incomes do not reach £150 per annum, are entirely exempted. Now, if the plea of Sir Robert, that an equivalent was received, were rendered valid, and a bargain were struck with the consumers to this effect:—"At present the consumers in Great Britain pay in taxation, called customs, an average of so much per head per annum, in proportion to their consumption of these articles, not to their ability to pay for them. It is proposed to substitute a tax called an income or property tax, averaging 20s. or 30s. per head less than the customs tax, to be levied according to the property and income of each individual. Hereby each consumer will gain so much per annum." If it could be clearly shown that every one received a *quid pro quo* of his share of the income tax, and the tax were made to bear proportionately upon real property, as compared with incomes,—the objections against this tax would in a great measure vanish, and the tax-payers would gladly compound on terms so much to their advantage. Of course none but paupers would be excluded from the operation of the tax, because all would compound favourably; the operatives, however, who, as the greatest consumers, had previously contributed the most per head to indirect taxation, would, under the property and income tax, contribute the least.

The net produce of a property and income tax, levied universally, it would be difficult to estimate. If not sufficient at the present rate to furnish an equivalent to the produce of the customs, it would suffice at least to abolish all taxes upon the necessaries of life, and any remaining deficiency might be supplied by a moderate tax upon a few luxuries of the greatest consumption, such as tobacco, wine, &c. But the total abolition of all customs duties would be cheaply purchased by the substitution of a property and income tax, furnishing the same revenue to Government: retaining merely a register duty to pay the expenses of Government regulations of exports and imports.

These notions are in advance of public opinion, and several steps in Free Trade must be gained before they can be entertained. We must first have the total abolition of all protective duties whatever. All pretences for protection (whether for anti-slavery colonies, home agriculturists, or home manufacturers) must be taken away! When protective duties shall be entirely abolished, import duties will be considered as merely a revenue question, and the conclusion must be arrived at, that a moderate duty is the most productive,—combining the advantages of the greatest possible consumption with the greatest possible revenue. One step further, and we shall arrive at our previous conclusion,—that all import duties operate as a bar to consumption,—that they create to the community a much greater loss than the amount of revenue collected, and are a very unwise means of taxation.

CHAPTER VI.

APPLICATION OF THE RECIPROCITY SYSTEM TO THE HOME TRADE—DIFFERENT CLASSES OF PRODUCERS—PROTECTION—SHOULD BE EQUAL—IF EQUAL, IS NOT PROTECTION—OVER-PRODUCTION AND UNDER-PRODUCTION—MALTHUSIAN OBJECTION TO FREE TRADE.

It is surprising that the advocates of commercial treaties should have confined their attention to the regulation of foreign interchange, and never looked nearer home. If reciprocity be a desirable system as applied to the foreign trade, why not extend it to our domestic transactions? What is good in the one case cannot surely be an evil in the other!

The two great interests of the home trade, between which it is desirable that a treaty of commerce should be drawn up, are the manufacturing and the agricultural. Suppose it arranged between these high contracting powers that the same *ad valorem* duties which are placed on foreign produce for the protection of the one, shall be imposed on foreign manufactures for the protection of the other. At the first glance this would seem a most equitable arrangement; but the question is,—would it secure those mutual and equal advantages which were contemplated by such a treaty? If the manufacturer, depending upon his monopoly of the home market, refused to exert his faculties and restrained his production in order to enhance the price of his goods;—if, by using the word over-production as a bugbear, he sought to render goods scarce, and to keep up a high remunerating price;—if, by the aid of his protection, he raised the price 30 or 40 per cent. above that at which the farmer could purchase the same goods from the foreign manufacturer;—if such were the position of one party, whilst meanwhile the farmer had most wonderfully increased the production of the soil by all the means in his power, partly by his excessive industry, partly by judicious investment of capital, and more especially by the aid of science,—if through these agencies agricultural produce had multiplied beyond the demand of the home consumer, and found a vent in foreign markets;—if such were the condition respectively of the two interests, on which side would the balance of advantage preponderate? The objection would be raised against the manufacturer, that the protection rested entirely with him. Nevertheless he might forcibly argue, that the tariff protected both alike,—that protection was absolutely necessary to the institutions of the country,—that without it the wages of labour could not be maintained,—that the important *vested interests* of factories, the outlay of capital made on the faith of legislative enactments, required the tender consideration of Government,—that the distress of the farmers arose solely from speculation and over-production, which compelled them to sacrifice their produce in foreign markets,—moreover, that it was of the most vital importance to the health and decency of her Majesty's liege subjects, that they should be totally independent of foreigners for a supply of clothing; otherwise this country might be reduced to the lowest depth of degradation during a time of war, from the want of coats, vests, pantaloons, &c., and the various paraphernalia of ladies' apparel. What could the farmer reply? "That the measure of protection was the price he had to pay for his goods to the home manufacturer, above that at which the foreign manufacturer offered to supply him the same goods; whereas he must supply the manufacturer with corn cheaper than the foreigner, otherwise he, the farmer, could not afford to export and meet the foreign grower in his own markets,— consequently that protection was one-sided, and operated to the benefit of the non-exporting manufacturer, but to the injury of the consumer of clothing;—that to blame over-production as a cause of distress, was to arraign the bounty of Providence, who had blessed the farmer's labours, and granted good harvests."

The preceding arguments would exactly apply to the state of things on the continent of Europe and the United States, where the manufacturing interest is fostered at the expense of the agricultural. The argument is not weakened when reversed and applied to the state of things in Great Britain.

How strangely sounds the charge of over-production when brought against the British manufacturer, and assigned as a chief cause of the late distress! "There has been too abundant a harvest of goods: machinery has been too productive." As well might the Portuguese accuse his sunny sky and fruitful vines of yielding him too exuberant a vintage;—the Russian charge with over-growth his indigenous forests;—or the inhabitant of the western valleys of the United States blame the exhaustless fertility of his alluvial soil.

But from whom comes this charge of over-production against the manufacturers of England? Why, from the very parties who chiefly profit by it,—from the consumers of clothing,—from the landowner. But against them is retorted the graver charge of *under*-production of food. During the period of severe, unprecedented distress, through which we have passed, hundreds have perished for lack of food, whilst the owners and cultivators of the soil have failed in producing an adequate supply, and yet, like the dog in the manger, have interdicted their countrymen from supplying themselves from abroad; or, in plainer language, they neither grew it themselves, nor would they let others grow it. If the productive power of agriculture had progressed with the same speed as that of manufactures, —if the same improvements had taken place,—it is manifest that the population in general would have derived a mutual advantage from this multiplied provision against their wants. Unfortunately the supply of food has not increased in proportion to the increase of the population, whilst manufactures have far exceeded that proportion; hence a progressively larger and larger quantity of clothing has had to be exchanged for a progressively diminished quantity of food. With much justice do our hard-worked operatives exclaim, that machinery has done little for them. They do not look beneath the surface, but attribute the evils of their condition to that machinery which, under more favourable circumstances, would relieve their toil. The true cause of complaint would be more readily ascertained, if wages were paid in kind, and every workman received his share of the produce of his labour. That share has been doubled by machinery, and the workman would now receive from his employer at least twice as much of cloth or other manufactures, as would formerly have fallen to his lot. But were he now to take this double quantity to the shopkeeper, he would find to his amazement that he could receive no more food, nor perhaps so much, as he formerly obtained for half the quantity of goods. That labourer must be wilfully blind who did not hence perceive why machinery had been of no service to him. It had not gone far enough. It should have been equally applied to increase the productions of the soil as of the loom, and in that case the double quantity of cloth would have purchased a double quantity of food. The labourer would then receive twice as much of the necessaries of life as before the application of machinery.*

The tirades of hired democrats against the extension of foreign trade, which carry popular feeling along with them, have much point and aptitude. Thanks to our absurd system of protection, commerce has hitherto contributed more to the

* In common parlance we often talk of our ability to supply the whole world with clothing, as if there were no limits to our productive powers. But, in fact, the raw materials of manufactures, whether wool, cotton, silk, or hemp, whether vegetable or animal, are directly or indirectly the produce of the soil, and have no tendency to increase in greater proportion than articles of food. The increase in manufactures has arisen solely from the application of machinery and the economy of labour. If the same means were applied to agriculture, undoubtedly the fertility of the soil and the extent of land under cultivation, might be wonderfully increased. When we presume to clothe the world, it is to be hoped that others will use equal exertions to feed the world.

luxuries of the rich than the necessities of the poor. Starvation and luxury stalk side by side throughout our land.

Do the bold yeomen of England call out for *protection?* It is a child's cry,—a woman's plea! They who consider themselves the pride and strength of the country, to sue for protection from the pale mechanic, the over-worked factory child! Shame on such drivelling! Let them throw away their crutches and exert themselves like men!

But suppose Government continues to them that protection; the same advantages should be conceded to all other classes. Protection should be equal and universal, or not at all. If one class only be protected, all others may expect from a just Government the same benefits, and if all are *equally protected*, this is tantamount to no protection. Take the case of the farmer. By the aid of the corn laws he may obtain prices for wheat higher by 20 or 40 per cent. than are realised on the continent. Supposing the legislature could secure to the manufacturer equally high prices,—*i. e.*, high in proportion to what the same articles could be purchased for abroad,—what advantage would either party gain from high prices? They would receive more for their produce, but would have to give more for every purchase they made. Consequently at the year's end they would find themselves not wealthier for high prices, and would have to bear all the expense of the government machinery of protection.

Now, manufacturers cannot dispose of their goods in the home market. They are obliged to sell to the foreigner and deliver at his own door full as cheap as the foreign manufacturer can offer them. It is clearly impossible, therefore, that they can realise 30 or 40 per cent. above the continental prices, like the farmer; and from so-called protection they can derive no benefit. Hence protection, being partial, is unjust. One remedy presents itself. Let the agricultural interest engage to take *all* the goods from the manufacturers at 30 or 40 per cent. above the foreign price,—the latter may then engage to take all the farming produce at the same premium.

It remains only to notice the Malthusian objection against

Free Trade, which tinctures more or less the tone of its modern opponents. "Of what use is it," say they, "to extend trade? You may increase the population, but you make the people neither wiser nor happier. Manufacturing towns are plague-spots—a pest to the kingdom, and a cause of general demoralization. Even if you succeed in raising wages, rendering employment more abundant, or adding to the means of subsistence, your mushroom population will assuredly multiply beyond your measures of support. Improvident marriages have ever characterised your factory people."

There is some truth in these remarks, mixed with mischievous error. For argument's sake, grant that it is unwise to increase the population,—it is at least benevolent to better the condition of those actually in existence; but all exertions would be in vain unless trade were opened, and a greater demand for labour created. Should every advance in wages, every addition to employment, and abundance of provisions, fail to improve the state of the people, and every attempt be counteracted by the still greater increase of population,—provident marriages must be inculcated by a careful system of general education. Some would attempt to throw the whole responsibility of this education upon employers. But surely the burden of finding food both for body and mind cannot fairly be thrown upon the same individuals. The latter is more peculiarly the province of the clergy, of the ministers of the various denominations of Christians,—or, of the Government; for what object is there so important to the well-being of the community at large?

There are comparatively few improvident marriages contracted amongst the middle classes. Young men of good education and correct principle see the folly of undertaking the responsibility of a wife and family until they have the means of maintaining both in some degree of comfort. True affection shrinks from the idea of placing a beloved object in a state of impending wretchedness, and rendering her life one continued scene of domestic drudgery or slavery.

It is by no means impossible to extend these notions to the

uneducated portion of society. A system of general education, combining with elementary instruction the inculcation of religious feeling and moral restraint, would do much towards effecting so desirable an object. Other societies are required for young men, when they leave the school-room, to form correct habits, give a healthy tone to the mind, and instil maxims of economy and prudence in after life.

But this discussion must be left to the more responsible agents of education.

CHAPTER VII.

SUMMARY OF PRECEDING ARGUMENTS—THE COMMERCIAL POLICY OF GREAT BRITAIN SHOULD BE TOTALLY INDEPENDENT OF THE CAPRICES OF OTHER NATIONS—FOUNDED ON A BASIS OF IMPARTIAL, UNPROTECTIVE, UNFETTERED SYSTEM OF FREE TRADE—CONCLUDING ADDRESS TO MANUFACTURERS.

In the preceding chapters I have endeavoured to show—

I. The utter hopelessness of obtaining reciprocal tariffs from other countries, and the dangerous delay of waiting for them.

II. The folly of placing our sole dependence upon the colonies.

III. That the aim of our commercial policy, viz., to force exports and exclude imports, is founded in error.

IV. The unwise prejudice against foreigners draining us of gold, and the false alarm of foreign rivals driving our manufactures out of our markets.

V. The unfavourable effect of customs upon commerce.

VI. The application of the reciprocity system to the home trade.

Having thus glanced at the current objections against Free Trade, which have been so often refuted by abler pens than mine, I would fain ask those men of business who differ from me in opinion upon the preceding topics, and who still maintain that we ought not to relax our restrictions without corresponding concessions from contracting powers, "How long shall we wait?" If a period could be named with certainty when their hopes might be realized, there would be some ground for patience. But, independently of the very questionable advantages of these treaties, the most sanguine begin to despair of seeing them carried into execution. We are indebted for the important advantages of the Chinese tariff, not to any diplomatic efforts in the old track of negotiating treaties, but simply to the force of our arms and the energetic determination of Sir Hugh Pottinger. Such an attempt to modify the tariffs of our belligerent neighbours might be attended with unpleasant consequences.

Public opinion is gradually paving the way for great changes in our commercial code. The unsatisfactory conclusion of our negotiations with Brazils, and our twice-raised and twice disappointed hopes respecting Portugal, have ripened the growing opposition to such vain diplomacy.* These treaties have been held out as baubles to amuse the people, and to stave off those measures of free trade which otherwise would, ere now, have been forced upon our Government. What have the most strenuous exertions of successive administrations done for us when directed to improving our foreign relations? So far as the shipping interest is concerned, mutual advantages have been secured, but beyond this their very efforts have apparently had the contrary result of inducing foreign powers to combine against British manufactures. Let the Government, then, cease its baffled attempts! Let Britain take a dignified, independent position! Let her freely admit the products of every quarter of the globe, perfectly regardless of hostile tariffs! To the enterprise of her own merchants and the self-interest of foreigners, she may safely confide the task of forcing her exports. This course will best contribute to the national wealth, and provide that which is a desideratum with all governments,—the sources of an ample revenue.

Manufacturers have been accused of selfishly retaining their own protection, whilst they leagued together for the

* Since these sheets were committed to the press, positive information has been received, that the negotiations with both these Powers are definitively broken off.

purpose of destroying that of the landowners;—they have been accused of introducing machinery, to the displacement of hand labour, and the great injury of the operative;—they have been charged with wanton cruelty in reducing wages to the point of starvation;—and furthermore, some of them bear the imputation of a desire to reduce wages still lower by agitating for a repeal of the corn laws.

First, as to the protection given to manufacturers, they utterly repudiate it! Any protection upon goods which are exported, and which, with the disadvantage of a heavy duty, undersell the foreign manufacturer in his own market, is inoperative. Reduction of wages is beyond the control of the employer; when trade is brisk, it is an impossibility; and when depressed, it is a choice whether he shall keep up wages and be driven out of the market by competitors, or pay the current rate, so as to enable him to sell at a market price, and continue employment to his work-people. That machinery has not the effect of displacing hand labour, but the contrary result of increasing the demand for labour and improving the condition of the operative, has been already proved: in those districts where machinery is most extensively used, *there* the population has most rapidly increased, and the average wages are the highest. As to a reduction of wages by the repeal of the corn laws, it is a self-contradiction. The object aimed at is a steady importation of foreign corn, which must of necessity be followed by a steady demand for our manufactures, in payment; a greater demand for labour will be the consequence, and if so, higher wages. The condition of the operative will be doubly benefited by a low, steady price of flour, and by a steady employment coupled with high wages; whilst the farmer will derive an indirect advantage in the improved means of his customer. Home produce will find a ready market, and increased consumption will take off both home and foreign produce.

In conclusion, I would respectfully beg leave to address a word to my brother manufacturers upon our present position and prospects. We have just passed through a long, gloomy period of commercial distress. Like a hurricane at sea, it hath left many sad wrecks; some vessels have foundered, and will be no more heard of; others have sunk in shoal water, and may possibly be raised again; even those who sailed in deep water under experienced captains, and foreseeing the coming storm, took in their spare canvass, have been forced to to lay to, sustaining many casualties, whilst they have made no way. The gale has at length blown over, and once more we have fine weather and a fair wind. There are already symptoms of putting out too much canvass. Let not our past experience be thrown away. Before any trade can be safely carried on to the extent which the necessities of this country require, our *imports* must be as unshackled, as unlimited, as our *exports*. The merchant may then venture boldly through the meshes of foreign tariffs, satisfied that his own Government will not rob him of his returns on the threshold of his own door. The very parties who accuse us of over-trading, tell us in the same breath that our foreign trade is taken from us by the foreign manufacturers! We shall have no fear of exporting too much, if we import to the same extent: no fear of selling too much, if we take care to get paid for what we sell. It is our own tariff which has brought on the hurricane, and it is our own tariff alone which is under our control. Let us give up the idea of moderating foreign tariffs,—a task beyond our control,—and directing our energies to that which is practicable, let us use every legitimate influence for the total abolition of protecting duties, and the reduction of all import duties to the lowest possible point. Let us earnestly endeavour to give a steady, permanent character to our commerce, by rendering it *free* in the fullest sense of the word,—*free* from the political changes of our own party administrations,—*free* from the vacillations produced by futile attempts at commercial negotiations,—*free* from parental bias to those spoiled children, our colonies,—*free to the whole world.*

THE CORN LAWS.

AN AUTHENTIC REPORT

OF THE LATE IMPORTANT DISCUSSIONS IN THE

Manchester Chamber of Commerce,

ON THE

DESTRUCTIVE EFFECTS OF THE CORN LAWS

UPON THE

TRADE AND MANUFACTURES OF THE COUNTRY.

WITH

NOTES AND PREFATORY REMARKS EXPLANATORY OF THE

CHARACTER AND POSITION OF SOME OF THE MEMBERS WHO WERE

PRESENT, OR TOOK A PART IN THE PROCEEDINGS.

LONDON:

RIDGWAYS, 169, PICCADILLY.

MDCCCXXXIX.

The meetings of the Manchester Chamber of Commerce in December 1838, following closely the successful campaign for the incorporation of Manchester,[1] served to stimulate the transformation of the Manchester Anti Corn Law Association into the National Anti-Corn Law League. According to Henry Ashworth

Agreeably to a requisition to a President of the Manchester Chamber of Commerce (Mr. George Wm. Wood, M.P. for Kendal), a general meeting of the members was held on the 13th December, 1838, to consider the effect of the law on the importation of Corn, and, if thought advisable, to petition Parliament for its repeal. At the meeting the President read a petition which he had drawn up, setting forth very fully the evils occasioned by the operation of the Corn Law; but during the discussion which followed, it became evident that he and some of the directors were divided in opinion, and that the President was more inclined to *modify* than to *repeal* the existing law, and the prayer of the petition which he had prepared was accordingly to that effect. It was the largest meeting of the Chamber which had ever assembled, and the discussion, after continuing for some hours, was adjourned to the following week (the 20th December), when the attendance was still more numerous, and comprised the most eminent manufactures and merchants of the district. During the interval, Mr. Cobden, Mr. J. B. Smith, and I, prepared another petition, praying for '*the Repeal of all Laws relating to the Importation of Foreign Corn and other Foreign Articles of Subsistence*,' which was submitted to the meeting for approval. The debate again extended over five hours, and the merits of the rival petitions were amply discussed. During the whole of this protracted sitting there was evidence of a deep and concentrated interest, amounting even to a feeling of solemnity. The amended form of petition was moved by Mr. Cobden, seconded by Mr. R. H. Greg, and carried by a majority of about six to one, and this was followed by the non-election of the President, and, at the next annual meeting of the Chamber, by the appointment of Mr. J. B. Smith to the office.[2]

Prentice, who had also been present, reported in the *Manchester Times* (22 December): 'The facts stated by the different speakers, coming as they did from some of the most intelligent of our merchants and manufacturers, appeared to make an impression on the chamber such as we have never before witnessed in any assembly, and we are confident that they cannot fail to produce a similar feeling throughout the whole manufacturing and commercial community of the Kingdom.'[3] In January 1839 the League was founded.

[1] See V. A. C. Gatrell, 'Incorporation and the pursuit of Liberal hegemony in Manchester 1790–1839', in Derek Fraser (ed.), *Municipal reform and the industrial city*, Leicester University Press, 1982, pp. 16–60.

[2] Henry Ashworth, *Recollections of Richard Cobden, M.P., and The Anti Corn Law League*, London: Cassell Petter & Galpin, [1876], pp. 20–1.

[3] Quoted by Prentice in his *History of the Anti Corn Law League* vol. 1, p. 88.

PREFACE.

WHILST entreating attention to the important facts disclosed in the accompanying revised report of the late proceedings at the Manchester Chamber of Commerce, the question may naturally be anticipated, "Why were not these alarming circumstances made public before?" The answer is, that nearly three years ago the Directors submitted to Government samples of British and Foreign manufactures, with the prices and qualities of each carefully described, proving, that in several articles, such as prints, ginghams, &c. our goods were superseded in neutral markets by the greater cheapness of the Saxon and Swiss manufactures. The reason why the Members were slow to proclaim at a public meeting of the Chamber their own adverse situation and gloomy prospects, and thus advertise to the world the cheaper markets of their rivals, may easily be understood. It is not an easy task to induce Englishmen to believe in the superiority of their foreign competitors; and still less so to persuade them in a body to make public confession of their own inferiority. The circumstance, that the members of the Manchester Chamber of Commerce consist generally of the more prosperous and intelligent class, and are therefore the last to suffer inconvenience from the rivalry of foreigners, operates also as an impediment against any premature or rash movement of that body.

In proportion as these circumstances account for the tardiness of the public demonstration of the Chamber, must they be admitted to augment the force of the present movement. Here is an assembly of men of every political party, comprising seven county magistrates, the mayor and eight aldermen of the borough of Manchester, and including in their number the most extensive manufacturers in the kingdom —one individual present giving employment to six thousand persons, and another with his brothers owning thirty steam engines, whilst six of the assembled capitalists could be enumerated, whose assessments to the poor-rate averaged 2,000*l.* each — here is a body of intelligent and experienced men, who make known to the world that their industry is decaying beneath the rivalry of foreign manufacturers, whilst they declare it to be their solemn conviction that "this is the commencement only of a state of things, which, unless arrested by a timely repeal of all protective duties upon the importation of corn and other foreign articles of subsistence, must eventually transfer our manufacturing industry to other and rival countries." This verdict solemnly and deliberately given by a body of men the most competent to decide the question, is now submitted to the tribunal of public justice, to await the judgment that will determine not alone the fate of our commerce, but the destiny of this powerful empire.

REPORT OF PROCEEDINGS,

DECEMBER 13, 1838.

In compliance with a requisition signed by nineteen of the Directors of the Manchester Chamber of Commerce and Manufactures, to George William Wood, Esq. M. P. President of the Chamber, a special general meeting of the Chamber, at which the attendance of all its members was specially requested, was held on Thursday the 13th of December, "to take into consideration the propriety of petitioning Parliament for the repeal of the existing Corn Laws." The meeting was very numerously attended, being the largest assemblage of its members since the extraordinary meeting held on the subject of an application from Liverpool for pecuniary assistance from Government.

Mr. George William Wood, M.P. President of the Chamber, was called to the chair, and, after reading the requisition and notice convening the meeting, he said he had been requested, as the president, to lay before the meeting, on behalf of the directors, the form of a petition which they had unanimously adopted, as one which in their opinion was suitable to be sent by the Chamber for presentation to parliament on this occasion. He had been further desired to explain the views which had actuated the directors in the preparation of that petition; and though any partisanship from that chair would be exceedingly improper, it might be allowable, perhaps desirable on this occasion, to open the subject on behalf of the directors, since no difference of opinion existed amongst them, and he should therefore have to state nothing but that in which they all concurred. It appeared to him that no time could be more propitious for the consideration of this question than the present, when the country had for some years enjoyed low prices, when the expectations and habits of the farmer were familiar with those low prices, and when rents had already accommodated themselves to this state of things. The chairman then entered at length into a consideration of the nature, operations, and effects of the corn laws of 1815 and 1828, with notices of the nugatory statute of 1822. He quoted passages from Mr. Canning's speeches, delivered in 1827, condemnatory of the previous law of 1815, and also referred to Mr. Grant's speech explanatory of the designs of the framers of the present law. Its avowed object was to secure stability of price; but to adopt a system which forced us to depend mainly upon the products of our own soil for the food of our people, was surely not the way to promote that stability. To give access to as many markets as were attainable, and of as varied a character as possible, appeared to him the most likely way to attain stability of price. This could only arise from the adoption of the principle of commercial freedom—by putting the trade in corn upon the same footing as that which regulated all the other great branches of our commerce, and under which they had long flourished. The farming capital of this country, by the great vicissitudes of price (occasioned by the act of 1815), succeeded by extreme low prices, twelve or fifteen years ago might be said to have been wholly annihilated, and it was not until lately that the farmers had recovered from that shock. Such a visitation upon any great interest could not but be productive of national mischief. On the other hand, the effect which must be produced by high prices on the condition of the working classes of the whole country was fearful to contemplate. Those who remembered the periods of scarcity thirty years ago, from successive seasons of lamentably bad harvests, the enormous prices to which wheat rose, and the sufferings which the people endured in consequence, must shrink from any thing that could tend to bring about a return to such a condition. But the effects of this kind of legislative interference were not confined to what happened at home. It produced a most injurious effect on our foreign relations. We could not expect foreign states to value or seek to cultivate a trade with us in corn, when the demand for it was so uncertain, and so liable to be stopped as suddenly as it arose. To set them an example for adoption, which was, in fact, prohibitive, if not in perpetuity, at least for a long period of time, was to encourage them to follow a similar course with respect to those manufactures, on the export of which so much of the prosperity of this country depends.—(Hear.) The merchants and manufacturers of this town were suffering at this moment from the German league; which was a system similar in kind, though not equal in degree, to that by which our importation of corn was governed. They sought to protect, by high duties, their home manufactures, in the way we seek to protect by high duties our growth of corn at home. The manufactures of the United States had their origin in similar restrictions. In consequence of our engaging in war with America, she was thrown upon her own resources; manufactures were established; they received legislative protection; then came high duties; and the manufacturing interest of America had reached the high pitch it had now attained, in consequence of the hostilities between the two countries. On one occasion a proposition was made by the president of the United States to abandon their system of prohibitive duties, and to adopt one of moderate duties (having reference only to finance, and not to the protection of manufactures), provided we would adopt a similar course with respect to grain. We refused, and adhered to our prohibition with respect to American flour; and America maintained her position with respect to our manufactures.—(Hear, hear.) It would not be just to conclude his observations, without a brief reference to the arguments used by the advocates for the present system of the corn laws. We were told by them, that it would be dangerous to trust to foreign countries for a supply of food. But to a certain degree we did so now; for it was universally admitted, that, taken in the long run, this country does not grow corn enough for the support of its inhabitants, and that in an unfavourable season we must have recourse to other countries to supply our deficiency. Surely we were less likely to be injured than now, by a system, which, instead of leading to an import of a million quarters of foreign corn in one week, should give us a steady, regular, and healthy trade in foreign corn, bringing it in gradually as consumption went on, and which should be to foreign states that kind of demand for their produce which could alone encourage them to value the trade, and provide for the supply. A regular trade in foreign corn would be a greater security against the danger of foreign commerce than the present system. If we were to adopt and carry out this principle of prohibition,—if there were to be no dependence of one state upon another for the supply of national wants,—if we should be driven to live upon our own resources in all things, international commerce could not exist, and one nation must ever be a stranger to another. By adopting the opposite system of free intercourse, we should indeed create a dependence, but that dependence was mutual; and he apprehended that it was according to the intention of a gracious Providence that this state of things should exist. So far from its leading to hostilities and war, it was the surest guarantee for peace. —(Hear, and cheers.) This dependence was not one-sided; for if we depend on other nations for corn, they had to depend on us for what, to them, was more valuable than corn. It was thus that international commerce fructified, not only in the country into which, but in that also from which, it flowed. It was said again, that the repeal of the corn law would be injurious to agriculture. He was one of the last men to wish to see a great national interest suffer, or to be less prosperous than any other interest in the country: but the assertion proved too much, if any thing; for, if the prosperity of agriculture had to depend upon such a state of things as he had described (including prohibition and all its consequences, as a high price of bread to our labouring poor), then he would say that a somewhat lower state of prosperity to agriculture would be a less evil than such a state of things flowing from its highest prosperity. But he did not believe, that a scale even of low prices, provided they were steady, could be injurious to the farmers of this country. (Hear.) What affected them was great vicissitude in price; and they would have a better assurance of being free from such casualties when corn was cheap, than when subjected to such vicissitudes as had prevailed during the period from 1815 to the present time. Exclusive taxation was another ground alleged by tne landed interest why protection should exist. On that subject it was satisfactory to know, that, during the last few years, much had been done for the relief of the land from its exclusive burthens. [The honourable chairman adverted to the new poor law, as a great relief and permanent advantage to the landed interest; to the permanent commutation of tithes act, converting tithe into a fixed land-tax, and exempting from this tax all future capital expended upon the land; and to the transference of a considerable portion of the county rates to the national expenditure.] On these grounds, therefore, though some things remained which might be considered as pressing upon the land, the landed interest had received a great relief, from the sense of justice entertained by the country and by parliament; and this ground of the argument for high prices, therefore, could not be urged with justice to any thing like the extent it might have been some years ago. With respect to its operation, he knew not whether the sentiment he was about to express would be concurred in by all who heard him; but he did think, that in whatever degree it could be satisfactorily shown that the land had been subject to exclusive taxation, from which the other interests of the country were exempt, and that those other interests had no other exclusive taxation to countervail those charges — to that extent, as an additional charge upon the growth of corn at home, that interest might fairly be considered entitled to protection to the amount of that charge.—(Hear.) That, he thought, was all they could ask; it was all, he was sure, which the country ought to allow them. He had thus endeavoured to explain his views on this important question, and he believed he had spoken in accordance with the views of his fellow-directors. He would conclude by presenting the draft of the petition which had been prepared by the directors in the manner he had described. — (Applause.)

Mr. Samuel Fletcher (a county magistrate), in moving the first resolution, said, he did not approach the subject as a question at all bearing upon party politics, nor with the design of placing in invidious contrast the agricultural and trading interests of the country, for the purpose of advancing the one at the expense of the other. He considered them so closely identified that they must rise and fall together, and on this ground he questioned the policy of any partial legislation. If they required protection, let it apply equally to the commerce and the agriculture of this country. He questioned, however, if the interests of both, and of the country, would not be best advanced by leaving them to take care of themselves, freed from all legislative interference.—(Hear.) It was considered on all hands, that the principle of the corn laws was so bad, that they had failed to afford the farmer the protection he sought from them, while they had placed the importer of foreign corn in a position exposed to all the temptations and hazards of gambling speculation. The idea of rendering our country independent of others for a supply of food, was nothing more or less than a new edition of the old fable of the belly and the members. He disliked the term *independence*, whether applied to individuals, countries, or nations; for it had pleased God to make us all dependent upon each other. A mechanic might determine to be independent of his tailor; but whatever might be thought of his determination, we should think but little of his wisdom, in such an employment of his labour and time. The dangers attendant upon the repeal of those laws, he thought, had been very much exaggerated. Some persons had said to him, "If you repeal the corn laws, rents must fall; the circulating medium will be reduced; government will not be able to collect the taxes; the mortgagee will not be able to get his interest, and you will paralyse the whole nation." But the value of the land in this country was not to be measured by any protection supposed to be derived from the corn laws, but by the wealth of the country. In a wealthy country like this, land could never be at very low prices; for the wealth obtained by commerce would seek to invest itself in land, and thus keep up the level. He regretted that the consideration of this national question had been deferred from time to time by the legislature, till, at length, want seemed coming upon us with the power of an armed man. He moved, "That a petition be presented to the house of commons, at the commencement of the ensuing session, for the repeal of the existing corn laws."

Mr. JOHN MACVICAR (an East India and China merchant), fully coinciding in the opinions expressed by the president, and by the mover of the resolution, had great pleasure in seconding it. The resolution was put from the chair, and passed unanimously.

The CHAIRMAN then read the draft of the petition, as follows:—

"*To the Honourable the Commons of Great Britain and Ireland in Parliament assembled.*

"The Petition of the President, Vice-President, Directors, and Members of the Chamber of Commerce and Manufactures of Manchester, agreed to in a Special General Meeting, held on the 13th day of December, 1838.

"Humbly showeth,—

"That your Petitioners feel it their duty to call on your Honourable House to bestow its early attention on the present position of the corn trade.

"Wheat has again risen to a high price, and much apprehension exists of its becoming still dearer.

"The existing corn law has not proved satisfactory to the people. Its provisions will now be scanned with a jealous and scrutinizing spirit, and the principles on which those provisions rest will have to undergo the further consideration of parliament.

"From the period when the country was happily restored to the blessings of peace, it has been a leading object of national policy to break down monopolies, to remove restrictions, and to promote a free interchange of commodities with other states, in the well-founded belief that the national prosperity would thus be placed on its most stable footing.

"The corn trade has been made a striking exception to this wise policy, and has been trammelled with restrictions. Your Petitioners are not aware of any satisfactory reason why this trade should be regulated on principles so different from those applied to other branches of commerce. They believe the exception to be unnecessary, and consider it to be permanently and most extensively injurious.

"To prohibit the importation of foreign corn in a country not permanently growing enough for its own wants, which was the object of the corn law of 1815, or to subject its import to heavy taxation, which was the intention of the law of 1828, must produce the natural consequence of all monopolies, and materially augment the average price of bread; although the injurious effects may, in particular seasons, be more or less counteracted by harvests of unusual abundance.

"A cheap supply of human food is one of the main sources of a people's welfare.

"To interfere with this cheapness is to place a barrier to the gradual acquirement of those comforts of life, by the industrious poor, on which their own social and moral condition, and the nation's true dignity and strength, so much depend.

"Steadiness of price, in the cost of human food, is another important element of public welfare.

"Great changes in the price of corn, such as have occurred since the passing of the law of 1815, are pregnant with evil: rapid and large reductions of price destroy the farmer's capital, and bring ruin on the dealer. An opposite extreme grievously impairs the needful comforts of many in the middle classes of life, and brings to the poor a complicated mass of helpless and lasting suffering—their furniture disappears—clothing cannot be replaced—their food becomes coarser and more scanty—debts accumulate—and penury and wretchedness ensue.

"The best security for a cheap and steady price of corn will be found in ready access to many and varied sources of supply.

"The attempt to limit that supply to the produce of our own soil must produce much needless fluctuation, and will bring upon us at intervals, when our harvests fail, what, in the emphatic phrase of an eminent statesman, would be '*a famine price*.'

"To seek to overcome the evil tendencies of a bad system by the complicated frame-work of heavy graduated duties, fluctuating inversely with every change of price (as attempted in the law of 1828), must prove unsuccessful, inasmuch as the endeavour is not within man's agency to accomplish.

"Beyond the injury done to the immediate well-being of the people by the existing corn-law system, other evils exist of a different character.

"The friendship of foreign powers is alienated by a refusal to receive their produce; they will not value, and are little likely to provide for, an uncertain and capricious demand, disappearing as suddenly as it springs up; restriction on our part, leads to restrictive laws on theirs; rival manufactures arise, and protecting duties are imposed to foster them. Capital becomes extensively invested; the evil gets beyond the reach of remedy; and jealousy and prohibition occupy the place of international confidence, and of natural and healthy commercial intercourse.

"But the mischief is not confined to the countries where our evil policy first plants it. Those who start as competitors at their own homes become rivals in foreign markets.

"Twenty years and more of European peace has given an impulse to peaceful arts among the continental states, which has been diligently improved.

"Our former pre-eminence in the universal cheapness of our manufactures is already passing away, and though old recollections and national pride may make men loth to give ear to accounts of such changes, they have been long forcing themselves on the notice of those who directly experience their effects.

"If, from mistaken notions of an unassailable supremacy, we are indifferent about the price of human food, and require our manufacturers to eat dear bread, whilst our foreign competitors procure theirs at a cheaper rate, our industrious population will unavoidably be driven back in the scale of civilization, to a level with those whom they have hitherto excelled in physical comforts, and we shall speedily undermine the foundations on which both our agricultural and manufacturing industry repose.

"Another evil of the present system is the diseased state into which it necessarily throws the trade in foreign corn. Long intervals of inaction are followed by fits of great excitement; speculation and gambling are its dominant characteristics; and fortunes are won and lost as averages rise or fall.

"It remains to notice the two chief arguments urged in favour of the system.

"1st, The danger of foreign dependence for a supply of food is dwelt upon.

"There is a security against this in the ordinary workings of self-interest. Sellers profit along with buyers, and have an interest not less strong to prevent any rupture of the connection.

"Tendencies to war are checked, and war itself is prevented, by those friendly relations of mutual dependence which grow up between nations bound to each other by the ties of a regular and profitable commerce.

"There is another security in the number and variety of countries where corn can be bought. If one channel of supply should be closed by accident or misfortune, many more will remain; and it is not for the nation which boasts of being mistress of the seas, to distrust her power to retain and protect her maritime commerce.

"This alleged danger of foreign dependence, however, be its amount what it may, exists at present; and it would be diminished, not increased, by the introduction of a more regular system.

"2dly, The necessity of securing, by prohibitory duties, a remunerating price to the growers of corn, is also dwelt upon.

"An uniform standard of remuneration could not be established, inasmuch as it must be dependent on the quality and situation of land, and on the capital and skill employed in its culture, with which the legislature cannot deal. Whatever was done would be arbitrary in its operation, favouring some, falling short of the fair expectations of others, and fluctuating with the changing opinions of the times.

"The claim of the farmer to remunerating protection is not stronger than that of the manufacturer, and they should be placed on a similar footing.

"Your Petitioners address your Honourable House on this subject in no spirit of partisanship. They do not desire the exclusive advantage of a class, but the equal good of all; they wish to see 'the trade in corn conducted as far as possible on the principles of other trades, in a sober regular course, and not by perpetual jerks and impulses arising out of extraordinary emergencies; to see it flow in a regular equable current, supplying the real wants of the country without overwhelming it."

"Your Petitioners hope, that your Honourable House will take measures in accordance with these sentiments, and with the opinions they have ventured to offer to your notice.

"And will ever pray, &c."

Mr. William Neild (calico printer, of the firm of Thos. Hoyle and Sons), moved, "That the petition now read be adopted by this meeting, and be signed by the chairman, on its behalf." If, as had been said, agriculture and commerce were twin-brothers, he did think that the former regarded himself rather too much as heir-at-law. He had never been jostled about by that fair competition to which his brother had been subjected, and which had spread our commerce to every part of the habitable globe, and increased the prosperity even of the agricultural interest, far beyond what it ever could have acquired without the assistance of the commercial energies which had been brought to bear upon it. Within seventeen or eighteen years, printed calico was reduced 75 per cent. in price, or from 100 per cent. to 25 per cent., from various causes, the most powerful of which was competition. Had the agricultural interest been fairly subjected to such competition? It was true that machines could be multiplied, and acres could not; but he was assured by celebrated agriculturists, that there were means of making the land vastly more productive, and there were cases in which, by proper management, the produce of the land had been doubled, and even trebled. As commercial men, we had great reason to complain of partial legislation for the agriculturists, and it was high time that the legislature gave to this question the consideration it deserved.

Mr. Richard Birley, vice-president of the chamber, seconded the resolution.

Mr. J. B. Smith (Mr. Smith is a retired merchant and a county magistrate), and Mr. J. C. Dyer rose; and the latter having given way,—

Mr. J. B. Smith said he felt called upon to add a remark or two at this stage of the proceedings on what had fallen from the president in his introductory address. He (Mr. Smith) had the honour to be a director of this Chamber as well as a member. Now he understood the president to say, that the petition which he had presented spoke the sentiments of the whole of the directors. He (Mr. Smith) begged to say the petition did not speak his sentiments. (Hear, hear.)—[The President said he certainly understood that Mr. Smith had agreed to the petition on the day before.]—He certainly did agree to what he then heard, but some passages had been since added. He believed it was in the prayer of the petition that passages had been added from which he could not but dissent. The inference to be drawn from that prayer was, that this Chamber approved of a protective corn law of some sort—an inference which he could never allow to be drawn from any document purporting to bear his sanction. (Hear, hear.) He did not hesitate to say, that he could not approve of any protective duty on corn, and that in his opinion the whole course of legislation on the subject had been from beginning to end one of the most scandalous instances of landowners legislating for their own benefit at the expense of the people, that was to be found in the history of legislation in any country of the world. (Hear, hear.) In the early history of corn law legislation — at the revolution of 1688, when the country grew more corn than could be consumed—the landowners passed an act giving a bounty of five shillings upon all corn exported to foreign countries; thus enabling the foreigner to obtain British wheat at a cheaper rate than the inhabitants of this country themselves could purchase it at. From 1740 to 1750 no less a sum than 1,515,000*l.* was paid* in this way out of the pockets of the English people in the shape of bounty, for the exclusive benefit of the corn law legislators; and when it was recollected that the bounty system continued not for those ten only but for one hundred and twenty years, he would leave the meeting to form an estimate of the amount that must have been taken out of the pockets of the people during that period for the benefit of the landowners. (Hear, hear.) Mr. Smith proceeded to trace the history of prohibitory duties on corn from 1773 to the passing of the prohibitory laws of 1815. — By the law of 1773 the bounty duties were relinquished and protective ones substituted. By that law the importation of wheat was prohibited up to 48*s.* when it was admitted at 6*d.* per quarter duty. This was the most favourable corn law we ever had. From that time our population and manufactures began rapidly to increase, and enabled us to consume our corn at home; prosperity smiled upon the country, prices rose, and the agriculturists in 1791, taking advantage of that prosperity, passed another law by which the duty was raised from 6d. to 24s. 3d. per quarter. In 1804, prices having risen in consequence of the war, they passed another law, by which the duty of 24s. 3d. per quarter was imposed till the average price reached 63s. Then came the law of 1815, the year after the peace, when prices began to fall, for they had obtained during the war as much as 120s. a quarter. Then the landlords passed a law prohibiting foreign corn till the average reached 80s. per quarter. In those days our worthy president was an agitator (hear, hear), and he remembered hearing an excellent speech from him declaiming against the injustice of that iniquitous law. The excitement of that time had never been equalled within his memory. Crowds of people assembled and beset the houses of parliament, which had to be guarded by soldiers whilst the law was passed. That law might be said to have been passed at the point of the bayonet. He believed that it was the only instance in which a law was so carried in the British parliament, and he hoped it might be the last. (Hear, hear.) This law, however, was found not to answer the purpose of those for whom it was framed, and then came the Duke of Wellington's law of 1828, by which, instead of prohibiting corn till it was 80s., it was admitted on a graduated scale of duties. This law was given as a great boon, by which we were to have an importation of grain at all times. Corn was admitted when the average price reached 40s. at a duty of 46s. 8d.. What an insulting mockery. By the corn laws of 1773 we were allowed to import corn when the average price reached 48*s*. on payment of 6*d*. duty; by the boon of 1828 we might import it by paying 38*s*. 8*d*.! — (Hear, hear.) In fact, up to 60*s*. a quarter we still pay a duty of 26*s*. 8*d*., and it was not until the market price had attained to 70*s*. that it was admitted as low as 10*s*. 8*d*. duty, and 73*s*. that it was admitted at a duty of 1*s*. This was the landowner's boon, and he would appeal to the meeting if he was not justified when he said, that the British parliament, had, under the forms of constitutional law, adopted a system of legislation in reference to corn which no despot had ever dared to attempt. (Hear, hear.) Now it was important to see the effects of this law upon our commerce. The effects of excluding foreign corn had been to induce foreign nations to impose heavy duties upon our manufactures. We had disregarded their remonstrances against our unjust exclusion of their produce in exchange for ours, and we might now turn to look at the effect of our selfish policy. In 1820 we exported to Russia 13,203,857 yards of cotton cloth; in 1837 our exports to that country were reduced to 847,022 yards only. (Hear, hear.) In 1820 we exported to Prussia 5,442,535 yards of cloth; now we exported not a yard. (Loud cries of hear.) To Germany in 1820, we exported 47,658,285 yards; in 1837 our exports to that country had fallen off to 38,581,533 yards. The effect of our prohibitory system had been that, notwithstanding the great increase in the population of Europe since the peace, our exports to Europe had actually fallen off, and were less by 20 per cent. in the last five years than during the first five years of peace. Our exports to Northern Europe, by far the most populous, civilized, and wealthy portion of the globe, were less by 7,400,000*l.* in the five years since 1832, than during the first five years after the war. Nor was this all; a more fearful state of things had arisen: those countries had become manufacturers themselves, and we, instead of being manufacturers of cotton goods for them, had become merely the spinners of their yarn, while our poor weavers were reduced by it to a state of wretchedness and suffering, which admitted of no hope. To show the truth of this last statement, he would call attention to our exports of cotton twist. In 1820 we exported to Russia 8,762,347 lbs., while last year the quantity exported amounted to 23,910,019 lbs. To Germany and Prussia in 1820, we exported 11,682,683 lbs.; last year 36,109,100 lbs. To the United Netherlands in 1820 we exported 232,474 lbs. of cotton twist, while last year our exports of that article had risen to 17,457,232 lbs. (Hear, hear.) These were our exports to Northern Europe, and our trade was not oaly going to destruction there, but we were fast losing our ground in Southern Europe, where a similar policy was being adopted to that pursued in the north, and we should find, that while in 1820 we exported no twist to France, in 1837 the exports amounted to 354,025 lbs. In the same manner our exports had increased during the same period to Gibraltar from 61,182 to 280,114 lbs.; to Malta and the Ionian Islands from 108,464 to 371,760 lbs.; to Italy from 1,291,261 to 9,118,938 lbs.; to Turkey from 542,093 to 4,047,871 lbs. Total exports to South Europe in 1820, 2,003,000 lbs.; last year, 14,172,708 lbs. (Hear, hear.) But the exportation of raw materials was not confined to cotton alone; labour was so much cheaper on the continent, that true as the needle to the pole, manufacturers were finding their way to the cheap food. In 1820 our exports of woollen yarn was only 3,924 lbs., in 1836 it was 2,546,177 lbs. (Hear.) The same process was going on with respect to linen yarn, and on examining the exports it would be found, that while in 1820 we exported not a pound, our exports in 1836 were 4,574,504 lbs. The total export of cotton yarn in the same period had increased from 23,032,525 to 105,106,529 lbs.; and we found now that warps were sent abroad sized and dressed ready to be put into the loom; thus affording every facility for the most unskilful workman to weave them into pieces. Mr. Bazley had just mentioned to him that even cops were sent out in casks ready to put on the shuttle. The effect of this upon our labourers was to deprive them of half their work — We exported more cotton yarn than would be sufficient to manufacture all the cotton goods we exported to all parts of the world; and if instead of exporting yarn we exported it made up into goods, which we should do but for the corn laws, there would be employment for double the number of hand-loom, and double the number of power-loom weavers employed in this way at present. This was a most important consideration, and sufficiently accounted for the deplorable condition of our poor weavers. (Loud cries of "Hear, hear.") But our exportation of cotton yarn was only on sufferance; the spinning of our rivals was rapidly increasing. On looking at the consumption of cotton in foreign countries he found, that while in 1808 the United States consumed only 100 bales of the raw material, in 1836 she had converted into manufactures no less than 237,000 bales. (Hear.) France, in 1832, consumed only 262,719 bales, whilst in 1836 her consumption amounted to 353,005 bales; and there were no less than sixty cotton mills in course of erection. In Austria also a rapid increase was taking place in cotton manufactures, and in 1837 she had 650,000 spindles at work, and 100,000 more in preparation. Similar progress was making in Bohemia, the Tyrol, Lombardy, Naples, and Salerno. Now, after these statements, it would not be surprising to find that the same results were taking place in our trade in other commodities as in our cotton trade. (Hear.) He had recently been to Birmingham, Wolverhampton, Leicester, and Derby, where he had picked up some facts relative to the staples of those towns which it might be useful to mention. The export of hardwares and cutlery from this country in 1824 was 12,285 tons, and in 1830, 16,275 tons, being an increase of 33 per cent.; while, what was most important, was, that in the same period, the exportation of bar iron, pig iron, and castings, had increased from 34,591 to 106,467 tons, being an increase of 300 per cent. The Sheffield people complained that there was no increase in their export trade; but look at the increase of raw materials; in 1820 the export of unwrought steel was 326 tons; in 1834 it was 1,709 tons, an increase of 550 per cent. With these vast exports of raw iron and unwrought steel, added to the export of coals, the foreign manufacturers were enabled to make articles at a cheaper rate than in this country; and it was important to notice the great increase in the export of coals coincident with the increase in that of raw iron and unwrought steel. In 1820, the export of coals was 158,672 tons; in 1835, 546,338 tons. By these means the foreigner was enabled to make and export cutlery at a less price than ourselves. He (Mr. Smith) thought by such facts as these he should be able to convince the Chamber that foreign competition was not as had been represented—all a farce; and that it would be their duty to take a much higher ground than had been taken in the prayer of the petition before the Chamber. (Hear, hear.) He had received a letter from a gentleman at Wolverhampton who wished to have been present at this meeting, but was prevented by unavoidable business, containing some important statements regarding the trade of that town, from which it appeared, that in relation to the German manufactures, a great number of articles which were formerly made in Wolverhampton, such as scythes, sickles, coffee-mills, pepper-mills, common knives, hinges, common locks and bolts, which were formerly exported to Germany, could now be purchased so much cheaper in Germany, that the merchants of Wolverhampton purchased in that market instead of manufacturing themselves, for re-exportation to foreign countries. (Hear, hear.) A merchant of Birmingham said, that for years past they had been constantly losing the sale of some article or other which they had formerly supplied to foreign markets—that in Constantinople they were cut out of the hardware market by the Russians, while in Portugal and Spain the wares of Germany and France were supplanting those of England; and what was more extraordinary, that the wares of those countries were imported to supply our own markets. Even the article of *Brummagem* buttons, which one would think were cheap enough, were imported from France, and after paying a duty were sold for less in the London market than they could be made for in Birmingham; while the article of gilded toys, which formerly gave employment to numbers of persons, had ceased to be manufactured in Birmingham, and were imported from France. At Leicester, one of the largest manufacturers had told him, that he had bought a quantity of foreign worsted hosiery at lower prices than he could make it, and that the quantity of woollen yarns now exported was sufficient to give employment to 10,000 stocking makers all the year round. This of itself was sufficient to account for the distress felt in the hosiery trade. In Derby similar statements were made to him, and the furniture trade was suffering from the importation of foreign rosewood aud mahogany goods, which were imported and offered for sale by public auction. A gentleman in Manchester indeed had corroborated this statement, and said that he knew houses where such articles were regularly sold in Manchester. America was exporting machinery to Russia, and a gentleman in Birmingham said he had a relation in Russia who had engaged himself to an American company who were establishing cotton weaving and spinning manufactories there, the machinery for which was supplied by the United States. (Hear, hear.) Another article which we were losing the supply of was cotton hosiery; for not only was Saxony manufacturing as large a quantity as ourselves, but while we exported only 430,000 dozen pair, they exported 1,500,000 dozen pair per annum. The Saxons supplied as much cotton hosiery to the United States alone as we did to all the world. He held in his hand a beautiful specimen of their manufacture of white cotton gloves, which cost only 3*s.* 6*d.* per dozen at Hamburgh. He held in his hand also another specimen of gloves of foreign manufacture, and one of similar quality of the manufacture of this country, but while the price of the English goods was 6*s.* per dozen, those of the Saxon manufacture were purchased at Hamburgh for 3*s.* 2*d.* per dozen. He had before him another specimen of beautiful stockings of Saxon manufacture, which at Hamburgh sold for 12*s.* 4½*d.* per dozen, while the stockings of the same quality of English manufacture which he held in his hand, could not be had for less at Nottingham than 23*s.* per dozen. It was a lamentable fact, that Saxon hosiery and gloves were now regularly imported and sold in this country at lower prices than they can be made here, and will undoubtedly shortly entirely destroy this large branch of our manufactures. (Loud cries of hear, hear.) Now he would put it to any gentleman whether foreign competition was a farce, after the statement of facts such as these. (Hear, hear.) Could there be a doubt of the pernicious effects of laws which enabled the Saxons thus to undersell us in the manufactured article, the raw material for which they purchased in the same market as ourselves (Cheers); and when it was recollected that the yarn was spun in England, taken there for the purpose of being converted into goods, which were brought back again after a land carriage of nearly 700 miles, and sold at the low rates he had already quoted? He could not but think, that after statements like these, the meeting would agree with him it was the duty of this Chamber to speak in a more decided tone to the legislature (Hear, hear). In speaking to Mr. Porter, to whom he was indebted for many of his statements, and whose book he would recommend every man to read, that gentleman said—" the more he looked into the subject of our present policy the less he dared to think of it—its consequences were so fearful." (Loud cries of "Hear, hear.") Our population was increasing, while the means of employment and of subsistence were decreasing—could any one think of the consequences without seeing the perilous situation in which we were placed? (Hear, hear.) It was true, as the Chairman had already stated, that the landowner's monopoly had been the cause of all this; and we had the best evidence that our corn laws had been the means of establishing manufactures in America. The British minister at Washington, Mr. Addington, in reference to the tariff, wrote to Mr. Canning as follows:—" I have only to add, that had no restrictions on the importation of foreign corn existed in Great Britain, the tariff would never have passed through either House of Congress, since the agricultural states, and especially Pennsylvania, would have been opposed to its enactment." The Prussian ambassador had in the same way frequently remonstrated against the exclusion of their corn and timber; but had our ministers ever had the courage to mention this, when complaints were made in Parliament of the Prussian-German league? This was the time for the Chamber to speak out upon this question. If our ministers did not know our wants, and did not know how to legislate for them, they were unfit to govern this great commercial country—(hear, hear,)—and if on the other hand they were aware of those wants, and knowing the justice of them, lacked the courage to bring forward measures of relief, then they were undeserving of our support. (Cheers.) Nothing was more unsatisfactory to him (Mr. Smith) than the late interview of Mr. Poulett Thomson with the directors of the Chamber of Commerce. He happened to be present at that interview, and he could not but notice the invariable reply which Mr. Thomson gave to every question of monopoly brought under his notice—"It is a very important, but it is a very difficult question." (Hear and laughter, and applause.) True, it was difficult to reconcile monopoly with free trade, and the same difficulty would exist to the end of time. (Laughter.) But had not Mr. Huskisson greater difficulties to contend with, when he first broached the principles of free trade? What a mass of ignorance, interest, and prejudice was arrayed against him. No wonder that at that time people were startled at the sweeping changes about to be introduced into the protective policy which had existed for ages; but far different was the case now, we had had thirteen years' experience of the effects of free trade; and when we looked at the benefits which free trade had conferred upon the country, we ought to demand the extension of it to every branch of our agriculture, manufactures, and commerce. (Cheers.) Perhaps he might be allowed to speak here of a few of its results. In 1819, to appease the clamour of the English agriculturists, a duty of 6d. per lb. was laid upon foreign wool. They said that wool had fallen in consequence of the large importation of foreign wool, and the object of the duty was to raise the price of the English wool. Fortunately (not for them but society) it failed in its object. It succeeded, however, in ruining the manufacturers of Yorkshire, but so far from the price rising, it fell to a lower figure than it had been known for 200 years before. In 1825 Mr. Huskisson was the first man to propose a reduction of the duty from 6*d*. to a 1*d*. upon wools above 1*s*. per pound, and to ½*d*. upon all below it. The result was, that while in 1820, when the protective duty was in force, our imports were only 9,000,000 pounds, in 1835, ten years after the reduction of the duty, they had risen to 42,000,000 pounds; and the price of British wool rose to double the price it fetched during the monopoly. (Loud cries of "hear.") He would appeal to his friend Mr. Tootal, if the benefits derived by the silk trade from a similar policy were not equally satisfactory, the duty on raw silk being reduced from 4*s*. in 1824 to 1*d*; and the duty on thrown silk being reduced from 14*s*. 8*d*. to 3*s*. 6*d*. The result was an increase of imports from 2,399,000 pounds to 5,315,000 pounds, thus giving employment to double the number of people previously engaged in this manufacture. Another measure of Mr. Huskisson's was the reduction of the duty upon coffee from 1*s*. to 6*d*., by which the consumption rose from 8,000,000 pounds in 1825 to 22,000,000 in 1830. Now ought there to be a difficulty as to the line of policy we should pursue, after results like these? (Hear, hear.) Another important question with us was the protection of monopolies by discriminative duties. They would all be aware, for instance, that the duty on foreign sugar was 63*s.* per cwt., while the duty on British colonial sugar was only 24*s.*; that on foreign coffee 15*d.*, while on British it was only 6*d.*; and on foreign timber 55*s.* per load, while the duty on Canada timber was only 10*s.* Now we have a treaty with Brazil, which would expire in 1841, and the Brazilians complained very loudly (as the Prussians had done), that we would not take their sugar and coffee; and they say, "If you don't take our produce, we won't take your manufactures." And that was a very reasonble proposition. Was it surprising they should complain when they saw our ships enter their ports laden with our manufactures, and return empty? (Hear, hear.) And what was all this for? Why, to protect the West India interest! He did not understand the difficulties to which Mr. Thomson had alluded when down here; but he had a suspicion, and the matter was now explained by seeing the papers this morning, where he had read the answer of the Board of Trade to a petition from merchants interested in the coffee trade, proposing that the duty on colonial coffee should be reduced from 6*d.* to 3½*d.*, and on foreign coffee from 15*d.* to 7*d.*, a measure which the Board says it cannot recommend.

Mr. Birley thought this was not the question before the meeting.

A Member. I think many gentlemen will be of opinion with me, that the facts Mr. Smith has been stating bear materially on the question before us, and it would be desirable to hear them.

Mr. Smith believed the meaning of Mr. Thomson's difficulty was, that they meant to stick by the monopoly system. He had little doubt, however, "the difficulty" would by-and-by be settled by the Brazilians in the same way as the Prussian league had been settled, and that our unjust exclusion of Brazilian sugar and coffee would be retaliated by their prohibition of our manufactures. (Loud cries of "hear, hear.") He would not, after these interruptions, further occupy the attention of the meeting; he believed he had said sufficient to show that our corn law legislation had been one of most scandalous injustice, and he thought they should so state in their petition, with the addition, that while we sought for abolition of the corn laws, we were not so unjust as to ask for protection on manufactures. (Applause.)

MR. HENRY TOOTAL (extensive silk-manufacturer, of the firm of H. and E. Tootal) said, that the prayer, and some other sentences of the petition, had been added since the day before; but the spirit and substance of those sentences had been stated by the president before he left the chair, and it was formally put to the directors, whether that statement was in accordance with their views, and whether the sentiments then expressed, and to be embodied in the addition, also met their concurrence. Those sentiments, in his (Mr. Tootal's) opinion, were embodied, as they were represented by the president. (Hear, hear.) Mr. Smith had given his unqualified assent to the petition, and stated that it met his concurrence, except as to one thing omitted, without which he said he thought it was incomplete.

Mr. J. B. SMITH explained, that what had been added since, was what he disapproved of.

forward some facts on the subject, but would now abstain from doing so at any length, seeing that gentlemen had already done it so much more ably. He could have wished to see a strong demand for the absolute repeal of the corn laws, on the simple ground of justice, embodied in the petition. Nothing could be plainer than that principle of eternal justice—that every man had a right to exchange his labour for food, without restriction of any kind; and he wished to see this fundamental view of the question powerfully urged. There were strong interests opposed to this, for the landowners knew the present systemto be necessary for the support of their high rents. They asked only what it was monstrous injustice to refuse, that they might be allowed to take cheap food for their cheap manufactures. It was no way surprising that the central and richest portion of Europe should cease to take our manufactures, seeing how pertinaciously we had refused to take their produce in return. The outlets of the Rhine and the Elbe ought to send us their corn, cattle, and other commodities, as well as wine and other luxuries. The Chamber had been long and interestingly employed in discussing this subject, and he could not help urging that it was a question too important to be handled with nice delicacy, through fear of shocking the nerves of our rulers. It was a question of national vitality, for it was evident that our manufactures could not flourish, unless we took food freely in exchange for them. We were fettered not merely by a corn law — we must remember that we had also, beef, pork, mutton, and fish laws, all tending to burden manufactures and keep up rents. He would have them always to keep in mind the injustice of this monopoly, and to demand and be content with nothing short of its absolute repeal. Nothing but universal agitation would effect their object, and it was strange that Manchester, and the country at large, should have remained so long asleep on the verge of such awful danger, as that with which we were threatened from the corn laws. Though painful, it was necessary they should look the subject fairly in the face. He had observed the thoughtful looks of members, while Mr. Smith was detailing his alarming array of facts, illustrating the falling off in our exports. Still he knew, from sources of information on which he could rely, that no power in Europe could yet compete with England, if she had only a fair chance. But what could we do under our present heavy burdens? We ought to struggle to retain that superiority which we possessed, and to demand most strenuously those concessions from government, which were necessary to the salvation of the country. In reference to the prohibition of the import of beef, pork, &c. alluded to above, it was worthy of remark, that in the preamble of the bill enacting it, Huskisson's customs' consolidation bill, it was actually stated to be for the encouragement of trade! (Hear, and laughter.) Could any thing more atrocious in legislation be conceived? It rested with the British people to send representatives to parliament, who would legislate on principles better calculated to promote the true interests of the country. They had not hitherto done so, and the more was the shame. We had some trade with the South of France, because we took their wines, and with Italy, because we took her silk. With the United States we had an extensive trade, because it supplied us with cotton. We were also allowed to take trunks of trees, and, in fact, any thing from Canada and elsewhere which we could not eat. But our trade, it was evident, could not but be very limited, where our imports were confined to luxuries and raw material. There was no raw material so important as beef and bread. Let food be received from abroad, and then full employment will be obtained; and when the essential wants of the working classes shall have been supplied, he would not grudge the rich their luxuries, but first of all let them provide for the ample feeding of the people. It was said that our island could produce corn enough for the whole of its population. Perhaps it might yield as much as would keep the people in existence, but to be only half fed was to be but half alive, and he would repeat, that an ample supply of food ought to be provided. (Hear.) It was giving the people food that would most effectually restrain vice. He felt that he ought to apologize for these generalities. It was by going into details that the subject was best elucidated and enforced, and there were many gentlemen present who could make their knowledge bear upon it. Our trade with Northern and Central Europe and the United States, would have been at present double what it is, had we all along taken food from these countries in exchange for our manufactured goods. He did not think it was yet too late to recover our ground, provided that a universal and energetic demand should now be made for our relief. Perhaps it was not expedient for him to make any further remark, but he would suggest, that the Chamber might make its influence more effectually felt in this matter, were it to take the lead in calling a public meeting for the discussion of the subject. If there were any arguments to be brought against the abolition which they advocated, he thought a very small amount of knowledge and of talent would be sufficient to confute them, and to induce a large majority of the people to enter zealously into their views. A petition emanating from a public meeting would have more force. He lamented the tardiness of the steps taken by that Board for the repeal of the corn laws, but he rejoiced to see the feeling which now existed on that subject, and he hoped they would not relax their efforts till their object was accomplished. He thought if it were put to any plain man who went to a baker's shop for bread, whether he would have two or three loaves for his 2*s.*, he would only laugh at the folly of the question; and the absurdity of doubting in regard to the policy of the corn laws was equally glaring. If they asked the manufacturer whether he would have a glut of unsaleable goods in his warehouse, with his people only in half work, or have a brisk demand and his people fully employed, they might easily guess the answer. If they wished manufactures to prosper, they must take every means to obtain a repeal of the monopoly of food. It was lamentable to think that they should be obliged at that time of day to send lecturers throughout the country to enlighten the people on a subject which bore so deeply on their interests. In reference to the gloomy anticipations as to the results of foreign competition, he would again say, that if the question were now to be taken up as it ought to be, the danger might yet be avoided; and he did wish to see the petition express the opinion, that it was opposed to the eternal principles of justice, to continue a monopoly in the trade of corn and other articles of subsistence.

Mr. COBDEN (of the firm of R. Cobden and Co., calico printers, employing one thousand hands; author of pamphlets, "*Russia*" and "*England, Ireland, and America*, by a Manchester manufacturer") said, that it appeared to him, whilst listening to the petition just read, that the Chamber had gone back from the opinions expressed in the petition of last year upon this important subject—an opinion that he confessed had been much strengthened by the remarks that fell from the chair. (Hear, hear.) The Chamber had last year advocated an absolute freedom of trade.—[Mr. C. read from a printed copy of a petition that had been sent from the Board last year, a passage praying that the trade in corn and in all other commodities might be freed from all *protective* duties, leaving only such taxes as might be deemed necessary for *revenue;* and that every obstacle to the free operations of capital and labour, might, as far as possible, be gradually repealed.] It did appear to him, that if at a time like the present, when considerable interest, and indeed excitement, existed upon the subject, the Chamber should send a petition less decided in its tone and character than last year, a very unfavourable and unjust opinion would be formed of the zeal and intelligence of that Board. (Hear, hear.) With these views he hoped the petition might undergo some alterations. Indeed, looking to the mass of valuable facts just given to them by Mr. Smith, and which, he was sure, had made a strong impression on the minds of all present, as well as to the clear and forcible arguments of Mr. Dyer, coupled with the fact that had been elicited of some discrepancy in the minds of the directors;—looking to these circumstances, together with the fact of the evident haste with which the petition had been drawn up, he could not help recommending, that an adjournment of this meeting for a week, in order to afford time for the preparation of another petition, would be advisable. (Cheers.) The ground taken up last year, that of demanding a total repeal of all protective duties upon corn, and at the same time of deprecating all protection upon foreign manufactures, was the only one consistent with justice or safety to ourselves. Look at the different operation of protective duties upon manufactures and the products of land. He would suppose that in his own article of prints, by means of a prohibitive law, the profits could be raised a thousand-fold their present rate. How long would it be before such an amount of capital flowed into the trade, as, by competing with the present owners of printing machines, and print works, would reduce the profits to the same level as other trades? (Hear.) In a country such as this, where a boundless extent of capital was yielding only three or four per cent., it was folly to suppose that by artificial means, any trade could long be made to pay more than an average rate of profit. The effect of all such restrictions could only be to narrow the field of industry, and thus in the end to injure instead of benefiting the parties intended to be protected. But look at the very opposite position in which the owners of land stood. He would suppose that a law could be passed to raise the price of wheat to a thousand shillings a bushel. Now what would be the effect of this, but that the capitalists who now get their ten per cent. profit in London or Manchester, would immediately send their sons to bid fifty per cent. over the farming tenants of Norfolk; and if these were still in the way of getting higher profits than other trades, then other competitors would again appear, to bid fifty per cent. over them, until Lord Leicester's farms had reached the full market price, and yielded only the ordinary rate of profit of all other trades. (Hear, hear.) But mark the difference in the situation of the landowner and the calico printer. Whilst additional mills and print works might be erected to meet the demand for, and share the profits upon calicoes and prints, not one acre of land could be added to the present domains of the aristocracy. Therefore every shilling of protection on corn must pass into the pockets of the landowner without at all benefiting the tenant or the agricultural labourer: whereas on the other hand no extent of protection could possibly benefit the manufacturer. He felt ashamed to make observations so trite to the intelligent body around him. They were quite unnecessary, because they knew very well the laws which governed the rate of profit upon capital according to the field of operation. Yet they constantly heard in the House of Commons, the Marquis of Chandos and others urging the policy of high duties for the protection of tenants and agricultural labourers! The landlords had been living upon the capital of the farmers nearly ever since the peace; and when he heard them talking of benefiting their tenants by protective duties, he thought of the saying of Voltaire with reference to the monks of his day—"that he wondered they did not laugh in each other's faces from under their hoods when they met in the streets;" he wondered the landlords did not burst into laughter when passing the corn law, under pretence of benefiting the tenants and labourers. (Hear, hear.) A good deal had been said by Mr. Smith, and by the worthy president, upon the subject of the past history of the corn laws. He thought they had very little cause to rail at the aristocracy, on account of their protective laws, previous to 1825, for the legislature had given about as much protection to the trades as they desired—silk, lace, and gloves were all virtually prohibited. The landlords did not even allow themselves to export their wool, and even if found within a certain distance from the sea shore, it was liable to seizure. But in 1825, Mr. Huskisson introduced the principle of Free Trade, and declared that the cabinet of Lord Liverpool would not sanction any duty for the purpose of protection, beyond thirty per cent. Mr. Huskisson distinctly avowed, that, if that protection was not sufficient, the trade ought not to be pampered with a higher rate of duty. When, in 1827, the same cabinet was forced, reluctantly, to take up the subject of corn, and were urged, by Mr. Whitmore and others, to apply the same principle to that, which they had applied to manufactures, Mr. Canning, in the name of the ministry, was driven to the admission, that if the trade in corn was to be legislated upon at all, it ought to be regulated upon the same principle as other commodities. But when they brought forward their Corn Bill, the ministers were found to have abandoned their own principle altogether, and instead of an *ad valorem* duty of only thirty per cent., they imposed a graduated scale of duties, fluctuating according to the prices in the home market, and which has been equal to an *ad valorem* duty of one hundred per cent., upon an average, ever since. He quite differed from the opinion expressed by the worthy president, that the corn law of 1827-8, under which the country now suffered, was a relaxation of the one which was passed in 1815. On the contrary, he was prepared to show that the law of 1827-8, is an aggravation of that of 1815; in fact, it never was intended to be a relaxation, but was passed with a full knowledge that it was a severer law than the previous one. To understand this subject clearly, it was necessary to refer to the very different state of the currency in 1815 and 1828; at which latter period, it had undergone an appreciation of about twenty-five per cent. That this point was very well understood by the confederates — he might call them conspirators — who passed the present law, was very evident to all who read the proceedings in parliament of that time. Indeed, the alteration in the currency was urged by the Chancellor of the Exchequer, Mr. Robinson (who let the cat out of the bag when hard pressed by Sir E. Knatchbull and the fanatics of the agricultural party for a complete monopoly) as a reason for passing the bill; and Sir F. Burdett, who was in favour of the high duty on corn, consoled his party by telling them, that whilst the currency law remained in force, they would not be worse off by the change. An appeal to the duties at the two periods, fully justifies this opinion. In 1815, corn was admissible duty free at 80*s.*; and by the law of 1828, it is admitted at a shilling duty, when the price in the home market reaches 73*s.* Taking into account the change that had taken place in the currency, by which the sum of 80*s.* in 1815, had been made equivalent to 60*s.* in 1828, the landlords actually raised the monopoly some fifteen per cent. higher by the change. In further proof of his position, he referred the meeting to Mr. Porter's excellent work, "The Progress of the Nation"—a book that all ought to possess—in which it was clearly shown, that in the years subsequent to the law of 1828, the people of this country had consumed a less number of pints of foreign corn per head, taking into account the increase of population, than they had done previous to that change. He joined with Mr. Smith, in expressing indignation at such scandalous robbery, in the name of legislation; and he thought it became the duty of the Chamber of Commerce to declare energetically, that it knew and felt the extent of the injustice inflicted upon the trading community. Agreeing with Mr. Dyer, that it was useful to submit to the meeting such facts as came under one's personal observation, he would add, that he had made the tour of Germany lately, and had given some attention to the progress of manufactures in those countries through which he had passed; and without going again over the statistics of Mr. Smith, further than to corroborate generally what he had stated, he would refer to a branch of industry that was making great progress, and which had struck him as one of the most ominous signs he had witnessed. He alluded to the great increase in the manufacture of machinery abroad, under the auspices of English mechanics. Previous to the time of passing the corn law in 1828, the manufacturers and spinners of this country, anxious to share the monopoly of the landholders in some shape, pressed for a prohibition of the exportation of machinery, and it was granted. The artizan, who had been previously interdicted from emigrating, now demanded a law to enable him to carry his labour to the best market, and this of course was granted. And here we see the invariable effects of trying to make selfishness harmonize with the public good. The artizan left this country to teach the foreign spinner how to organize his mill, and was then sent home to reap the effects in a restricted market for his industry. But now the demand arises for the makers of machinery, and the same process was going on to instruct the foreigner in making spinning frames, that was formerly done in spinning cotton. Whilst at Dresden he was shown over a large machine-making establishment, by an Englishman, who took him into a large room filled with machinery for spinning flax, with Gore and Wesley's patent improvements—this, said he, was brought out from England, at an expense of 35,000 dollars, for models, and I am engaged to superintend the copying it. At Chemnitz, also in Saxony, he visited also a large establishment organized and conducted by English mechanics for the manufacture of machinery. And it happened, that on the very day he was there, the place was decorated with evergreens and laurel branches, for the purpose of doing honour to the King and Queen of Saxony, who paid a visit to the premises. He found at Prague, in Bohemia, an establishment belonging to an Englishman, for making machinery for manufactures. And at Vienna there were two of our countrymen accommodated under an imperial roof, carrying on a similar trade. At Elberfield and Aix-la-Chapelle, he also found large machine-making businesses carried on by Englishmen. At Liege there is a similar concern, the largest in the world, belonging to Mr. Cockerell, who was born at Haslingden, in this county, and who employs nearly four thousand hands. And at Zurich, he found the large establishment of Mr. Esher, with an Englishman at the head of the foundry, and another at the head of the forge, casting five tons of iron a-day brought from England, into spindles, rollers, and wheels, for the spinners and manufacturers of Austria, Saxony, or Bavaria. In almost every large town there were English mechanics instructing the natives to rival us. Now he contended, that every one of those artizans was expatriated from their native country by act of the British parliament. They carried their labour abroad, because our corn law will not allow them to exchange the results of their industry for the corn and food of other countries. He quitted the continent at Antwerp for England, and he would tell them what were his feelings after walking through the deserted Exchange of that once famous emporium, and looking at its almost deserted harbours, in which by the way he observed American, not English vessels, which had been the bearers of the coffee and sugar of Cuba. Whilst looking at these evidences of departed greatness, and reflecting upon the cause of the decay of Antwerp, of the atrocities of the Spanish general Alva, who banished the skilful weaver and the capitalist of Belgium to foreign countries, he felt a conviction, which he still was sorry to entertain, that the rulers of this country were pursuing precisely the same policy as the Spanish governor in Belgium; or Louis XIV, by the revocation of his edict of Nantes—that our aristocracy was playing over again the same part in a different character—and unless prevented by the efforts of the suffering people, it would end as in Belgium, in the ruin of the empire. (Loud cheers.) After entreating his hearers not to suffer themselves to be deluded by any other plan which the aristocracy might with a view to lead them upon a wrong scent propose to do, whether by war or diplomacy, to benefit trade; but exhorting them to keep a steady eye upon the corn law, which was the real and only obstacle to an increase of their trade, he concluded by proposing, if it met the views of the company, to offer a resolution, without at all meaning any disrespect to the directors, that the Chamber should meet again next week, to pass a petition, praying for the total repeal of all protective duties whatever. (Cheers.)

Mr. Edmund Ashworth (brother of Mr. H. Ashworth, and carrying on extensive spinning establishments, under the firm of H. and E. Ashworth), in seconding Mr. Cobden's amendment, said, he thought that even though they should require another meeting of the Chamber, if their time should then be as profitably employed as it had been on that occasion, few would regret the necessity of their coming again together. The petition seemed to read as if there were some tampering with the question, and he thought it should be worded with more decision. On that account he seconded the amendment that the meeting should be adjourned, and that a committee should be appointed to draw up a petition which would more fully embody the sentiments of the Chamber. And he did not think that by pursuing this course the least disrespect would be shown to the directors, because there had been matters brought to view since they met, which were calculated to affect the expression of their opinion on the subject before them. Mr. Fletcher had said he approved of the petition because it was moderate in its tone. He (Mr. Ashworth) opposed it on account of its want of energy. If that Chamber were really intelligent, ought it not to speak fully out? If their sentiments were strong they ought to express them strongly. At present the country was governed by the landed interest, and there were merchants ignorant enough to be led away by the sophistry put forth as to the paramount value of our home market to the manufacturer. Only a fifth of the cotton fabrics produced were consumed at home, and of the twenty millions of cotton goods annually exported, more of it was in the shape of yarn than would yield five millions sterling to our workmen, supposing it to be woven into cloth. He hoped the meeting would see the reasonableness of adjourning, in order that a more stringent petition might be prepared.

Mr. Cobden said, that, only the day before, he had received a call from the most extensive agent in Leipsic for the sale of all articles of Saxon and Bohemian product; and he (Mr. Cobden) had given him introductions to the American houses, for the purpose of his transacting business with them in the sale of his products. He would venture to predict, that, in five years, the agents of Saxon houses would be established in Liverpool and Manchester for the sale of their products in these markets.

Mr. Samuel Fletcher thought, that, by adjourning the meeting, the Chamber would lose much time; and, concurring with Mr. Smith and Mr. Dyer, he thought all they aimed at was sufficiently embodied in the prayer of the petition.

Mr. J. C. Dyer said, that the substance of last year's petition might be embodied in this; without which, he thought the present one feeble and ineffective.

Mr. Wm. Gibb (wine and spirit merchant), said, the directors, doubtless, wished to draw up a petition satisfactory to every party, and to ask for something which they might get; and he thought it better to go for half a loaf, than to ask for a whole one and get nothing. (Disapprobation.)

Mr. Wm. Rawson thought that any thing short of the total abolition of the corn laws would not save us five years.

The Chairman regretted that he had so inadequately expressed his own intention and the wishes of the directors, as to lead to the petition being so much misunderstood. Its prayer was, that the existing corn laws be repealed; not one word was said of either protective or prohibitive duties on corn.

Mr. COBDEN said, that if the petition was so framed in its wording as to be misinterpreted by himself and various other gentlemen present, that was some proof that it was not sufficiently strong, precise, and clear.

Mr. J. C. DYER thought its length gave it feebleness and indecision.

Mr. H. TOOTAL, avowing himself a zealous advocate for free trade, and as desirous for the repeal of the corn laws as Mr. Smith, expressed a wish that the petition might be adopted.

Mr. HENRY ASHWORTH (a cotton spinner and a county magistrate), said, he thought every attention and delicacy had been manifested towards the directors; but he questioned whether, if they pressed for any further expression of sentiment, they would find the meeting so much in their favour as they expected. He strongly urged the postponement of the meeting.

Mr. GEORGE SANDARS (a corn merchant), expressed his total dissent from the amendment. He believed the directors, with one or two solitary exceptions, did not wish for the total and immediate repeal of the corn laws, and he thought it impolitic to aim at that.

Mr. SAML. STOCKS (cotton spinner and bleacher), should be glad to have a committee appointed to act with the directors, in drawing up a petition to be laid before an adjourned meeting.

Mr. WM. NEILD urged the importance of unanimity, and thought all that was wished might be expressed in the petition before the meeting without adjournment; but he would submit to the directors, whether it was well to press the subject forward, after the opinion expressed by different parties present.

Mr. Richd. Roberts (cotton merchant, chairman of the bank of Manchester), thought, great advantage would be secured by the opportunity of consideration afforded by a week's adjournment; and he wished to impress the sentiment, that the manufacturers were not taking a one-sided view of the question, but were endeavouring to secure the best interests of the whole country. He should support the amendment.

Mr. John Spencer (manufacturer) thought a week's delay would enable the Chamber to embody the principle of last year's petition to the fullest extent in its present petition.

Mr. M'Clure (wholesale dealer), came with the full intention of opposing the motion for a repeal of the corn laws, expecting that it would be unqualified, and, therefore, under existing circumstances, an injustice to one portion of the community; but he should support the petition because it was moderate.

Mr. Fletcher and Mr. J. C. Dyer again spoke; and the Chairman said, that, before putting the question, it was right clearly to ascertain the views of the gentleman who moved the amendment. If he rightly understood its purport, it was to this effect,—that the corn laws be abolished: that no duty whatever should afterwards exist upon corn; and that all duties existing upon any manufactures should at the same time be entirely repealed.

Mr. Cobden. All protective duties.

The Chairman. What I am in doubt about is,

whether Mr. Cobden wishes that the removal of the protective duty on grain should be gradual or instantaneous.

Mr. Cobden. I should not deem it necessary to express any opinion upon that point; and none was expressed in the former petition.

The Chairman said, though he could not, as an individual member, consider the request for a delay as unreasonable, he thought that to adopt it in the form of an amendment, coupling it with instructions and conditions, would embarrass the course of the Chamber; and he thought it better, therefore, to come to a decision at once upon these two views, rather than adjourn upon instructions, evidently upon diversified views.

Mr. Rupert Ingleby (copper merchant), suggested, in the event of adjournment, that the petition should be printed, and a copy sent to every member of the chamber.

After some further discussion, Mr. J. C. Dyer suggested that both motions should be withdrawn.

The Chairman said, he had offered that suggestion to Mr. Cobden in private, and that the Chamber should adjourn, having passed the first resolution (that it would petition), but Mr. Cobden had declined to accede to it.

Mr. Cobden said, personally he had no objection; but he was in the hands of the meeting.

Mr. James Fernley (cotton spinner and manufacturer), hoped both motions would be withdrawn, and the meeting be adjourned.

Mr. Cobden would consent to that, if the petition were identical with that of last year. He subsequently consented to withdraw his motion; to which Mr. Ash worth, the seconder, also consented. — Mr. WILLIAM NEILD, as the mover of the original resolution, consented to withdraw it: and the meeting, having given its consent to the withdrawal of both motions, passed a resolution, on the motion of Mr. RICHARD ROBERTS, "that the meeting be adjourned to this day week [next Thursday], at the same place and hour."—On the motion of Mr. ROBERTS, seconded by Mr. J.C. DYER, thanks were voted to Mr. G. W. WOOD, for his able and impartial conduct in the chair. The proceedings then closed, a few minutes before four o'clock, the Chamber having been assembled about five hours.

REPORT OF PROCEEDINGS,

DECEMBER 20, 1838.

THE special general meeting of the Manchester Chamber of Commerce and Manufactures, adjourned from Thursday week, the 13th inst. was resumed on Thursday last; and so great was the interest excited in the town and neighbourhood, by the discussion of the former day, that, in the interval, we are informed, ten or twelve gentlemen became members of the Chamber. The attendance on Thursday last was even more numerous than at the former meeting, and we should consider it the largest meeting of the Chamber for the last eight years.

On the motion of Mr. GEORGE SANDARS, seconded by Mr.* Alderman MACVICAR, GEORGE WM. WOOD, Esq. M.P. president of the Chamber, was again called to the chair. He stated the circumstances under which the meeting was originally convened and adjourned, and said that the directors had felt it their

* In the interval between the two meetings, the municipal elections for the recently incorporated borough of Manchester took place.

duty to meet as early as possible after the previous Thursday, to consider the course which they had adopted anterior to that meeting, and the observations made in the course of the discussion at that meeting; and they had desired him to state, that, finding that objections were made to the concluding paragraph in particular of the form of petition, as laid before that meeting, and that objections were also taken to the prayer of the petition, as being somewhat informal, they had considered that matter, and had desired him to report that they wished to substitute for the two concluding paragraphs of that petition, the one which he would now read. — [We give the two cancelled paragraphs first, followed by that proposed to be substituted.]

(Cancelled Paragraphs.)

"Your Petitioners address your Honourable House on this subject in no spirit of partizanship. They do not desire the exclusive advantage of a class, but the equal good of all; they wish to see 'the trade in corn conducted, as far as possible, on the principles of other trades, in a sober regular course, and not by perpetual jerks and impulses arising out of extraordinary emergencies, to see it flow in a regular equable current, supplying the real wants of the country without overwhelming it.'

"Your Petitioners hope, that your Honourable House will take measures in accordance with these sentiments, and with the opinions they have ventured to offer to your notice.

"And will ever pray, &c.

(Substituted Paragraph.)

"Your Petitioners address your Honourable House on this subject in no spirit of partizanship. They do not desire the exclusive advantage of a class, but the equal good of all. They desire not to retain for themselves any protection which they protest against allowing to others; but are anxious to see every department of our national industry left to rest on its own resources and native energy. Considering therefore, as upon the strongest grounds they do, that the operation of the corn laws is disastrously injurious to all their fellow-countrymen, who earn their daily bread by their daily labour; — that it is sapping the foundations of our national prosperity, by the unjust advantage it confers on the rival manufactures of other countries; — that it is thus vitally opposed to the prosperity of our commerce and manufactures; — and considering, moreover, that our agricultural prosperity is closely connected with those two branches of national strength, and must flourish as they flourish, and fall as they decay, — your Petitioners earnestly conjure your Honourable House that the existing corn laws may be repealed."

The matter was now before the Chamber, to be dealt with as should be thought most expedient, and likely to promote the success of the great object under consideration. The directors had no desire or idea of dictating to the general meeting what ought to be the form in which they should express their sentiments; but they did consider it their duty to be prepared with some form of petition which they considered suitable to the occasion. It was for the Chamber to deal with their suggestion and recommendation, as it merited; and they wished the Chamber to consider that they acknowledged, in this Meeting, the most unlimited power to act independently of any thing they had suggested; not doubting that an assemblage so intelligent, respectable, and enterprising, would do that

cheapest rate, and which is the most accessible to us, in exchange for the export of our manufactures. The landlords, to whom the benefit of the monopoly was secured, had a certain number of persons dependent on, and *fed* by them, and these were neutral in the question; these persons cared not whether food were dear or cheap, but all *our* domestics, and the parties employed by us, were interested in our prosperity. If we fell, they fell with us; therefore it was the "lords of the soil," who like vampires lived upon the blood of the nation, and were solely interested in keeping up the monopoly. The universal people were interested on the other side. The acts of legislation upon this subject, were specimens of extreme ignorance and selfishness, eminently disgraceful to the legislature that passed them; and, as an individual, he would not consent to shrink from the expression of the indignation which he felt, in consequence of the mischief thereby inflicted upon the country. It was said that we ought to offer a boon in return for the granting of this great and essential right,—that we must concede the repeal of protective duties on manufactures. He would say, that the first duty of all legislatures was to provide for the supply, from the best markets, of cheap and ample food for the whole people. This we should demand as a principle of justice, and not of compromise. If our manufactures could stand competition, having all protecting duties repealed, he should be rejoiced to see them so placed, and he thought legislation ought so to be directed as to come ultimately to that condition; but he did not think it right for us to mix up the two questions. Whenever any imposts upon manufactures operated injuriously or to the disadvantage of any class of men, even of the landlord class, then he should be glad at once to see them relieved from such impost. That we were now in a condition to remove all protective duties from manufactures was not true. He was happy to say that it was so with respect to the great manufactures of this town and district; but there were other branches of manufactures in other parts of the country, for the removal of all protection from which it would be cruel for us to pray. Take, for example, that large class of manufacturing industry employed upon the material of leather, as coach and harness makers, saddlers, boot and shoe makers, in which trades there were a great number employed, especially in the rural districts. The landlord had secured a heavy duty upon foreign green hides, and a heavy duty upon foreign bark, both for his own protection; and it was therefore necessary that there should be a duty upon manufactured leather, so long as the duties securing the landlords' monopoly price for the raw material are continued. We could judge for ourselves; but we had no business to go all over the country, and say that every protective duty on every manufacture ought to be removed, in order to obtain the removal of the injurious monopoly in corn. He must protest against the principle of giving any thing for the removal of this crying injustice, and contend that we ought to demand its removal as a simple unqualified *right*. If we did not make this demand in language not to be misunderstood, we might seek in vain to obtain our object; we should have a demand for a high duty set up, and this would be acceded to by many of those ordinarily called "liberals," and "friends of the people," one of the most eminent of whom had actually proposed a duty of 10*s.* a quarter, *gradually* to be reduced; which, in fact, was to submit to robbery to the extent of 25,000,000*l.* a year, for the estimated consumption of corn in this country was 50,000,000 of quarters. Were we to begin by taking off a small fragment of the mischief, and wait ten years for its total removal, while in the mean time our people might die of starvation? To concede any thing in the way of a duty on corn was to compromise a principle, which, he thought, would be no credit to a community so deeply interested in having simple, plain, and unqualified justice — the right to exchange the produce of their industry for cheap food, wherever it could be got. He had some objection even to adopt the phrase of a late eloquent statesman (Mr. Canning) — one of the most expert makers of good jokes and bad laws that ever disgraced this country — he would however take his phrase "antagonist principle," and say, that that principle should not be as Canning put it in parliament, "absolute prohibition on the one hand, and overwhelming supply on the other," the latter being an absurdity, but it should be put to the whole people as cheap and abundant food on the one hand, and scanty and dear food on the other; scanty, because we are prevented obtaining it from any other than British growth; and dear, for the purpose of keeping up the landlords' rents. It was said, that this was not a political party question. He hoped it was not such now; but when he looked back at the majorities in the House of Commons repeatedly recorded in favour of this monopoly, he saw they were chiefly Tory majorities. He was willing, in courtesy, to admit that the great majority of landowners being Tories, might account for this, and that it might be, as it undoubtedly is, a landlords' question. And certainly very large landlords of the Whig party seemed mysteriously to come about, and ally themselves to the Tories, when any question was raised about cheap food for the people. But he hoped and prayed, that this was no longer to be made a party question by any set of men. Let it be a British question—a question of humanity, of justice, and one of which it is dangerous to delay the decision—dangerous to submit quietly (nor would the country submit quietly) to its perpetuation. He would move, as a rider to the petition, the following amendment: —

"That your Petitioners submit, that the acts of 1815 and 1822, relating to the importation of corn, and more especially the existing law, of 1828, passed with a full knowledge of the pernicious effects of the former acts, are instances of ignorant and selfish legislation, which stamp with indelible disgrace the parliaments that passed them; and the continuance of this law, fraught as it is with cruel injustice to the industrious consumers, is inconsistent with the duty which all governments owe to the people, of keeping open to them the best and cheapest markets for an abundant supply of food; and this law is alike opposed to the principles of humanity, and to the peace and welfare of the country."

He had not conferred with any gentleman on the subject, or asked any one to second his motion.

Mr. J. B. Smith having seconded the motion, for the sake of discussion, without pledging himself to the course he might take thereafter,

Mr. Alderman COBDEN said, in the course he took he had no personal feelings to gratify; on the contrary, his respect for the directors and their president would have inclined him to concur if possible in their recommendation. He could not, however, view this as a personal question; but one of paramount and vital importance to the community around us and to the country at large. He would confess that he felt disappointed that the directors had not come forward with a new petition; it was with that expectation that he had withdrawn his amendment of last Thursday. And it would be in the recollection of those who had attended on the former occasion, that the speakers who advocated an adjournment, did so with an express desire that the petition to be prepared for this day should contain some of those important facts that had been brought in a condensed form before the Chamber by Mr. Smith and others. (Hear, hear.)

Mr. Alderman TOOTAL here interposed on the part of the directors, and reminded Mr. Cobden, that Mr. Smith had on the last meeting expressed himself willing to accept the petition, with the addition of the prayer now added.

Mr. Alderman COBDEN continued: Much as he respected Mr. Smith, and greatly as he felt himself indebted to him for his labours in the important subject in hand, he could not defer to his opinion on such a point. He reiterated his disappointment that the directors had not incorporated some of those facts, without which the arguments in the petition would have no more weight, however ingeniously urged, than a thesis drawn up by some tyro in political economy at a university. (Hear, hear.) The reasoning was that which had been given by Adam Smith, and every other political economist since his time; but that reasoning would have no weight in the quarter to which this petition was to apply. The facts brought forward by Mr. Smith, as to the progress of manufactures abroad, and those relating to the progress of mechanical establishments abroad, should be referred to; and if any gentleman present doubted those facts, and doubted the proofs of them in the hosiery produced to the Chamber, that was an excellent reason why the Chamber should again adjourn; for those facts should either be ascertained or disproved, and, if ascertained, then forced upon the attention of government and the legislature with all the authority which this Chamber could give to them. There was another question which had been glanced at, and which was very much misunderstood, which ought to be referred to,—he meant the great commercial league in Germany, upon which our national prejudices and pugnacity had been very much invoked, but upon which those who had the guidance of public opinion had studiously avoided the truth. That great league, so far as regarded its own people, was a benign measure; it was calculated to unite the German family in one bond by the establishment of a common tariff, and ultimately one common standard of weights and measures, and one system of money. (Hear, hear.) It was a union formed for the first time in the annals of the world, without a political bond. (Hear.) It was not an alliance of princes for their own purposes of aggrandizement, involving the disputes of legitimacy—not a mere parchment treaty of diplomatists, that might be torn in pieces any moment, as thousands had been before—but a bond of union, a commercial confederacy, a partnership entered into between the German people, for the purpose of facilitating their trade; allowing travellers to pass the frontiers into every country from Belgium to Russia, from the Tyrol to the Baltic, without let or hindrance, without being stopped at barriers in the shape of custom-houses, in the interior, as was formerly the case, three or four times a day. But we were told by those who guide public opinion, that the German league was formed as a hostile measure towards England, forsooth; that the Prussian cabinet had no other object in it than to annoy and harass us. It was thus that our bristles were set up, and we were sent abroad with our nationality misdirected, to fight against Russians, Prussians, or against any people or principle in the world, so that it only diverted us from the real cause of all our mischiefs—the landlords' corn laws. (Applause.) That German league had for its object the settling of one uniform tariff for the whole country, but that was not to be fixed for a perpetuity. Every three years a congress of the leagued states met together, and arranged the commercial terms of that tariff for the next three years. When travelling lately within the pale of that league, he had made it his business to inquire minutely into its operation; he procured semi-official introductions, with a view of ascertaining the truth; and it was his firm conviction, from what he heard every individual say with whom he conversed, even including the Saxon manufacturer, throughout Prussia, Saxony, Wirtemburg, and Bavaria, that it was in our power at any time to effect a reduction in the duties upon our manufactures. All intelligent men concurred in saying—"Repeal your corn law, and we will remove the duty on your goods." He would give in his own words the saying of a person of great intelligence in Prussia, upon this subject, "If you will send us," said he, "a *commercial* agent, to represent a *commercial* people, and competent to agree to, take in exchange for your manufactures our products, we shall have no difficulty in arranging an extensive trade together; but whilst you send us an *agriculturist*, to represent an *agricultural* people, we cannot hope to deal with you, for we are agriculturists ourselves." (Hear, hear.) The extent to which that vast league was operating to our injury might be judged of, from the fact, that it comprised 26,000,000 of the most intelligent and the richest people of the continent, containing four monarchies with their capitals, and a score of minor independent sovereignties, each having a nucleus in its capital for the consumption of luxuries and articles of considerable cost in the fabrication; so that we must see the extent to which we were injured, and to what extent that league was calculated to foster the industry of a state like Saxony, whose manufactures now, instead of being confined to the consumption of two millions and a half of people, had the whole range of a country comprising twenty-six millions. This was a most important element in the competition we must now expect from Germany. Those who were now manufacturing in Berlin, Leipsic, or in any other part of the country, would have access to the whole of the markets of Germany. But the league not only stimulated them, but had security to give to them.

(Hear, hear.) Hence a feeling of confidence had sprung up; they had overrun the country with rail-roads, joint-stock banks were established; and this confidence was so great as even to sustain paper money. All those evidences of security and confidence were mainly the growth of that commercial league, and all that security and confidence would become elements in a powerful competition with ourselves, since we had hitherto, of all nations, alone possessed and enjoyed this confidence and security. The Dresden and Leipsic Rail-road Company had permission to issue 500,000 dollars in paper, one of which notes he held in his hand. These were absorbed and circulated immediately, payable as they were on demand, though (as one of the intelligent directors had told him), five years ago, not one dollar of those notes would have kept in circulation. (Hear.) Surely some reference should be made, in our petition, to the great progress making in internal improvements abroad—as ordinary roads, rail-roads, and those other improvements of which we had hitherto had the monopoly in Europe. We had this no longer; rail-roads were being constructed in almost every part of the continent, and Belgium was more completely intersected with rail-roads than any other country in the world. They were now constructing in Prussia a line of rail-road to run through the empire; in Saxony they had nearly finished one from Dresden to Leipsic, and that from Magdeburg to Leipsic was in a forward state; so that probably by the end of next year, we should be able to go by steam from Hull direct to Leipsic. This communication gave to the stocking manufacturer of Chemnitz an equality, at least, with our Nottingham manufacturers. Russia, and even Switzerland, were busily engaged in constructing rail-roads; and this ought to be referred to in the petition, as one reason why we could not afford to be left in our present adverse position in point of food. But one prominent object which we should have in view, should be to point out to the government of the country the impending evils which hang over the working classes in this densely populated country; and he did not hesitate to say, that nothing but invoking the alarms of government would have the slightest effect upon their measures. Surely it became us, who were situated in the centre of this multitude of labourers,—who might at any moment be thrown out of employment, and of the consequent means of subsistence,—to read the signs of the times before they could be seen in London, and to give warning in time. Why are these incendiaries agitating the district? Why do thousands and tens of thousands muster at torch-light meetings? Think you that men would leave their homes, their fire-sides, at this season, their tables, with something comfortable upon them? No; they go to these meetings because they are distressed and impoverished, and because surrounding you there is an immense mass of human poverty and suffering. It became, then, our duty, and no less our interest, to represent to the government the impending evils of such a state of things. We were in the midst of these dangers; this would be the theatre of the tragedy whenever it was acted in this country; and that tragedy must be enacted, if those corn laws were not repealed. Therefore were we bound to speak out our fears of the dangers that surround us, and therefore was it deeply our interest to do so.—(Hear.) Though of a sanguine temperament, he was not sanguine enough to think that any thing we could do or say would have the slightest chance to avail with those who had the power in their hands to legislate for their own exclusive interest, irresponsibly to the people at large. But unless an effort were made by us, commensurate with these impending evils, the responsibility would not be with those, who, living in London, or fox-hunting, or running abroad, would have no means of knowing the danger; but that responsibility would rest heavily upon ourselves. (Hear.) He had prepared a petition, which he would read, though he would not move its adoption. Mr. Dyer, if he pleased, might withdraw his amendment, and support this petition; but at all events he threw it before the meeting as a petition which (he spoke of the matter only) appeared to him more adapted to the exigencies of our condition than that prepared by the directors. In offering it to the meeting, he threw to the wind all personal considerations, and should despise the man who could not act from public motives for the general welfare, without the slightest regard to personal feeling. By the course which Mr. Dyer had taken, it would be seen there was no concert or collusion between them; and he (Mr. Cobden) would simply read the petition, and leave it in the hands of the Meeting, taking no part in the discussion upon its merits. Mr. Cobden then read the following petition:

"Humbly showeth,

"That your Petitioners deem it their imperative duty to call the immediate attention of your Honourable House to the consideration of the existing laws affecting the free importation of food.

"That your Petitioners would premise, that your Honourable House is already acquainted with the nature and extent of the cotton trade; combining, as it does, a larger amount of capital, with greater enterprize and skill, and giving more extension and better regulated employment than any other branch of manufacturing industry. This source of increasing population and wealth, which is now become essential to our well-being as a nation, owes no sort of allegiance to the soil of England; and if it has grown up with a rapidity unparalleled in the annals of trade, history affords us many examples to show how speedily it may, by misgovernment, be banished to other shores.

"That your Petitioners view, with great alarm, the rapid extension of foreign manufactures; and they have, in particular, to deplore the consequent diminution of a profitable trade with the continent of Europe; to which, notwithstanding the great increase in population since the termination of the war, the exports have actually been less in value during the last five years than they were during the first five years after the peace: and whilst the demand for all those articles in which the greatest amount of the labour of our artizans is comprised has been constantly diminishing, the exportation of the raw material has been as rapidly increasing.

"That several nations of the continent not only produce sufficient manufactures for their own consumption, but they successfully compete with us in neutral foreign markets. Amongst other instances that might be given to show the formidable growth of the cotton manufacture abroad, is that of the cotton hosiery of Saxony, of which, owing to its superior cheapness, nearly four times as much is exported as from this country; the Saxons exporting annually to the United States of America alone a quantity equal to the exports from England to all parts of the world; whilst the still more important fact remains to be adduced, that Saxon hose, manufactured from English yarn, after paying a duty of twenty per cent. are beginning to be introduced into this country, and sold for home consumption, at lower prices than they can be produced by our own manufacturers.

"That further proof of the rapid progress in manufacturing industry going on upon the continent, is afforded in the fact, that establishments for the making of all kinds of machinery for spinning and weaving cotton, flax, and wool, have lately been formed in nearly all the large towns of Europe, in which skilled English artizans are at the present moment diligently employed in teaching the native mechanics to make machines, copied from models of the newest inventions of this country; and not a week passes in which individuals of the same valuable class do not quit the workshops of Manchester, Leeds, and Birmingham, to enter upon similar engagements abroad.

"That the superiority we have hitherto possessed in our unrivalled roads and canals is no longer peculiar to this country. Rail-roads, to a great extent, and at a less cost than in England, are proceeding in all parts of Europe, and the United States of America; whilst from the want of profitable investment at home, capital is constantly seeking employment in foreign countries; and thus supplying the greatest deficiency under which our rivals previously laboured.

"That, whilst calling the attention of your Honourable House to facts calculated to excite the utmost alarm for the well-being of our manufacturing prosperity, your Petitioners cannot too earnestly make known that the evils are occasioned by our impolitic and unjust legislation, which, by preventing the British manufacturer from exchanging the produce of his labour for the corn of other countries, enables our foreign rivals to purchase their food at one-half the price at which it is sold in this market; and your Petitioners declare it to be their solemn conviction, that this is the commencement only of a state of things which, unless arrested by a timely repeal of all protective duties upon the importation of corn, and all foreign articles of subsistence, must eventually transfer our manufacturing industry into other and rival countries.

"That, deeply impressed with such apprehensions, your Petitioners cannot look with indifference upon nor conceal from your Honourable House the perilous condition of those surrounding multitudes, whose subsistence from day to day depends upon the prosperity of the cotton trade. Already the million have raised the cry for food. Reason, compassion, and sound policy demand that the excited passions be allayed, otherwise evil consequences may ensue. The continuance of the loyal attachment of the people to the established institutions of the country can never be permanently secured on any other grounds than those of universal justice. Holding one of those eternal principles to be the inalienable right of every man freely to exchange the results of his labour for the productions of other people, and maintaining the practice of protecting one part of the community at the expense of all other classes to be unsound and unjustifiable, your Petitioners earnestly implore your Honourable House to repeal all laws relating to the importation of foreign corn and other foreign articles of subsistence, and to carry out to the fullest extent, both as affects agriculture and manufactures, the true and peaceful principles of *free trade*, by removing all existing obstacles to the unrestricted employment of industry and capital.

"And your Petitioners, &c."

Alderman COBDEN continued — All that he should add with reference to the two petitions was, that he accepted the addition which had been made by the directors to their former petition as a full adoption of the principle of free trade in corn, for which he contended; but he wished it had been rather less ambiguously expressed. Whatever emanated from the Chamber now, would be regarded with interest, not only here but in London and elsewhere: and if they wished by their proceedings to influence the Cabinet, and particularly their Right Hon. Representative, the petition should be clear, energetic, and precise. He was bound to confess his dissatisfaction with Mr. Thomson upon this question. He must confess he thought he had attempted less for free trade whilst representing the free traders of this borough, than Mr. Huskisson had done whilst representative of the monopoly interests of the old borough of Liverpool. According as we decided, he would be influenced in his public conduct. He would perceive that whilst we asked for nothing but what was for the interest of the nation at large, he was bound to be the bona fide representative of our interests, and not bow himself before a landed aristocracy. (Cheers.) He was led to make these remarks partly from what he had learned whilst in Berlin upon the subject of the German tariff. He was there told that the Prussian Embassy in London had again and again told our Cabinet, that our corn law was the sole obstacle to the arrangement of a commercial treaty between the two countries. He would read an extract from a letter he had just received, from a gentleman at Berlin, whose intelligence and means of access to the first sources of information disposed him to place implicit confidence in his authority.—"I have spoken," says the writer, "to one or two leading men in the finance bureau, and the result of our conversation has been, that in their opinion, if we choose to alter our corn law in England, and to admit the corn of Prussia at a fixed duty, there can be no doubt that Prussia would reduce the duties on British manufactures *at least one-half:* and of course this would apply to the whole Union, and to a population of twenty-six millions. This contains an indirect answer to your question, and shows that our corn laws originally led to the legislative enactments of Prussia, and through her influence to a system of retaliation through the whole of the North of Germany. One official man told me, that he knew the Prussian ministers in London had repeatedly told Mr. P. Thomson that your corn law was the stumbling block to a trade between the countries." (Hear, hear.) Mr. Cobden concluded by advising the meeting to show, from the energy of their proceedings that day, that they had a proper sense of their rights, and thus secure from Mr. Thomson the exclusive services of a representative.

The CHAIRMAN, after stating that he did not understand the adjournment to be made for any such purpose as the preparation of another petition, explained that the present proceedings were not in order, as there had been no motion for the adoption of the amended petition of the directors.

Mr. Alderman MACVICAR moved, that the form of petition prepared by the directors, and presented to the last general Meeting, with the alterations now proposed by them, be adopted by this Meeting, and be signed by the president on its behalf.

Mr. Alderman TOOTAL seconded the motion.

Mr. J. C. DYER said, that since he had prematurely made his motion, another entire petition had been offered to the Meeting, which, in his opinion, expressed more fully and correctly the opinions which ought to be expressed by this Chamber; and, instead of moving the paragraph which had been read, he would, with the permission of the Meeting, withdraw that, and move the adoption of the petition presented by Mr. Cobden, in the form of an amendment to Mr. Macvicar's motion. He would suggest an additional train of considerations, exhibiting the justice of our claim to the absolute and total repeal of the corn laws. Up to within seventy or eighty years ago, this country produced corn and food enough generally to feed the people. The introduction of labour-saving machinery, and the successful inventions which gave rise to, and so repeatedly pushed on to success, our manufacturing system, tended most rapidly to increase our population, which had been nearly twice doubled within that period; and food for the sustenance of this increased population had, in a great measure, been drawn from the home soil. The consequence was, that the people had been short fed—had paid heavily for their food—and had been much damaged in their progress to general prosperity, by being restricted to the home supply of food. The laws relating to the supply of food, being made by parties interested in supplying it at a dear rate, was the cause of this condition of the people. But suppose, for the sake of argument, an opposite state of things had prevailed; that the power of making the laws had passed into the hands of the manufacturers, bankers, capitalists, professional men; and that, instead of our becoming a great manufacturing people, our numbers had dwindled; suppose that the agriculturists had cultivated the land, and produced much more food than the people could consume, and that, in order to take up the entire supply produced by the home soil, a great portion of it were sold at extremely reduced prices, and much waste happened, and that little or no *rent* could be obtained by the landlords, with such a depression of prices and glut of the home market for food; — then, suppose the manufacturers and merchants to say to the agriculturists — "Gentlemen, you shall not have a yard of broad cloth, or a piece of calico, or a parcel of hardware, or any description of manufactures, except from our shops and warehouses, and at three times the price charged by our neighbours on the continent. We have a *right* to the home market, and you have no *right* to go abroad, and buy cheaper than you can at home." The consequence would be, that corn would be a drug in the market; other nations, flourishing in manufactures and commerce, would wish to buy our corn, but could not pay for it; not from want of money, but because we would not (in this case) take any of their manufactures in return; and the English agriculturist could therefore have no export trade, or relieve himself from extreme low prices, unless the *manufacturing monopolists*, who, in this supposable case had made the prohibitory laws, would consent to repeal them; ought not the injured parties, in the case here supposed, to denounce such legislation as grossly selfish and unjustifiable, and to unite their energies to cause the removal of laws so cruel and oppressive as applied to the *landlords;* and was not the actual case of the manufacturers at present, the exact converse of the case supposed? He thought, then, that we ought not to flinch from an absolute demand for the repeal of all duties on corn; and he would repeat, that if it should happen that farmers having long leases should suffer by the instantaneous repeal, all such cases would have a fair claim to national indemnity. He thought the meeting ought to adopt that petition, which left no doubt of the great danger of continuing in our present course, or of the indignant and resentful feeling which its continuance would foster in the public mind. He entreated the Chamber to adopt that form prepared by Mr. Cobden, as that which was most energetic and expressive of its opinion.

Mr. R. H. Greg (of the old firm of Samuel Greg and Co., the most extensive spinners in the kingdom, consuming in their numerous establishments the one-hundredth part of all the cotton spun in this country. Mr. R. H. Greg is a county magistrate, and is the author of a pamphlet containing a large amount of valuable information upon the subject of factory labour here and abroad, written in reply to an article in the Quarterly Review upon the 'Ten Hours Bill'), rose with some hesitation to second the amendment for two reasons:—1st, He had not been present at the last meeting; and 2dly, As he had not till that moment heard the petition or heard of it, he ought to apologize for taking it up in what might appear so hasty a manner. But the first petition had been before the public during last week; and he thought, in its general character, it had rather too much of the nature of a thesis, as Mr. Cobden had said, and was too quiet or moderate. He saw in Mr. Cobden's petition (speaking of its general character) not only more facts stated, which was important, but there were great vigour and earnestness pervading it. It had been remarked by a great man and great writer, that no great body of men ever had justice done to them, except through motives of fear and intimidation. Such, unfortunately, was human nature, that you cannot get attention paid to your sufferings unless you show you are in earnest, or unless, to use the term for want of a better, you threaten. That was the case as to the catholic question: had it not been for the threatening, or, to use a vulgar term, "bullying," we should not have obtained that measure. So it was with the reform act, and so it would be with the corn laws. This question was a case of life and death, not only with the masses in this neighbourhood, but he believed it to be one of life and death as regarded the prosperity of England. (Hear, hear.) There was an immense mass, he would not say of ignorance, but of interest united against us; and we had no chance of getting a repeal of those mischievous laws, except by union amongst ourselves, and putting on a most determined aspect, and assuming a most determined tone. For this reason he preferred the general tone of Mr. Cobden's form of petition. As to the general question, he would observe, first, that he thought too much had been said about the power of competition of foreign manufacturers in a market common to them and us; but there was one question which preceded that, and was, in fact, of more importance, but which, he thought, had not been sufficiently dwelt upon—namely, that every country has its protecting duties, the effect of which was to give to each country the entire supply of its home market; and what, in fact, was that, but to cut us out first from one market, then from another, and finally from all? (Hear, hear.) We know that, as to the 26,000,000 of people in Germany, it is utterly impossible for us to compete with them, under the 1*s.* 6*d.* per lb. duty; nor could we with America, with the duty of 15, and even 20 per cent., after the ultimate tariff is carried into execution. This, then, was plainly our fate, whether we could compete in common markets or not, we should first be excluded from one country, then from another, and then from all. This important question was independent of foreign competition. To add one or two facts to those mentioned by Mr. Smith and Mr. Cobden, as to the rapidity with which foreign manufacturers supply themselves with the means of competition, he (Mr. Greg) had had furnished to him, in the beginning of last year, a list of orders for machinery to the amount of 500,000*l.* in the hands of Mr. Schlumberger, Mr. Esher, and a very few others, all foreign machine makers of Belgium, Switzerland, and Germany. (Hear.) That was proceeding with very great vigour, and it might readily be supposed, that that gap which yet remained to be filled up in the supply of their own market, would very rapidly be filled up. The competition was already felt in our own market. His

(Mr. Greg's) house had last year to break up 200 looms, which formerly supplied an article for one of those markets. And this year they had broken up 200 looms more, which supplied another article for another of those markets. (Hear.) With such facts before him, he was compelled to think that a timid, mild, reasoning, and moderate petition, was not likely to make any impression on the government or the legislature. With regard to the markets of the world, that, though a more remote, would ultimately be a very serious question. Switzerland, the only country abroad that supplied her own consumption, now exported nearly three-fourths of all she manufactured; though no country (except Austria perhaps) was worse situated for an export manufacturing country; having no port, and many disadvantages. Yet nearly three-fourths of all she spins, she manufactures and exports to foreign countries. The spinning-mills on the continent were increasing most rapidly. Last year his (Mr. Greg's) brother visited a great variety of those establishments, and he reported that the machinery in their best mills was fully equal to ours. That machinery was made by their own machine makers, though it cost something more than ours, which was owing merely to the immense profits that their machine makers were now making, which formed a very large proportion of the whole cost of that machinery. But competition would soon reduce prices to their proper level; and their mechanics, getting 12*s.* a week, would do as much as ours at 30*s.* a week, and produce machinery, notwithstanding the increased price of metal there, at as low a rate as in this country. The rate of production in their mills, including the extra time worked, exceeded the rate of production here, in any mills of which he had any cognizance. (Hear.) Their (the foreign) mills averaged from 19 to 21 hanks of 40s twist per day, and there were mills turning off 18 hanks of 60s twist. An English mechanic from that part of the continent, who was in this country last year, told him (Mr. Greg) that he had visited a mill where 18 hanks of 60s twist was spun; he saw this done himself, and he said, "I had no conception, Sir, of the rate they are going on in these countries; and my word for it, Sir, before seven years are over, you must look about yourselves, or you will be beaten." (Hear.) With respect to the medium qualities of cloth, into which labour enters to a certain amount, there was no doubt in his (Mr. Greg's) mind, but that Switzerland and Germany would completely beat us out of any common market, after supplying their own home consumption. As to America, not only that could and would be done, in those particular articles where the raw material formed a large portion of the cost, and in which they did actually beat us; but also in our strongest point, where our large establishments, and large capital, told more than where labour formed a larger part of the price. Mr. Smith had not mentioned the case of America, and he would, therefore, read over the exports from America. He had a large packet of American grey cloth, and all different kinds of printing cloth, on which he knew that, in 1836, when we were getting here *5d.* or *6d.* they were clearing a dollar per piece. The exports of their own manufactured cloth from the port of New York alone were, in 1823, 1,700 bags; in 1825, 1,600; in 1827, 2,500; in 1828, 1,900; in 1829, 2,800; in 1830,

5,300; in 1831, 3,000; in 1833, 13,000; and in that part of 1834, of which he had a return, 10,000 bags, valued at two millions of dollars. In 1835, the export was valued at 2,856,000 dollars. He had no returns for the last two years; but he knew that, in the eighteen months including half of 1836 and the year 1837, the Americans had exported 20,000 bales of their own manufactured cloth round the Cape of Good Hope, and 16,000 bales of cloth to South America. (Hear, hear.) As to the profits on these articles, it was sometimes said that the Americans could not compete with us in plain cloths, but must sell without profit. A gentleman, who had established a mill at Lowell, and who was formerly well known to some gentlemen here, stated that he had cleared there, in great part by these exports, 200,000*l.*; and gentlemen might be sure the Americans would not export at the rate stated, if they did not get a profit by it. The same gentleman, who was the owner of the mills at Lowell, said to him (Mr. Greg), "We have pushed these *low domestics* beyond the mark, and now we are turning our attention to spinning low numbers of twist for the German market." (Hear, hear.) These were facts which, for some time past, had filled him (Mr. Greg) with alarm; but what most alarmed him was this,—that our own manufacturers and merchants—those who ought to know better—who knew or ought to have known these facts—were not only ignorant of, but utterly incredulous as to these facts. That was the most alarming feature of our case. It was not so much the interest of the landed gentry that kept us in this condition, as our own ignorance or indifference on the one hand, and the union of the landed interest on the other. These circumstances had been acting on his mind and the minds of his partners so powerfully, that some time ago they had made a determination to have no increase whatever of their establishments in this country, but in any further increase to look abroad. (Hear.) They had been on the point more than once, and should be again, of forming establishments out of this country—in Germany, and probably in America—such were their convictions, that they intended to act upon them in this way. Then came the question, If this was the state of things, what could be done? How could we retrace our steps, and extricate ourselves from this difficulty and danger? He was certainly almost hopeless respecting our capability of extricating ourselves; but his strong conviction was, that the only chance of escape lay in the repeal of the corn laws; and the progress of the operation of such repeal would be just the reverse of what had taken place. The corn laws had first deprived our customers of the means of payment, not from poverty, for it was not a question of price, but we said to them, "Gentlemen, we won't take what you offer us in payment; we don't like your bill; we don't like your cash." We would not take what the foreigner had to give us. The next step was to make him a manufacturer, of course; the next was to give him cheap food; and the next, to give ourselves dear food; and this was the way in which our ruin would be consummated, if we obtained no remedy for the evil. The repeal of the corn laws would reverse these steps: the first would give us cheaper food; the next would give the foreign manufacturer dearer food;

the next would create customers for those who now have none; the next would create, or increase if it already existed, an agricultural interest abroad, which would act as a counterbalance to the preponderance of their manufacturing interest, saying to them, "We want to sell our corn; the English are very good customers of ours; and we will not have these very high duties imposed on them." If we exchange our clothing for food, which, after all, was the great interchange between different commodities and different countries, one which never could end or be limited in amount, both being necessaries of life, millions of people might exist in countries where they do not and could not now exist; even millions might exist in this country, that never could have existence under the present system. Supposing we doubled our population, or had another twelve millions to feed, who should consume not one quarter of English wheat, but entirely foreign corn, what would be our condition? First, that double population would consume double the quantity of butcher's meat, of milk, butter, potatoes, &c.; there would be double the quantity of occupation land wanted—(hear); and thus the value of land, instead of declining, would actually advance; so that there was no fear for the landowners, except in their continuing the present impolitic laws. We should have half the amount of taxation, with a double population; and with that reduced taxation, there would be double the demand for all English agricultural produce (save corn), which the agriculturist would ever have the monopoly of, or nearly so. If such circumstances would give us a prosperous condition, every approach to it would put us in a more prosperous state. He thought, therefore, we should not alarm the landed interest more than necessary; for, after all, it was more important to have a return for our goods than even to have cheap food; for if government furnished us with food for nothing, we could not trade with those countries whose produce we would not take. (Hear.) He seconded the amendment, believing that the spirit of Mr. Cobden's petition was more likely to excite interest and attention, and to do good, than that prepared by the directors.

At the suggestion of Mr. George Sandars, the Chairman read both petitions at length, for the better information of gentlemen not present at the former meeting, and that both might be fairly before the present meeting.

Mr. Benjamin Pearson (commission merchant), in reference to Mr. Cobden's observations respecting Mr. Poulett Thomson, said, that how far that right honourable gentleman had discharged his duty, he (Mr. Pearson) was not prepared to say; he did not appear there as his advocate; but it was right for the public to know, that Mr. Thomson saw, as clearly as any man, the difficulty attending our foreign commerce from the operation of the corn laws, and had admitted that he constantly met this difficulty in every attempt to form a commercial treaty with other countries. He had acknowledged that that was the grand obstacle to any satisfactory treaty with Prussia, and he deeply lamented the indifference shown in this town. Mr. Thomson was aware that he had both the cabinet and parliament against him; and he was, to his

(Mr. Pearson's) knowledge, greatly surprised at the supineness manifested here, saying, "I have never been supported by the people of Manchester." (Hear.) When the question was put to him, "What is the remedy for this?"—"Such is the state of public feeling, the want of interest experienced, that I have no hope of any repeal of the corn laws, but through a famine." (Hear.) He (Mr. Pearson) thought we were already approaching to a state of very great suffering, which he did not see could be lessened, and feared must go on increasing. Every one must admit how much better it was to concede to justice than to clamour. It was the duty of government and parliament strictly to investigate the subject, and to give what belonged to the people. But how could we expect parliament to take up the subject, if a full and clear statement was not made of the facts by the people of Manchester? Approving as he did of the sentiments of the first petition, he thought that of Mr. Cobden much better calculated, under existing circumstances, to make an impression on the legislature, and he had heard it moved and seconded with great pleasure.

Thomas Potter, Esq., mayor of Manchester, said, that he had been a farmer from the age of sixteen to twenty-eight, at which time there were no protective corn laws in operation; and he had an opportunity of knowing all the farmers within perhaps ten miles of York. They were then a rich and happy body, the only individuals not prosperous being idle or unskilful men, who mismanaged their land; but, to the best of his knowledge, every industrious farmer, acquainted with his business, was prosperous, and was accumulating money. His father occupied a little farm; but, though a scientific farmer, he never took any active part, and he (Mr. Potter) had taken the management of it from the day he left school, at the age of sixteen, and he continued to purchase a hundred head of cattle, and five or six hundred sheep, every year. His father had expended a great deal of money, and had at one time some difficulty to make his way, but he died worth fourteen or fifteen thousand pounds; and when he (Mr. Potter) and his brother gave up the farm, they came to Manchester with upwards of seven thousand pounds. The effects of the corn laws had been ably exhibited by his friends Mr. Smith and Mr. Cobden: these laws were passed by the landed interest, the owners of the soil; but it was evident that the farmers had not profited by them, for, generally speaking, no one would dispute that the farmers were a much poorer race than at the time to which he had referred. It was clear, therefore, that this was a tax raised solely for the benefit of the rich, while it injured the farmer, and was oppressing and starving the poor. Ought such a state of things to exist? He believed that it could not exist long; it was impossible; and he felt convinced that it was injurious even to the landed interest themselves. Disclaiming all party feeling, and with the best feeling to every gentleman present, he must say, that, looking at the two petitions, he considered the former one as too tame, and should certainly support that prepared by Mr. Cobden, as much more suitable to our circumstances.

Mr. G. Sandars could not allow that opportunity to pass without saying a few words. He regretted to see their want of unanimity. An unanimous petition from that Chamber would have great weight with government. The difference, however, was so slight, that he hoped it would be got over, resolving itself as it did merely into a question of time. They all advocated a repeal of the present corn laws, but some of them, and he was among the number, were for substituting, in the mean time, a fixed duty to be gradually reduced, while others would not consent to any. He had been represented as a friend of monopoly, and as advocating the cause of the agriculturists. He had spoken on behalf of their interest as he would have done for any interest which he conceived to be threatened with injustice. The absolute and immediate repeal of the corn laws would cut down the landed interest to the extent of 50 or 60 per cent. Compensation to the mortgagee and the holders of long leases had been talked of. If they carried out the principle of compensation, they would require to expend a sum larger than the national debt. (Loud laughter.) He knew that there were many here who would not agree with him, but these were his ideas, and he would not shrink from expressing them. He thought that in the first place the duty should be 15*s.* per quarter, to be reduced 1*s.* per annum till it reached 10*s.*; and afterwards, if it should be found safe, to go on reducing till it came to 5*s.* per quarter fixed duty; and ultimately it might be abolished altogether, if it were to appear consistent with the interest of the country. A great deal had been said about the loss of our foreign trade, as a consequence of our refusal to take corn in exchange for their manufactures. He believed there was a great deal of delusion on that point. The price of corn had been of late years as high in America as it had been here—(cries of oh! oh! President, order)—and it was well known that they had actually been importing it to a considerable extent. He thought there was a great fallacy in the nation about the benefit of cheap bread. (Laughter.) If, as had been said, three loaves, instead of two, would be got for 2*s.* in consequence of a repeal of the corn laws, another consequence would be, that the workman's 2*s.* would be reduced to 1*s.* 4*d.*, which would leave matters, in so far as he was concerned, just as they were. As to its effect on trade, it was not corn-growing countries that were our best customers. Poland did not take our goods; while Spain and the West Indies, which were the best customers for our manufacturers, had no corn to give us in return for them. The best way would be to endeavour to assimilate prices all over the world, by bringing those in other countries to a level with ours. Our manufacturers would thus be enabled to compete with those of other nations, who would, under these circumstances, be inclined, from their superior agricultural advantages, to invest their capital in producing corn. He expressed his regret that they were not unanimous. As a director of the Chamber, he had considered it his duty thus to express his sentiments. He would oppose the amendment. (Disapprobation.)

Mr. Alderman COBDEN wished, through the chair, to ask whether Mr. Sandars was really in favour of free trade, or of a system of protection.

The CHAIRMAN said, he could permit no gentleman to put a question to another as to his individual opinion.

Mr. Cobden said he wished to put the question to Mr. Sandars as a director of that Chamber. In that capacity he had given expression to certain opinions; and had, both on a former, and on this occasion, to some extent, identified himself with the board of directors. He thought it vitally important, that the members should know what were the principles entertained by the Board on so important a question as that of free trade. A petition had been presented from the Chamber nearly twenty years ago, embodying, to the fullest extent, the avowal of the principles of free trade; and he therefore wished to know whether Mr. Sandars merely spoke for himself, or as uttering the sentiments of the board of directors.

Mr. Sandars said he spoke only for himself.

Mr. Cobden wished to know whether the prayer, added to last week's petition, was really, what he believed it to be, for a trade totally free, and deprecating all protection, or a prayer for the repeal of these corn laws, leaving the subject to be debated, whether there should be hereafter a protective duty of 15*s.* 10*s.* or 5*s.* per quarter. It was of the strictest importance that the matter should be disentangled from any doubt, and made so precise and clear that no one could misunderstand it. He took the amended prayer of the petition to be an avowal of the doctrine of free trade, those who advocated which could not advocate a protective duty of any kind. (Hear.)

Mr. Sandars explained he was a friend of free trade, but not of a sudden transition from entire prohibition to entire free trade; the difference, as he had said, was merely one of time, and the opinion as to not going below 5*s*. duty was merely his own individual opinion.

The CHAIRMAN was not aware that any individual had assumed to himself the right to speak for the general body of directors, and the extent to which unanimity had been claimed for them was, that, out of the twenty-three directors, exclusive of the president, twenty-one signed the requisition; of the two whose names did not appear, one gentleman had been from home during the whole time. He understood, though not present at the deliberation of the board, that again they did the day before this meeting agree unanimously —[Mr. J. B. SMITH. No.]—at least *nem. con.* to recommend the alteration for adoption.—[Mr. SMITH. No.]—He thought it due to his own character, and the high station he held as president of the Chamber, not to permit his word thus to be questioned before the Chamber: if he said any thing erroneous, he would beg their pardon; but intending throughout to act with good faith and open candour, he claimed from them that support which he had never known an assembly of gentlemen withold from their chairman, when he averred a thing to be correct, and it was called in question. (Applause.) The record of proceedings, which had led him to state what had thus been questioned, was:—"Resolved, *nem. dis.* That Mr. Wood be required, on the part of the directors, to recommend for the adoption of the general meeting of the Chamber the petition already prepared, with the alterations presented by him."—[The chairman read the names of the directors agreeing to this resolution, including that of Mr. Smith.]—The directors had been asked what principles they avowed; his reply was, they avowed the principles set forth in the petition presented by them to the meeting, which, though stigmatized as tame, and weak, and long, had not yet, so far as he knew, been controverted on any one point, either of policy or principle. If this did not satisfy Mr. Cobden, he referred him to the principle upon which the Chamber had ever acted. It might have been more or less qualified in the manner in which it had recorded its opinions; but it had never stooped to promote the self-interest of its members at the expense of any other class, but rather sought to promote the general good of the whole community. The petition had by one gentleman been called timid; but he might be permitted to say, that timidity was a feeling that never influenced the mind of the individual who prepared it, when called upon to discharge a public duty.

Mr. J. B. Smith rose to say that he could forgive the warmth of their president, though under all the circumstances of the case he certainly must say, that he did not think he had been treated with that candour and consideration by him which he was entitled to expect. He could overlook his warmth, however, because he believed it arose from a misapprehension of the facts of the case. He believed the president had withdrawn from the meeting of the Board to which reference was now made, but had he been present and seen the course pursued by him (Mr. Smith) on that occasion, instead of saying that he supported the amended petition, he would have remembered that he expressly stated "that he would neither vote for it nor against it" (hear, hear); and therefore the president had no right to read his (Mr. Smith's) name to-day as one of those who agreed to the petition. He could, however, he repeated, forgive the warmth of feeling expressed by the president, because he believed him not to have been personally cognizant of what took place when the petition was put to the vote by the directors. (Hear, hear.) He (Mr. Smith) begged to remind the president, that he took with him and proposed a petition of his own to that meeting, and with regard to the amended petition he told the directors, that he assented to all the reasonings in it — that it was very good so far as it went, but that it only went to show the inevitable effects of the corn laws; but it appeared to him that we had proofs that those effects had been produced which the petition predicted, and that therefore it was not suited to the occasion. His (Mr. Smith's) petition began where Mr. Wood's left off. It began with a statement of facts, showing the evils already produced by the corn laws. It insisted, much in the same manner as Mr. Cobden's did, that we had already lost our foreign hosiery trade, and were likely soon to lose the home demand for hosiery; that we were constantly losing the demand for one or other articles of our manufactures, and exporting instead raw materials, cotton twist, raw iron, &c., whilst the alarming increase of machine-making on the continent were good grounds for fearing, that the loss of our export of manufactures would shortly be followed by the loss of export of cotton twist, and imperatively urged the attention of Parliament to this important question. He had since the last meeting, the adjournment of which he had not regretted, because it had been the means of arousing public attention and informing many on this question who had not before been led to think upon it, received the thanks of many gentlemen for the statements he had brought before them; and as these statements might be the means of inducing a spirit of inquiry upon the question, he was not sorry he had brought them before the Chamber, though he required no thanks, as he was impelled by a sense of duty to the course he was now pursuing. (Hear, hear.) He would, with their permission, take the liberty of laying before them some further facts bearing upon this important question. His attention had been called to an article in one of the Manchester papers of last week, which impugned the inferences he had drawn from the facts he had produced at the last meeting, and which attempted to show that our exports had greatly increased, and that we had nothing to fear, for that in 1815-16-17 the average *official* value of British produce and manufactures amounted to 38,573,973*l.*; while in 1835-6-7 the *official* value of our exports amounted to 78,376,033*l.*; and the inference the writer drew was, that our exports were at the latter period 40,000,000*l.* greater in value than at the former period, and that we had nothing to be dissatisfied with. Now either the writer of that article was grossly ignorant of the question, or his object was to mislead his readers. He ought to have known that there was a certain value affixed by the Custom-house to goods in 1694 called the "official value," at which all goods exported since that time have been rated, but which, of course, cannot indicate the real value, but only the *quantity* of articles exported. Now there was another account kept by the Custom-house of all goods exported, which was called the "declared value," which is the *real value* as given in by the merchants at the time of shipment. Now the declared or real value of the exports of the years 1815-16-17 was 45,000,000*l.*, while the official value was 38,500,000*l.*; and the official value of the exports of 1835-6-7, comprising double the amount of stuff, though amounting to 78,000,000*l.*, in real value amounted only to 49,000,000*l.*; instead, therefore, of the manufactures exported in the latter period being double the value, they only exceeded the exports of the former period in money value by 4,000,000*l.*, which proved that we were now exporting double the quantity of goods for the same amount of money. (Hear, hear.) This tended strongly to prove the correctness of the views he had expressed at the last meeting, and which he would further illustrate. He had endeavoured to show, at the meeting of last week, that the greatest increase in our exports was in unmanufactured goods, such as cotton twist, unwrought iron, and steel; that these articles were now sent abroad in the raw state, and manufactured by the foreigner, whereby the workman of this country was deprived of the employment he would otherwise have received by converting them into manufactured goods. He would now proceed to show how this had affected different branches of our trade. Last year (1837) the total value of the exports of cotton manufactures was 20,000,000*l.* Of these goods, one-half consisted of cotton twist, the value of which was only 6,000,000*l.*, whilst the value of the manufactured goods was 13,000,000*l.*; and therefore by the export of yarn instead of manufactured goods, we sustained a loss of 7,000,000*l.* in labour and profit. Now he would ask, what would have been the condition of our weavers and other artizans, if these 7,000,000*l.* had been left here in the shape of wages among our working classes, instead of going to remunerate the foreign labourer? (Hear, hear.) He should be able to tell them the loss to this country in the wages of the workman, in the exportation of the raw material instead of the manufactured article, by some facts connected with the exportation of hardware. According to Mr. Babbage, the labour expended on the manufacture of a quantity of bar iron worth 1*l.* into agricultural instruments increased its value to 3*l.* 5*s.* 7*d.*; of the same quantity into musket-barrels, 9*l.*; into swords, 16*l.*; saws, 14*l.*; files, 20*l.*; razors (cast-steel), 53*l.*; table knives, 35*l.*; needles, 70*l.*; pen-knives, 657*l.*; and buckles, 896*l.* Now only conceive the immense value of the labour lost to this country by being deprived of the manufacture of hardwares, which was sufficient to account for the distress in Birmingham, Wolverhampton, Sheffield, and elsewhere. (Hear, hear.) There was another strong reason why the petition moved by Mr. Dyer ought to have the support of this Chamber, in preference to that of the directors. It was the alarming fact, that while the exports of this country were nearly stationary, the exports of foreign countries were greatly on the increase. (Hear.) He had before him a table of the declared value of the exports in the years 1815 and 1836, of three different countries. He would begin with our own first: the exports of Great Britain, in 1815 amounted to 51,603,029*l.*; in 1836, to 53,368,571*l.* The exports of the United States of America in 1815 amounted to 28,500,000 dollars; in 1836, to 66,500,000 dollars; an increase of more than 200 per cent. (Loud cries of "hear.") The exports of France in 1815 were 23,750,000 francs; in 1836 they had risen to 74,000,000 francs; nearly 400 per cent.! So that while our exports had increased only four per cent., those of France had risen to nearly 400 per cent. in the same period. (Loud cries of "Hear, hear.") He would repeat, that these were alarming facts; and the increase in the manufacture of different articles in other countries was also rapidly progressing. He happened to have in his hand a return of the increase of Russian manufactures from 1821 to 1831, a period of nine years. In that period the cotton manufactures of Russia had increased 230 per cent.; silk had increased 25 per cent.; woollen had increased 30 per cent.; flax and hemp had increased 45 per cent.; tobacco and snuff had increased 150 per cent.; and the manufacture of soap 131 per cent. (Hear.) Some gentlemen expressed but little alarm at the danger of losing our manufacturing superiority, and congratulated themselves that the country was not ruined yet. It might be that those who were engaged in the spinning of cotton twist were doing well. ("No, no, no.") He saw that gentlemen dissented. The makers of raw iron and steel he understood were well employed, but those who were engaged in the fabrication of these materials into articles were complaining of the hardness of trade. (Hear, hear.) Now when he had occasionally met some of the directors of the Chamber, they had affected surprise, that, notwithstanding the loss of portions of our trade, we should have flourished so long, exhibited such signs of wealth, and asked how could it be accounted for? It might be accounted for, he would reply, by the fact, that it was difficult to ruin a country like this all at once, abounding in wealth and natural resources. (Hear.) But were gentlemen insensible to the hand-writing on the wall? (Loud cries of "hear, hear.") Might not what had been raised by the superior skill and industry of our countrymen be destroyed by bad legislation? (Hear, hear.) We had attained our present position chiefly by the enormous increase of our productive power, by our steam and machinery, at a time when other countries had not turned attention to its employment. This had enormously increased our wealth. But who derived the benefit of this? Had the working classes? (Hear, hear.) No; because they had been giving constantly a greater quantity of manufactures for the same or a less quantity of food, and because it had been exchanged, not for the food which they consumed, but for luxuries for the rich — (hear) — or for raw materials, or for blocks of wood, as Mr. Dyer had justly said, for any thing but what the people could eat. (Hear.) The increase of our productive power might be inferred from the fact, that in 1815 our steam power was equal to 30,000,000 of labourers, while at present it was equal to 600,000,000. (Hear, hear.) That it was this that had enabled us to sustain the enormous burthen of taxation, and as large a burthen in the shape of corn laws, under which we groaned, there could be no doubt. But whenever the time arrived that our competitors should attain to that point in mechanical power possessed by this country, then was the time that Britain's sun would set. (Loud cries of "hear, hear.") And every approximation to that state of things would be to our certain injury. It was therefore of the greatest importance that every obstacle to the increase of our industry should be removed. Let not gentlemen flatter themselves with the delusion, that we had little to fear at present, that at all events the loss of our trade would be gradual. Let them take warning from the facts which he had already laid before them, and listen to the past. In the year 1834 the Prussian league was established. In 1833, the year previous to that time, our exports of velvets amounted to 8,162,000 yards; in 1837, only four years afterwards, they had fallen to 4,638,000 yards. In 1833 our exports of cambrics and muslins was 12,754,000 yards, while in 1837 it amounted only to 6,193,900. In the year 1833 our export of nankeens was 18,000,000 yards, in 1837 it had decreased to 355,000. (Loud cries of "hear, hear.") A gentleman connected with the export yarn trade had told him, that, in stating Switzerland took off from us no numbers of twist below 100s, he had understated the fact, as very little yarn was exported to that country now under 120s, and of those, none but the very choicest qualities. Switzerland, too, had become a powerful rival in the export of cotton twist, not only manufacturing enough for herself, but competing with us in neutral markets, which competition was increasing every day, and in consequence of which his informant had lost some very excellent commissions. From various quarters since last week, and in consequence of that meeting, he had received a large amount of information. One gentleman had sent him a lot of patterns of American prints, which he was desirous should be exhibited to the members of the Chamber in the same way as the Saxon cotton hosiery; but any gentleman could see them after the meeting. A gentleman who had been in the United States three or four years ago, and who was complaining to one of his customers there that they had sent him no orders for hosiery lately, was told, "Oh, we get it so much cheaper from Germany." The English merchant, supposing that the low price arose from the market being overstocked at that time, and that people could not sell goods at that price without being ruined, persuaded his American customer to give him an order for 500*l.* worth of English hosiery, and to order that amount of Saxon hosiery at the same time. This was executed; and the reply to his inquiry as to the result was, that the English hosiery cost his American friend 25 per cent. more than the Saxon. There were gentlemen present in the Manchester trade, who had been in the habit of selling largely to American houses; and they told him that since the revival of the demand for America, many Americans had called on them to purchase goods, and they had shown to these Americans various articles which they had been in the habit formerly of selling to them, and had received the reply as to one article, "That article we now manufacture at home;" as to another, "What is the price?" "So and so." "Oh, we can beat you at home." "What is your price for this?" "So much." "Oh, we can't afford to give it." Such were the answers, in very many instances, of the American buyers. He was informed by one of the largest exporters in this town to the American market, that all descriptions of low broad cloth had now ceased to be exported from this country, being manufactured in America. He knew that the article of Negro clothing, in which he (Mr. Smith) dealt largely himself, when in business, was now manufactured in the United States, and its export thither from this country had almost entirely ceased. The Americans no longer took our grey unbleached cloth, sheeting, shirtings, and bed-ticks, no longer took our printed goods under the value of twelve shillings, except blacks and whites: what we now exported were all of finer qualities than those, and they were every day getting of finer quality, while the Americans were daily improving in their manufacture of prints, as would be seen by the specimens in his hand. In the low qualities of hardware they manufactured many articles superior to the English, and as cheap; and we were losing that trade in consequence, as to the lower qualities. They made also a low fancy pantaloon stuff, not yet sufficient for their own consumption, and hitherto that deficiency had been supplied from this country; but his informant stated, that this year that article might be bought so much lower in the German than in the English market, that all orders for it this season had gone to Germany. The Americans were beginning to manufacture kerseymeres for themselves, and what the same gentleman told him of the decrease in our exports of this article seemed so prodigious that he almost doubted the statement; and when he got home, he referred to such documents as he possessed, which were not the latest, but they convinced him that the statement was correct. He found, from the tables of the Board of Trade, that in 1820, we exported to America 13,217 pieces of kerseymeres; and in 1831, only 3,500 pieces. Of flannels, we sent to the United States, in 1820, 1,525,000 yards; but in 1831, only 104,000 yards. That article we had lost the sale of in America. Such was the progress of cotton spinning in the United States, that his information led him to expect that, in four or five years, they would be powerful rivals to us in the exportation of cotton twist. (Hear, hear.) It was an object at which they were aiming; and he had no doubt that they would accomplish it, notwithstanding the dear corn they ate, of which Mr. Sandars had spoken. For the last three years, the harvests in the United States had been failures, in consequence of which they had been importers of foreign corn, a very extraordinary circumstance in that great agricultural country, and therefore prices ranged from eight to ten dollars, instead of, as usual, from four to five, a circumstance of which perhaps Mr. Sandars was not aware. He (Mr. Smith) would not now longer occupy their time, but he might mention, that it was the intention of the Anti-Corn-Law Association to establish a museum for the purpose of exhibiting articles of foreign manufactures, and placing them side by side with English manufactures of similar qualities, with the prices of each affixed, in order that all Thomas-a-Didymusses who were hard of belief on this question, might have ocular demonstration of the truth. (Hear.) It was also their intention to have specimens of foreign coffees and sugars, and of every article upon which there was a discriminative duty, exhibited with its price, in order that the people might see the amount to which they were plundered by monopolies. It was disgraceful to the government and to the legislature of this country that such societies were necessary, but as they were so, it was to be hoped that every gentleman having this cause at heart would see the necessity of becoming a member, and subscribing to this institution. He would conclude with observing, that there was no interest, in his opinion, in the whole country, so much interested in the repeal of the corn laws as the agricultural interest. (Hear.) Even the landowner, who looked beyond the receipt of his next year's rent, must see that the destruction of the manufactures of this country was the inevitable destruction of himself. (Hear.) What must be the result of destroying our manufactures, but to throw the greatest part of the people out of work, and reduce them to a state of pauperism? How were they to be supported when manufactures no longer exist, but by the land? And what, then, will be the value of the landowners' estates, which the starving people will eat up like locusts, and even find these insufficient to save them from misery and destitution? (Hear, hear, and cheers.) He would not longer take up the time of the Chamber now: their president, he believed, was unwell, and perhaps it would be desirable if this meeting were adjourned, if other gentlemen wished to speak on the question, to give them an opportunity, and to give time for the better consideration of the petitions now before the Meeting. He had found it difficult himself to follow the reasonings of a petition when hastily read over, and he would suggest, that if the two were to be printed and placed in the hands of members till the next assembling of the Chamber, whether they might not be able to come to that calm and dispassionate decision upon them which was desirable.

Mr. Henry Ashworth said, that, after hearing all that had been now and at the last meeting of the Chamber said upon the corn laws, he could not help thinking that they reflected strongly on those who had framed and enacted them. Various opinions had been expressed as to the best way of getting rid of them. He thought petitioning was the most legitimate and proper mode. Some had talked of famine; but God forbid that the remedy should come in that form. The destructive effects of these laws had been fully described, and surely when they looked at the peril with which they were threatened from them, they would agree that it was not a time to send a petition to parliament on the subject only half expressed. The petition submitted to them at the last meeting was less convincing and energetic in its tone than the speeches delivered by members on the occasion. Though a misunderstanding seemed to have taken place as to the object of the adjournment, he for one had to say, that he understood the directors were to call in the assistance of other members of the Chamber, to aid in the preparation of a suitable petition. He hoped they would not be led away by a misplaced feeling of courtesy to vote for the directors' petition. They justly boasted of the unrivalled industry and skill of their working classes, and would they stand by without seeking to rescue them from the cruel oppression of these laws? He trusted their claims would not be forgot. The long hours of labour of which they justly complained were not fixed on them by their employers, but by the landowners, for whom they were obliged to work four hours of every day. He would vote for Mr. Cobden's amendment; and before sitting down he would beg to inquire of the president if the directors of the Chamber were unanimous in their sentiments on the question of free trade?

The CHAIRMAN. I am not inquisitor-general as to the opinions of the directors.

Mr. W. RAWSON (hosiery manufacturer of Nottingham, with a house of business in Manchester) rose to correct an error into which Mr. Cobden had fallen, in stating the proportion of the cotton hosiery yarn spun by the people of Saxony. His statement might indeed be correct as to the period, which was but recent, when he was in the country. But we could not tell what a day would bring forth, for a Saxon gentleman had told him a few days ago, that they were now spinning a portion of their hosiery yarn. He was himself a sufferer from this turn of affairs, and a gentleman had told him at the conclusion of the last week's meeting, that a sufferer was not a good judge in his own case. Now he thought, that the bare fact that suffering existed was a sure proof of the reality of the evils of which they complained. Up to 1824 he had been engaged in making cotton hosiery for the Saxon market, when they were obliged to yield in the battle of competition. From 1824 to 1833 they had struggled on, but at the latter period they had lost all the South American continent in every article of cotton hosiery made by the Saxons. In fact, they could not stand before Saxony a single moment after she had entered the field of competition. In consequence of our long wools, they had not much interfered with the Leicester manufacture, which consisted of worsted and woollen hosiery. But Mr. Smith, in his late visit to Leicester, was informed that worsted and woollen yarns had been purchased there by the Saxons, sufficient to employ 10,000 stocking makers for a year. He believed he could not be contradicted when he asserted, in reference to our white cotton hose, that not an article in that line had been sold during the last three years, from one extremity of South America to the other, at a loss of less than 30 per cent. From 1834 Saxony had, in this department, commanded every market in the world. If, as we had seen, they could beat us in our own market, after paying the importation duty of 20 per cent., and 5 per cent. expenses, it was evident we could not have the slightest chance when we met them on common ground. After what he had seen last week of Saxon manufacturers, and comparing them with what they were in 1814, he felt like a person awakening from a feverish dream. They could sell us goods of equal quality to ours at little more than half our price. He had given orders for a lot of goods from their market, which he would have at the proportion of 3*s.* 3*d.* to 5*s.*, duty paid. They were a kind of goods on which about 80 per cent. of the whole value was expended in labour; and it was cheap labour, arising from the cheapness of food, that caused this, to us, alarming difference in price. In the hosiery trade, with which he was connected, this element operated to a greater extent than in many others, but he, and others in that trade, were only a little in advance of the rest in the road to ruin. They might be compared to persons living in a valley in which an alarming flood was rising. The inhabitants of the table lands around were sceptical as to the progress of the flood, so long as it did not threaten immediately to invade their own dwellings. Unfortunately for them, they lived far in the valley; but he would tell them who might think themselves secure, that the rising tide would soon reach them also. This overwhelming tide of foreign competition would never ebb, but would continue to advance so long as the cheap food of foreigners enabled them to work at half the money price of labour. He feared he was trespassing too much on the indulgence of the Meeting, for he knew that an assembly of hungry people (the Meeting had now lasted from eleven till three) was not the place for a bad speaker to be heard. (Laughter.) Mr. Rawson continued: It would actually be better for the manufacturers of Nottingham, engaged in foreign trade, to throw their machinery into the Trent than to employ it while they laboured under their present disadvantages. But it required a great deal of moral courage to take such a step as that. They were, however, only the advance guard, and the evil, if not determinedly met, would speedily overwhelm them all. With all due deference to the merchants of Manchester, he thought the thundering of their labouring wains, incessantly pushing through their streets to convey the produce of their spindles to the looms and workshops of the foreign manufacturer, seemed as if destined to act as a continual monitor, not to be misunderstood. After the astounding facts which had been brought before them, to talk of any thing less than complete abolition would be a mockery to the branch of manufacture in which he was engaged, and a false beacon of delusion to those in other branches who still indulge in a false confidence.

Mr. Holland Hoole (of the firm of Lambert, Hoole, and Jackson, extensive cotton-spinners and export merchants) thought both petitions good ones, and could sign either or both, and that, if both were again referred to the directors to combine their views, it might lead to a unanimous petition. He felt strongly on the subject of the corn laws, and not without occasion; for the welfare of the establishment with which he was connected, the support of his family, and the continuance of his business, all depended upon the continuance or the repeal of the corn laws. (Hear.) Therefore, though differing from many present upon political questions, he did not differ from them upon this, which was not a political question. He had been informed by a gentleman of respectability, that a gentleman, who transported himself to Belgium some years ago with his capital, and commenced the cotton business, was over here a fortnight ago, engaging hands and purchasing machines, which he found no difficulty in doing; and he said, "We (meaning foreign manufacturers) have nothing to fear except an alteration in your corn laws. (Hear, hear.) If you'll let them alone for ten years to come, we can do without you, we can then set you at defiance." (Hear, hear.)

Mr. James Fernley would second the motion of Mr. Hoole for adjournment. ("No, no;" "Question.")

The Chairman said it seemed to be the wish of the meeting that the discussion should now close. He had been requested to state, that both Mr. Fletcher and Mr. Neild had been called from home to a distance by private business, which prevented their presence. One word as to the statement he had made, that the resolution of the day before was passed *nem. con.* Mr. Smith had stated that he was there, and did not vote against it; and, therefore, he (the chairman) apprehended that practically he was to be considered as assenting to it. He should consider it the duty of every one present to hold up his hand against a motion if he did not wish it to be adopted.

Mr. J. B. Smith thought, after he had explained how he had dissented, by stating that he would neither vote for nor against it, it was most unfair in the chairman to represent him as approving of it.

The Chairman said, he had no desire to act unfairly towards any gentleman, but was guided solely by the minutes of proceedings. He had listened to the discussion with very great interest, and considerable advantage; his anticipation that the subject would be duly taken up, had been more than realized by the proceedings of the meeting; and whatever their differences of opinion as to the most effective and stringent mode of conveying their sentiments to the legislature, no one could say that the inhabitants of this town, and the merchants and manufacturers who constitute its Chamber of Commerce, were indifferent to the question, or that they did not see in it a question involving the prosperity of the country, and the well being of the working classes. His feeling and conviction were as strong as any gentleman's present, as to its being a great and enormous evil, which must eventually, if not remedied, weigh us down. He believed consequences had already arisen which it was now too late to avert; and all he hoped was, that measures might be taken to prevent their being aggravated. Having confidence in the justice of the cause, and in the integrity and intelligence of the Chamber, he did not see the wisdom or necessity of assuming either a threatening or a bullying tone. Let them express their sentiments with manly firmness and independence; but let them not assume the attitude either of the threatener or the bully. He knew not whether it became him to answer any observations addressed to them reflecting upon the conduct of one of their representatives in parliament, in the discharge of his public duty: observations giving him credit for the efficient discharge of his duties had also been addressed to them; and he (the chairman) should not have alluded to the subject, had he not had occasion, as their president, to hold much intercourse with that right honourable gentleman upon questions of this nature; and believing that he (the chairman) knew thoroughly the prevailing views of his mind, and what course of policy he thought it right to pursue, he would say, that he had never found the slightest difference of opinion between Mr. Thomson and himself respecting the great principles of free trade, and especially respecting the corn laws. As one of that right honourable gentleman's constituents, he had watched with great interest and anxiety his course, as a public man and a minister of the crown, in reference to those principles here entertained upon these and corresponding subjects; and it did appear to him that Mr. Thomson had rendered important services to his country, in various measures which he had carried through parliament, and in the principles he had there avowed; and that in no circumstances had he compromised those principles by language or act. What he had done, had been performed quietly, and without boast; its amount might be small, but it was done upon sound principles and efficiently. He (the chairman) was very loath to draw comparisons between one public man and another; but when a comparison was drawn between the late Mr. Huskisson, and our own right honourable representative, to the disadvantage of the latter, he (the chairman) could not help feeling a strong desire that the gentleman drawing that comparison would do Mr. Poulett Thomson the justice to read Mr. Huskisson's speech in 1828, when he recommended to the adoption of the House of Commons the very corn laws this Chamber was now met to deprecate, and the reasons he avowed for the adoption of that law: and compare them with the speech delivered by Mr. Poulett Thomson in 1833, while holding a responsible office under government, that of Vice-President of the Board of Trade, — but not a cabinet minister, and not allowed by those rules which regulated even governments, to give currency to those opinions, as a subordinate minister of the crown, in opposition to the cabinet ministers. He did then make known to the premier of that day, and the members of the cabinet, that he should feel it his duty, in the discharge of the solemn trust he held as the representative of this great manufacturing community, to declare his opinions adversely to the cabinet on the question then under discussion. He rose and delivered a reply to a cabinet minister, directly refuting the statements and arguments of that minister, and he (the chairman) would ask

Mr. Cobden to read and compare those speeches. (Applause.) He apologized for dwelling on this subject; but he had felt it his duty, having had much official communication as the president of the Chamber, with Mr. Thomson, to bear his testimony to the fidelity with which that right honourable gentleman discharged his duties. (Applause.)

Mr. R. H. GREG explained, as to the terms threatening and bullying, that what he meant was that no great act of justice was ever granted to bodies of men, except through the influence of fear; and he believed without such influence we should never get the repeal of the corn laws.

Ald. COBDEN said, he rose in a spirit of conciliation. The president had avowed the petition of the directors to be from his pen. He found himself therefore in the situation of a rival towards him for the honour of writing a petition. (A laugh.) As his superior in wisdom and senior in years, he would yield to the president. He had no peculiar regard for his own bantling; but would give up entirely the phraseology and composition, if the *facts* were incorporated in the petition of the directors. (Cheers.) But he thought, after the important revelations that had been made during their discussions, the Chamber would fail in an important duty if it did not communicate the facts directly to the government and legislature. (Hear.) And he would just add, that he thought it quite relevant to the subject under discussion to discuss the public conduct of their representatives in parliament. He knew Mr. Thomson there as a public character only. He had shared his hospitality and kindness, but that was not the place for discussing his private opinions or conduct. Upon public grounds he claimed the right to complain of Mr. Thomson, with reference to his exertions in the cause of free trade, and on the corn laws. He claimed the right to comment freely upon his public conduct in public assembly, without being subjected to the rebuke, remark, or criticism of any individual, whatever his position might be. (Cheers.) He was present in the gallery of the House of Commons, at the last debate in parliament on Mr. Villiers' motion for a repeal of the corn laws, and listened to all the nonsense and absurdity uttered by the landlords on the occasion, whose followers shouted down Mr. Mark Phillips; and he felt his blood boil and tingle too on Mr. Thomson sitting silent upon the treasury bench, instead of wielding the influence, which, as a cabinet minister, and as their member, he possessed; and he was almost ready to rush from his seat, as he saw him leaving the House before the debate had closed, to entreat him to refute the fallacies of such speakers as the Marquis of Chandos and Mr. D'Israeli. For this he complained of Mr. Thomson. Probably if *he* were anxious to be received by Mr. Thomson with smiles, to visit at his table, or to ask personal favours, *he* should have been able to quote passages in his past life deserving of eulogy. He had no such object to serve; but as one of his constituents he claimed for himself and for every one of the electors the right of calling in question the public acts of their representative. (Cheers.) They had been told by Mr. Pearson, that Mr. Thomson had himself declared that he knew the corn laws to be the sole obstruction to a profitable commerce with Germany, which corroborated the fact he had previously mentioned upon the best authority in Berlin. Now what he complained of was, that when the ministers are taunted in the House by their Tory opponents with the decline of our trade with that country, Mr. Thomson is silent, and does not tell the House and the country that a repeal of our corn laws would enable him to effect an alteration in the German tariff, by which the duties upon our goods would be reduced one-half—the cotton goods from 150*s.* to 75*s.* the cwt.—by which, as he was informed by the first merchants in Frankfort, all our trade in manufactured goods with those quarters, would be restored to us. For this conduct, for shrinking before a landed faction, he was dissatisfied with Mr. Thomson, and he claimed the right of publicly saying so. (Cheers.)

Mr. H. Hoole here said he should press his motion for adjournment, and it was accordingly put and negatived by a large majority.

The President said, that he should now proceed to put the question, and he believed according to the custom pursued in parliament it was usual to put it in the form, "that the words of the original motion do stand part of the question."

Mr. J. B. Smith wished to know if the president meant to put the original motion or the amendment first.

The President said, by the mode he proposed to adopt, which was usual in parliament, the original motion would be put first, and if rejected, the amendment would then be before the meeting.

Alderman R. Roberts said, with all deference he thought the most regular course would be to put the amendment first. It might be usual to pursue the course proposed by the president in the House of

Commons, but in this Chamber it was customary to put the amendment first.

Mr. J. C. Dyer said he had no feeling about the matter, and did not care whether his amendment was put first or last. The usual way he believed was to put the amendment first, but so long as the Chamber came to a dispassionate vote upon it he did not care.

The President was persisting in putting the motion in the form he had first proposed, namely, that the "original motion do stand part of the question," when Alderman Cobden and Mr. J. B. Smith and several other gentlemen said they did not really understand the way in which it was about to be put.

Mr. Greg certainly did not see why it could not be moved in the usual form. (Hear, hear.)

Alderman Roberts said, though the course pursued by the president might be that of the House of Commons, yet as we here were merely men of "common understanding," and liked to know precisely what we were about—(hear, hear,)—he would suggest that the amendment be put first.

The President said he was of course in the hands of the meeting, and proceeded to put the amendment accordingly, when Mr. Cobden's petition was carried by a large majority, only about four or five gentlemen besides the directors opposing it. The result was received with loud cheering, and the meeting, after the mayor had been called to the chair, and a vote of thanks given to the president, separated, soon after four o'clock.

CHARLES WOOD, PRINTER,
Poppin's Court, Fleet Street.

ARTISANS,

FARMERS, AND LABOURERS.

"The power of King, Lords, and Commons, is not an arbitrary power.—They are the Trustees, not the owners, of the estate. The fee-simple is in *us*. They cannot alienate, they cannot waste. When we say that the Legislature is supreme, we mean, that it is the highest power known to the Constitution; that it is the highest in comparison with the other subordinate powers established by the laws. In this sense, the word supreme is relative, not absolute. The power of the Legislature is limited, not only by the general rules of natural justice, and the welfare of the community, but by the forms and principles of our particular Constitution. If this doctrine be not true, we must admit, that King, Lords, and Commons have no rule to direct their resolutions, but merely their own will and pleasure."—JUNIUS.

LONDON:
RIDGWAY, PICCADILLY.
MDCCCXXXIX.

ARTISANS, FARMERS, & LABOURERS.

It may be thought, that the reflections here thrown together, are altogether unnecessary, after the able speeches against the Corn Laws in Parliament. However, they were written for the most part previous to the discussion of those laws; and it appears to the writer, that they in some degree differ in the view taken of the question in Parliament; which induces him to offer them in this form to the public; not for the purpose or pretence of attempting to enlighten those who have considered the question more deeply perhaps than he has done, and have brought forward more facts to confirm the opinion of the injustice of those laws: but because they may help to alter the view taken of them by the farmers and agricultural labourers, into whose hands a small pamphlet such as this may fall, when the more elaborate speeches of Honourable Members of Parliament are out of their reach, or from their length, disregarded.

The fact is—The question of the Corn Laws is a simple one. It is simply a law of injustice! and the less men's minds are puzzled about it by Political Economists the better.

ENGLAND takes her station among the nations of Europe—not from her size—her natural dimensions—but from her population, her industry and her wealth; not her agricultural wealth!—for no nation, simply agricultural, has ever risen to such eminence as the station England now occupies.

She is not naturally great,—she is *artificially* great!

To what then—to what wealth is that station attributable?

To her commercial wealth! and her manufacturing industry!—for until England was a manufacturing and great commercial country—a country of shopkeepers, as Napoleon termed her, (for to the shopkeepers did he owe the grudge of her greatness—literally, her commercial wealth)—she did not hold the rank she does now; and even what agricultural superiority over other countries she may now lay claim to, she owes to the stimulus of Manufacturing invention, and to Commercial enterprize and prosperity.

Other nations are jealous of us—jealous of our energies—our commercial greatness! but they trouble not their heads with the class which is here dominant, whose power would overshadow the nation! They know nothing of our Aristocracy, except by the visit of an occasional lounger. I find, that in Turkey they are apt to give nick-names to the various nations of Europe, and that we are there called *Tschokadschi*, linen-drapers—(See M. de Tietzs's St. Petersburgh, Constantinople, &c. &c.) Lord Ashburnham, whose opinion Sir James Graham cited the other night as co-inciding with his own—"that England will be the most destestable country in the known world to live in, if the Corn Law is repealed, and her population becomes more manufacturing than it is at present"—will know, having lived for so many years in Turkey! if the expression of *Tschokadschi* is rightly quoted; and he may (but I should doubt it!) return there to reside, and take his friend, the Right Honourable Baronet, with him—when the law *is repealed*.

But I do not think the Right Honourable Baronet has cause for alarm. I can't say, that I think there is any likelihood of the beautiful country in which Lord Ashburnham's property (in Sussex) is situated, and where coal has not as yet, to the best of my belief, been found—that that, or any—the greater part of England! will, when the present noxious law *is repealed*, be *blackened* and *withered*, and likened to the country about Wolverhampton.

As little likely do I think it; as that the Honourable Member for Wolverhampton (Mr. Villiers) should change, and become like the Right Honourable Baronet, the Member for Pembroke (Sir James Graham), either in person or in politics.*

* The Honourable Member, Mr. Villiers, is fair, and has always been a friend of the people! The Right Honourable Baronet, Sir James Graham, is dark—was once a liberal—is now a Tory!

But to return.—

They take no note, they know scarcely anything, of our proud and over-bearing Aristocracy. In truth, our Aristocracy, as they have taken to themselves so much of the power of the State, are too apt to ascribe to themselves alone the glory and ascendancy of England, and to attribute to themselves the successes of the last war. They "lay the flattering unction to their souls," that it was by their means that it was brought to a glorious conclusion.

Now, not to disparage the gallantry of the Somersets! the Manners! the Ponsonbys! and the Clintons!—the younger scions of which noble families (with others too numerous to mention!) did not decline the battle, but distinguished themselves in the late war—I would ask, did they or their compeers, did *they* find "the sinews of war?" Who furnished the sums by which Austria was subsidized? by which an army was raised in Portugal? and arms put into the hands of the heroic Spaniards?

Let an Ex-Chancellor of the Exchequer, who was in office in Tory times, and during the income tax, declare, if our Aristocracy—our Government of that day—for in that day, as pretty much in the present, our Government was composed of the Aristocracy!—if they, however wealthy, could have furnished the means of prosecuting the war without the aid of the *commercial and manufacturing interest!* And yet now, when after many years of peace, that very commercial and manufacturing interest, from which they derive their increased revenues, which afforded them the means of bringing the war to a glorious conclusion, for lack of that encouragement which Government should have given to commerce, instead of offering obstruction to it as it has, cry out, in consequence of the lowness of prices and the dearness of provisions—threatening to annihilate the artisans,—they turn a deaf ear to their complaints, *will not listen to them even!* and refuse to abrogate that unjust and destructive monopoly, the *Corn Laws*, which they themselves devised in a season of unexampled prosperity, *for their own interest*, and carried in their then (and still, even since the Reform Bill) but too subservient Parliament. Our Parliament—no honest man can deny —*did legislate for the good of one class*—the agriculturists, the agricultural interest—that is, *their own interest*. But as a proof of how dependant the one interest is upon the other—how intimately connected they both are, the agricultural and the manufacturing—that last interest has, up to a certain time, borne the strain upon it; and despite the drawback of a bad law, has even further! in some degree, partaken of the advantages that accrued to the agriculturists from partial legislation.

But the time has come when a re-action has taken place. Our population has increased enormously, so much so, that we are sending agricultural labourers to the manufacturing districts. Foreigners are beginning to manufacture, themselves, in consequence of that *very Act* of the Legislature; and as the agricultural interest has thriven while they kept the manufacturers in profitable employ, at the time that they (the manufacturers) had a foreign market for their super-abundant produce, so now, if that market is lost to the manufacturers, the agriculturists will surely feel it.

They *will feel* it, if they do not relieve the manufacturer of the strain upon him.

As in a carriage drawn by a pair of horses, to which there is an unskilful driver, who makes one horse draw more than the other—*when one flags, both must stop*; if the weight is too great for one! So must the State Coach stop now, if the labouring beast (Sir Robert Peel has likened the manufacturer to a beast inferior to a horse) be not relieved of the strain!—foolishly put upon him, as regards the ultimate success of the journey; and unfairly put upon him as regards the other favoured animal.

In short, the agriculturists will find, that if the manufacturing interest partook of their whileom *prosperity*, so will they (the agriculturists) now share in the *adversity* of the manufacturers!

The Corn Laws act as a prohibitory law, against the introduction of foreign corn. Our own growth, except in years of abundance, that is after good harvests, is not sufficient; and it is only, when our manufacturers are in possession of foreign markets, that even then, in years of abundance! they can afford to buy a sufficiency of corn for themselves, their wives and families; and then only by exchanging a quantity of manufactured articles for an insufficient, or rather inadequate return of agricultural produce.

The barter, (putting the consideration of money out of the question) *has not been—is not just;* and the manufacturer is obliged to work double the number of hours that the agricultural labourer works, and not only he; but his children, and those of tender years! The fact then (as has been well observed) of my Lord Ashley's coming forward to protect them, by abridging the number of their hours of labour, is absurd: while he upholds these noxious laws, which are the cause of their extra work.

The fact is, then, that in order to keep up their revenue the landlords force the manufacturer to work so many more hours a day—in order to obtain a sufficiency of the common necessaries of life to keep himself and family alive.

For one drop of sweat by which the agriculturist eats his bread—the manufacturer in order to receive the same return must expend two.—But do the agricultural labourers themselves benefit by the high prices?

The landlords and farmers cannot prove it. Landlords undoubtedly do benefit greatly, and some farmers may: because they know the price of grain in the market throughout the year; and they can take an average and get their rents reduced: when they have not leases. But is it to be supposed that the hard-worked and uneducated labourer can take an average of the prices during the current year, and insist upon a certain average of wages equal to his just share of the profits of agriculture? The thing is impossible. He is paid by the day, and it matters not if prices rise for a time, he finds the difficulty in the increased price of bread: but he suffers in silence, and takes half a loaf rather than no bread: until the market is somewhat replenished, and he gets his loaf again; or to relieve himself he dips into the scanty purse into which he has dropped his earnings *(and this is the case only with the provident man!)* and diminishes the means he has provided against accidents and illness. The poor cannot uphold a struggle against the rich; except when they combine, and much affliction is endured before the poor labourers think of this or resort to combination. But do not landlords immediately avail themselves of high prices to raise their rents? I need give but one instance, and that of a man of high character and noble fortune—The Duke of Buccleugh! who (as the Newspapers assure us) *did* but a short time ago take advantage of the present high price and raised his rents in Northamptonshire; and sure am I, the opinion must be general among landlords, that it is justifiable so to do, when a man of His Grace's character does it.

The labourer may after that come to the tenant and say, "the price of corn is high," and "I am obliged to give eight-pence (or whatever the price is) for my loaf, you must give me more weekly wages." But the tenant says, "No—that I cannot do, for my landlord has taken the difference; and I am in the same situation or nearly! as I was before when the price was low, and my rent not so great. I won't raise your wages; and if you won't work for me for what you did before, I will employ another man." The landlords in general care nought. They leave it to the middle man (as it were in Ireland!) and the middle man (the tenant) screws the poor labourer.

It is upon the home market, say the landlords, that the manufacturers should depend, quite forgetting, that it is upon that very market in which the manufacturers themselves are their customers! that they (the agriculturists) too must depend; and yet they would, in their blindness, destroy this market, by causing manufacturers, who are losing their old markets abroad, and have an insufficient market at home for all their hands—an insufficient custom at home! to transport their capital and industry and best workmen to other countries. Capital and skill which, if the agriculturists met them upon equal terms, would find employment here, and for the many hands, which they will have thrown out of work if the Corn Laws continue.

It seems certain, that two-thirds only of our

manufacturers are wanted at home, that therefore one-third must find a market elsewhere. It is clear then, that one-third of our manufacturers—the producers of that superabundant quantity—if they do not find that market—must starve!

Now if our landlords could, by any means, draft the one-third of the manufacturing population, that are simple workmen, out of the country, and retain the capitalists with all the superior workmen, it might be very well their struggling to keep up their prices. But this cannot be. The men are not so easily transported; and *they assuredly will not starve. They ask for work!* But owing to the restrictions upon the importation of corn, they cannot get it; for foreigners have only corn to give us in exchange, and that, the very necessary the superabundant manufacturers require, they are prevented from importing!

Gentlemen, Landlords, Monopolists! You cheered on the people to exertion and industry for your own sakes during the war. They were prosperous, as were you!—They throve—they married—they begat children; and you *must not*—you *cannot* offer obstruction to their living. They have implored—(No! a large *Body*—the Chartists, knowing the uselessness of imploring an aristocratic Parliament, have held their peace.) But is it Peace?—You say it is—You cry "Peace where there is no Peace."—They have not implored—They hold their tongues.—To use a coarse phrase, they know it is no use barking.—But are you certain they will not bite? Oh! that we had a Minister, who could take a larger and more liberal, a more enlightened view of this question than has Lord Melbourne!

Our population is our wealth, if properly employed —the wealth of our agriculturists!—the consumers of their produce, and the cause of their producing more and more, by the improvement of their lands; without which, what would the broad lands of England be worth to the landlords?

Two-thirds of our manufactures are consumed in this country, as has been said, but one-third must find a market abroad.

Our Parliament—our Government with Lord Melbourne at its head! would starve one-third of our manufacturing population! Would to God he would take a larger—broader view of our situation. England has taken the lead in all political questions—has been foremost in extending civil liberty and religious over the world—has set the example of representative Government: if she has not the best *herself*. If she would still be the admiration of the world, and maintain her position, by her *great moral* example, she should submit perhaps to temporary disadvantage, (and all changes are productive necessarily of some evil, for a time!) and set the example of opening her ports. Other Nations *would—must*, after a while, follow in her footsteps, and ultimately such a measure *must be* of *material* advantage to her. Other nations would be obliged to do, in regard to her, as have Austria and France in regard to Switzerland; who, having persevered in free trade, has compelled the two Powers to reduce their duties, from 30 to 5 per cent. on her frontier. Tuscany is now rejoicing in free trade! and Mr. O'Connell, in his *most admirable speech (reported in the Newspaper of the 19th of March)* bears witness to its *extraordinary* and most *excellent* effect. Are we to be the last? not first, or among the first?

There never was a moment more favourable than the present—now after a long peace of twenty-four years! for the adoption of such an experiment, if experiment it may be called, which all enlightened men (and those practical commercial men, who are most likely to know its effects,) have admitted to be as just in theory, as it is likely to be advantageous in practice: if extended to the various nations of the world, having a direct tendency to amalgamate the interests of all nations; and prove among nations the well established fact among individual men, *that we are all mutually dependant upon one another!* But not among commercial men alone, but among Statesmen—even of Tory principles! this opinion holds. That this is the fact I need only cite the opinion of a very worthy man, an Ex-Chancellor of the Exchequer (before referred to) who for many years, in Tory times, managed our Finances, and who, although not remarkable for the general largeness of his views, was decidedly of opinion, that great blessings would flow from a universal opening of the Ports!* Some one among the great commercial people of Europe must begin, and is not England—the first in commerce and in fame—to set the example? She has flourished despite the restrictions upon commerce. How much more would she not thrive if unrestricted? It is in the market place at home, that people meet in friendly intercourse, and in commerce abroad, producing mutual good will, that people ascertain their several wants, and by communication learn to satisfy them. Instead of obstructing intercourse with other nations, an enlightened Government would invite them to an exchange of commodities.

Without international intercourse, Governments, for the most part anxious selfishly to obtain power and patronage (and *ours* seems to be of this class), may at any time excite their people, as has heretofore been the case, to disagreement and war.

But let the various nations of the earth meet together in amicable commerce, and mutual dependance one upon the other, as was doubtless intended by the beneficent Creator, and "the bow

* Mr. Canning would have said in his sarcastic way, "You got this communication by the heavy Van from Oxford!" What Mr. Canning's own opinion in regard to the Corn Laws *would now have been*, may be inferred by the vote given by his intimate friend and constant adviser, Lord Seaford, who, the other night, voted *in the minority* in the House of Lords!

shall in truth be broken, and the spear be snapped in sunder!"

Have we not a right to expect more from Lord Melbourne, as the consequence of the long peace, than the mere reduction of our establishments, about which he prated the other night—a reduction which, at this moment, owing to the non-intercourse of nations—productive itself of animosity between them, seems to have been ill-judged. This preparation *might not now have been necessary*: if our Government had taken advantage of the state of repose in which Europe rests, and had availed itself of the arts of peace, to encourage commerce, by taking off the duties upon foreign importation.

Manufactures we need not—what we need is food—food of the most necessary kind—that which supports our poor.

But to return to a point I would dwell on. It is needless now to dissemble the fact, as there is clear proof of the truth of it, and it is admitted by those who uphold the Corn Laws, that our home market is only sufficient for, or consumes only, two-thirds of our actual produce in manufactures! the remaining third then of our produce is lost, as a natural consequence, if we lose our foreign market; and the producers of that third, or one-third of our manufacturing population is condemned (if the Corn Laws are not repealed) to actual starvation!

But it has been said, we should not be dependant upon other nations.

Supposing that to be the fact, which I am persuaded is but a fallacy! that it is well to be independent of other neighbour countries: lest, in the event of disagreement and war, we should be prevented importing from them. Why has not Government, under this impression, proposed some grand scheme of relief to our own country, by populating our Southern Colonies—by sending out gangs of labourers under efficient agriculturists, to those regions which are so productive! with implements of agriculture—a scheme for establishing schools of agriculture here, and in those countries! where the science may be studied; so that, in coming years, we may not be dependent upon our neighbours, but upon our own colonists for any extraordinary supply of the staple of life, which we might require for our increasing population: whilst we should in return export our manufactures thither.

The quantity of wool imported from Australia has been yearly increasing. Why should we not, adopting a system, and properly encouraging emigration of labourers under able agriculturists, expect a sufficiency of corn, and other necessaries as well?

The commerce incidental to such a scheme would give employment to thousands of seamen; and would do more for our Navy than keeping an ordinary of seamen and coast guard.

But the present case is a pressing one, and I hold my opinion, *that our population is our wealth properly employed!*

In regard to the advantages we have derived from the peace. What are they?

Lord Melbourne and his predecessors may say, that the country *has* derived benefit from the peace. But what classes enjoy the benefit?

Our aristocratic Parliament, for their own purposes, have reduced the duties on foreign luxuries, —wine, fruit, &c. &c.: but they refuse to reduce the price of bread—a necessary to our people!

Honourable Gentlemen may pretend to deprecate the accusation, which some honest men in Parliament have fearlessly advanced against the monopolists—the agriculturists, (that is the *landlords!)* but the stigma attaches to them, and in vain do they attempt to relieve themselves of it. They *are* grasping, and selfish, and inconsiderate of the great body of the people! many of whom, however, the farmers and the agricultural labourers, they have succeeded in cajoling into the belief that *their* (the landlords') monopoly is for their benefit.

Witness the many petitions for this odious monopoly!

But do they think that those who see more clearly, and those, who are beginning to open their eyes to the truth, will submit to their arbitrement? and suffer themselves to be starved in a country which supports a wealthy Church—a Church, which proclaims, "That the labourer is worthy of his hire." That is, that a man who is willing to work, *shall be enabled to get his bread!*—a Church, that should concern itself in feeding the hungry, and should therefore, following the precept of their blessed Master, who proclaimed, that charity was the greatest of all virtues! assist in the abrogation of these laws against the importation of an article necessary to the poor of this country.

In regard to the necessary taxes, that is a State question! but a question which it is incumbent upon Parliament, and upon Government—supposed to consist of the ablest men in the country—to expound.

The agriculturists say, "that *they* pay the greatest proportion of the taxes!" Is that the fact? If so, as Mr. Ward very justly said, in his place in Parliament: "Our system of taxation should be revised." And in regard to the protecting duties which the manufacturers propose giving up! Are they essential to the revenues of the country, and the payment of the national debt?

If so—is it not possible to devise a levy of other duties, alias taxes, which, when all protection (the *unjust protection* of the agriculturists in the form of a Corn Law, which is starving our manufacturers,) is taken off, may equally affect both the manufacturing and the agricultural population, and support the credit of the crown and country?

This, and the question of leases held by farmers, who, holding them under the present Corn Laws, would suffer calamitously, if they were repealed without a just acquittal, as stated by Sir Robert

Peel; and the Tithe Composition Act referred to by Sir James Graham, are the difficulties.

An able Government should strive to overcome them.

"The ruin or prosperity of a state depends so much on the administration of its government, that, to be acquainted with the merit of a ministry, we need only observe the condition of a people. If we see them obedient to the laws, prosperous in their industry, united at home, and respected abroad, we may reasonably presume that their affairs are conducted by men of experience, abilities, and virtue. If, on the contrary, we see a universal spirit of distrust and dissatisfaction, a *rapid decay of trade*, dissensions in all parts of the empire, and a total loss of respect in the eyes of foreign powers, we may pronounce, without hesitation, that the Government of that country is *weak*, *distracted*, *and corrupt. The multitude in all countries, are patient to a certain point. Ill usage may rouse their indignation, and hurry them into excesses; but the original fault is in the Government.*"*

Far be it from me to say, that Lord Melbourne's Government is indisposed to do its duty, or that it is not superior to any former Government. But it must set about its work diligently, and without delay.

I finish in Mr. Clay's admirable and impressive words, for I am interested as he is. *My* only

* Junius.

personal interest is in land as is *his!* and I equally with him feel the advantages of an Aristocracy, that does not abuse a power, that is not rightly theirs according to the Constitution. *To be secure in property and in person they must be just.* Therefore do I advocate the repeal of the Corn Laws:—because, like him, I desire to see the Constitution of my country (King, Lords, and Commons,) permanent and secure. Mr. Clay, (the Member for the Tower Hamlets,) said, "that as regarded the Continent of Europe, our system of Corn Laws had shut us out from a wide field of beneficial enterprize—that it had converted friends into enemies, and customers into rivals. But a question of yet graver import, perhaps, remained. Did that system tend to render us less capable of competing with our manufacturing rivals in those markets where we meet on equal terms? We have wilfully and designedly, by enacting these laws, shut ourselves out, to a great extent, from European markets. Have we, by the same enactment, endangered our trans-atlantic markets? Now, in considering this momentous question, let them again take only the admissions of the supporters of the Corn Laws. The manufacturers say, that food is fifty per cent cheaper on the Continent than here, wages are consequently materially lower. At this disadvantage we cannot compete with our manufacturing rivals in American or Asiatic markets. The supporters of the Corn Laws, admitting that food is cheaper abroad, (as indeed they must, for it is their very proposition, that it is good it should be so,) reply yes; but your larger capital and greater skill, and the greater energy of our operatives, more than countervail this advantage, and it is not true, accordingly, that you cannot compete with the foreigner; and they refer us triumphantly to the increasing exports of manufactured goods. Now, in this view of the case, as stated by the parties respectively, there is one thing very remarkable, viz: the perfect coolness with which, on their own showing, the supporters of the Corn Laws would appropriate to their own profit that which is not theirs, viz: the whole advantages accruing from the superiority of the British manufacturer. [hear, hear, hear!]

"They say you can make a piece of calico for 50*s*., which costs the Swiss or German manufacturer 60*s*.; therefore you can give us the 10*s*., difference, and yet subsist. If the price of provisions in both countries were equal, you, the British manufacturers, would divide the extra 10*s*. among you, in the shape of larger profits to the master, and greater comforts to the operative, inasmuch as though wages might be something nominally lower, they would command more food; but you shall give the whole difference to the operative, in the shape of higher wages, and we will take it from him in the shape of higher priced food [hear, hear, hear!]. That was the case of the supporters of the Corn Laws, as stated by themselves, and upon that statement alone, he thought the manufacturing population would be entitled to demand the repeal of those laws. Up to this point the Corn Laws would seem only to be unjust; but would their effect cease here? Was not their injustice coupled, as in almost all cases, with the grossest folly—folly which would cause that injustice to be visited on the heads of its perpetrators? Could it be seriously believed, that we should always retain that superiority of capital and skill which enabled us at present to make head against the disadvantage of dearer food? If we could rely on the assertion of those who ought best to know the fact, we are already losing it; but he required no evidence to convince him that we could not long retain it. Capital will flow to the region where profits are largest—skilful workmen will migrate to the land where their wages will procure for them the largest share of enjoyment. The difficulty of transferring manufacturing capital, attachment to their native land on the part of our operatives, might retard this process, but its result was certain [hear, hear, hear!]. It was no answer to this argument to say that our export of manufactured goods was increasing. The wants of the new world were so vast, that without our aid they could not at present be supplied. But of this the House might be assured as a result from which there was no escape, that if by maintaining the price of subsistence here greatly above the level of other manufacturing countries they persisted in giving to the manufacturers of those countries a superiority of profit, they would, at a period more or less remote, see all our great staples transferred to other lands [hear, hear!]. The main feature of manufacturing industry, as contradistinguished from agriculture was this,—that whereas in agriculture the highest cost of production governed the price of the produce of the soil in manufactures, the price of the article produced at the lowest cost governed the price of all similar articles. Whereever, therefore, any manufacture can be carried on at the least cost, there will be its ultimate seat—elsewhere it will languish and decay [hear, hear!]. When the time shall come, as come it must, that the capital and skill of foreign manufacturers shall equal ours—one of two things must happen—either you must wholly lose your manufactures, or the wages of labour must subside to the level, or nearly so, of those paid by our foreign rivals. The natural advantages of England, in the possession of coal and iron for instance, and perhaps the native energy of our people, may always enable the capitalist to give somewhat higher wages here than elsewhere, but not to such an extent as to make up to the operative for any excessive difference in the price of food; and here he could not but advert to the monstrous doctrine that the operative manufacturer had no interest in the repeal of the Corn

Laws, inasmuch as if the price of food fell, wages would fall with it [hear, hear!]. That this opinion should be really and sincerely entertained by any persons—even by those whose humble station had afforded but little opportunity for mental training, was to him matter of surprise; but that it should find a voice within the walls of the House of Commons—above all, that it should find a supporter in the Right Honourable Baronet, the member for Tamworth, as must be inferred from his speech on the motion for hearing evidence at the bar, was to him (Mr. Clay) the subject of unbounded astonishment [hear, hear, hear!]. This most extraordinary proposition rested on the assumption that the capitalist has some power over the wages of labour. Nothing can be more certain than that he has no such power [hear, hear!]. The price of labour is regulated wholly by the supply and demand. If there be an advantageous field for the employment of capital, and the master manufacturer have many orders to execute, he will, in the fear of being outbid, give wages up to the very highest limit that will afford him a profit on his capital, and this he will do, however cheap may be the price of provisions.

"If, on the other hand, there be a limited field for the employment of capital, and the master manufacturers have but few orders to execute, there will be great competition among the workmen, and, whatever be the price of food, they will bid against each other for employment, down to the point of starvation [hear, hear!]. To talk, therefore, of the effect of a free importation of corn, and consequent reduction in the price of food, being to reduce wages, is to betray an entire ignorance of the laws, by which the price of labour is governed, to mistake the effect for the cause, and to confound the necessary order of events. Wages would not fall because the price of food fell, but, because in the struggle on which we were entering with the foreign manufacturer, wages must, of necessity, approximate to the foreign level [hear, hear!]. The repeal of the Corn Laws would mitigate to the English operative the effect of that struggle, possibly by giving a healthy impulse, and just direction to the manufacturing industry, as well of other countries as of this; it might be the means of averting that struggle altogether (hear!). The maintenance of the Corn Laws on the contrary, would render that struggle inevitable, and anticipate and aggravate its worst evils. The tendency of those laws is to lower the wages of labour, and increase the price of food; the effect of their repeal would be to raise the rate of wages, whilst it lowered the price of food (hear!). In conclusion, he would entreat of those Honourable Gentlemen, who more especially represented the landed interests in that House to consider well: whether it was prudent to reject year after year such motions as the present. This counsel proceeded from no unfriendly adviser. No one, if he might be permitted to advert for one moment to himself, could have less personal or selfish interest in this question. Utterly unconnected now, whatever he might once have been, with either commerce or manufactures, he had no other interest in the settlement of this great question, than inasmuch as his fortunes were mixed up with the fate and fortunes of the country. He would go further; he could say with perfect truth, that if there were one class in the prosperity of which beyond all others, he should be disposed to take an interest, that class was the landed aristocracy of England. He believed the existence of such a class to be essential to the stability of the constitution—of that mild and tempered form of monarchy which beyond all other forms of Government was capable of combining the utmost extent of freedom whether of person or opinion with the supremacy of the laws, the security of property, and the highest degree of social refinement (hear hear!). But it was precisely because he thought so highly of the value of the landholders as a class that he was alarmed at the pertinacity with which they clung to these useless—these worse than useless and disgraceful laws, (hear !). Look, said the Hon. Gentleman, at the advantages of the position in which you stand. Reflect whence these advantages are derived, and consider well whether by insisting on the maintenance of these laws, you do not place them all at hazard. The growth of the manufactures and commerce, and with them of the wealth and population of England, within the last three quarters of a century, is without a parallel in the history of nations—vast cities have grown up on barren heaths—every quarter of the land is filled with a thriving and wealthy population. Now, on what class of the British people does this unheard of prosperity confer the greatest benefit? Beyond all doubt on the landholders [hear, hear !]. As proprietors of the soil of Britain, you possess the greatest natural monopoly that the world ever saw [hear, hear !]. Every extension of trade, every advance of manufacturing skill, tends directly to your benefit. Every addition to the miraculous powers of the steam engine—every improvement in the spinning-jenny or the power-loom—is an addition to the value of your estates. "Vos sed non nobis" might almost be your language to the ingenious men by whom such improvements are effected; for the profits of any new invention can be retained by the inventor but until the knowledge of it is diffused; but if it add to the general health and population of the country, its permanent benefit is yours [hear, hear !]. It would scarcely be possible to over estimate the effect of the commercial and manufacturing prosperity of England, in the value of English estates; he believed it would be stating it too low to say that it had within a century quadrupled the rent and the value. Did Honourable Gentlemen know what was the value of good land in England a hundred years since ?

And what was its value now in the countries less auspicious to landholders than England? The rack rent of good land in England a century back did not exceed 5*s*. per acre, and now, with some very rare and trifling exceptions, it did not amount to one half or even a third of five shillings in any part of Continental Europe; indeed, over the greater part of Europe, as in the countries of the new world, rent could not be obtained, and the proprietor was forced to cultivate his own estates. To what circumstance could this difference of value be attributed, or why was an estate more valuable now than it was an hundred years ago in England, or than it now was in Silesia, or in Upper Canada? Could they imagine there was any other cause than the vast demand for every varied produce of the soil—not corn alone—which the wealth and population consequent on commerce and manufactures had created? (hear, hear!) It was well worthy of the observation of those who supposed that the rent of estates depended on keeping up the price of corn, that rent had risen altogether out of proportion to the price of corn; the average price of corn for the ten years since 1828, was 55*s*. 10*d*. an advance of not more than 37 per cent. on the price of the fifty years at the end of the seventeenth and the beginning of last century, viz. from 1675 to 1725, which was 40*s*. 8*d*., whilst rent had risen 300 per cent! What, then, was the obvious interest of the landholder? Above all things to protect, to preserve, to foster the commerce and manufactures of the country; but in maintaining the Corn Laws, as he had shewn, by the admission of the supporters of those laws, they cripple the growth and endanger ultimately the existence of those great interests. They limited the market for our manufactures in Europe, they endangered our possession of trans-atlantic markets (hear, hear!) But higher considerations than such as could be drawn from appeals to the selfish interests of any class, ought to influence the House in disposing of this question. Might not the continued existence of the Corn Laws tend greatly to enhance any danger to which our institutions were exposed, and to precipitate rash and ill-advised change? (hear, hear!) Did they think that the Corn Laws might be safely retained, because all classes of the people were not at present united in demanding the repeal?—because the great masses of the labouring population would not join in the agitation on this question? (hear, hear, hear!) Why, he confessed their holding aloof was with him the very strongest reason for immediate concession. Had the House remarked why they would not join the middle classes in demanding the repeal of the Corn Laws? Was it that they approved of those laws—that they were even indifferent to their existence? On the contrary, one of the very first acts of a Parliament elected according to what was called the People's Charter, would be the sweeping away of those laws; and they abstained, they said, from petitioning for the repeal, because, in a House constituted as was the present House of

Commons, the success of such petitions was hopeless. Again, they said—If we refuse to join the middle classes in procuring the repeal of the Corn Laws, they will join us in demanding the People's Charter. Let the House be aware lest it make good this prophecy (hear, hear!)—lest, in the utter hopelessness of seing justice done in this matter, it drove the middle to make common cause with the working classes, and to force on a change in our form of Government, as the only means of ridding themselves of what they felt to be an intolerable oppression. (Hear, hear!) Never yet, in the history of this country, had those classes combined without achieving the object at which they aimed. As yet, the members of that House had the time to prevent the alliance—as yet they might withdraw all the better portion even of the working classes, the honest and the well-intentioned, from the guidance of the visionary, the fanatic, the revolutionist, the incendiary. But it was mainly by their conduct on this question, that their faithfulness and competency as legislators would be tested. (Hear, hear!) If they showed that, although chiefly belonging to the landed Aristocracy, they looked, in legislating, to the interests of the whole community, they might preserve our present form of Representative Government. If, on the contrary, they clearly showed that they would regard only the interests or supposed interests of that class from which the representatives of the people of England have hitherto been taken

—then, as he believed, some great convulsion must ensue, and perhaps at no very distant period, in which assuredly it would not be the Corn Laws only that would be swept away. (Hear, hear!)"

I owe some apology to Mr. Clay for having transcribed so much more of his speech than I had at first intended. But I thought, upon reading it over again, that I could not do better than bring it again in another form before the country, or rather I should say, such as take the trouble to read this address. The arguments throughout his admirable speech are irrefragable, as are those in the speech of Mr. O'Connell, on a subsequent day—a speech, which redounds no less to his honour as a man, than to his well-earned fame as an orator. It should be read by every Irishman, as well as every Englishman, interested in the welfare of his country.

ANGLUS.

POSTSCRIPT.

In regard to lands being thrown out of culture after the repeal of the Corn Laws!

I do not believe, that that will be the case, and in confirmation of this opinion, I have the testimony of a gentleman of great good sense and practical knowledge as a farmer, in the County of Nottingham, who has a good deal of land in his own hands—his land being *exactly of that quality*, which it has been said by many—in order to cause apprehension to farmers and labourers, and to gain them over to their cause against the repeal of the Corn Law, would go out of culture *first of all lands (videlicet. strong clay land!)*—and his unhesitating opinion at the moment is, that at 45 shillings the quarter, or even at 40 shillings—he—a gentleman (and every body knows, that a gentleman's expenses in farming are greater than a farmer's!) *can continue to grow wheat with profit ; and that his lands will not go out of culture*, in the event of prices falling—even to that lower sum.

That is his opinion now.

And when the operation of a *Free Trade* comes into play, and its effects are seen in the diminished prices of articles consumed both by rich and poor —when the farmer pays less for the oats his horses eat--less for his timber and iron—less for his seed —less for his labour, and for the various articles of his domestic consumption—I am satisfied, that my friend's opinion will be more than confirmed, and that he will find, that the land (his land being heavy clay land—be it remembered !) may grow wheat even at a less return per quarter than 40 shillings, and *still* with sufficient profit to him, and to all employed in its culture.

And when prices are so reduced !—surely, in all fairness, the Fund-holder cannot object—*must consent* to a reduction of his per centage.

Money being the representative of a certain value—when the value of all articles in the market falls, more is to be had for it, and the difference then accruing to the possessor of funded property, should be equally shared by the public Creditor and the Debtor—the Nation !

Thus, supposing corn to be the standard of value, by which the price of all other articles is regulated, it being the article in most general consumption : If the price of corn falls, say, from 50 shillings to 40 shillings the quarter, and remains, as it probably would after a time *(with Free Trade !)* at a steady, fixed price remain, at all events without the sudden variations in price to which it has been subject, under the Corn Laws!—half the difference, half of the ten shillings should be remitted by the fund-holder—that is 20 shillings in the per centage upon every nominal hundred pounds in the funds, or one-pound should be remitted by the holders of five per cents., and so on, at a calculation through all funded stock.

The calculations to be made and accredited yearly, by Parliament, and in the face of the nation.

I don't pretend to a profound or accurate knowledge of financial matters; but this appears to me a fair proposal, and though it may be a simple one, it may not be the worse for that.

The more the science of Government, and all transactions—whether monetary or other—are simplified—the better.

Then in regard to the condition of the labouring class. I am distinctly of opinion, that, if—after the repeal of the Corn Laws—*after the rescinding of that partial and unjust enactment*—the poor labourer and artisan finds, that, notwithstanding the importation of foreign corn he cannot afford to buy a sufficiency of wheat for himself and family, he will, with the becoming spirit of independence, characteristic of an Englishman—a spirit not yet wholly estranged from this land—despite bad laws depressing him—acting after the example of the industrious and thrifty Scotchman—he will, I am firmly convinced, I say, prefer eating oaten or rye bread in his own cottage—he and his family—to accepting the wheaten loaf in an Union Workhouse; and that he will *undertake to labour for the landlord and farmer upon these terms—if necessary.*

He will feel then (that is *after the repeal of the Corn Law!*) that it is *the Will of Providence!*—that he is condemned by the Will of Providence (if so it may said) to eat a less nutritious food—not that I mean to affirm, that *it will be so*—for—if I have observed the decrees of that Just and Beneficent One aright—He grants to those of his creatures who seek honestly, and with unremitting exertion to obtain them, their reasonable desires, and assuredly seldom, except as a punishment for their own improvidence, takes from them or deprives them of what they have once enjoyed. Thus I trust the poor may in all times in this country eat wheaten bread, the food they have been accustomed to.

I have spoken of what his feelings would be: if the Corn Law was repealed!

What are his feelings now?

He, the labourer and artisan *now* feels under the infliction of that blighting law, that the *preventive* to his eating the better food, or enough of it! is the *will of the House of Commons!* falsely said to be representative of the People—backed up and strengthened by *the will of the House of Lords!!*

Hence his indignation! Hence his hungering after what neither the poor in Scotland, nor the poor in Germany, nor the poor in many other countries covet. It is the being debarred from obtaining it at a less cost—debarred by legislative enactment when he has the means in his hands (if the ports were open), that is the grief to him.

Repeal the Corn Law, and all will be content—as far as regards food: come wheat—come rye—come oaten cake—come what may—there will be contentment among the people of England! Of that I am satisfied—not immediately perhaps—for they are now roused, or rousing, to a sense of what is due to them—and there may elapse some time before they have forgotten the injustice hitherto done them. But that *justice*, though tardy, will bring contentment and happiness, needs no assertion of mine.

Gentlemen of England! this question should be no longer a party question—a disgrace to the Aristocracy! but should be entertained soberly and seriously; and with a view to do justice to all classes without favour or affection—discarding from your minds the thought of aggrandisement or wealth at the expense of the people.

The People of England, be assured, are tired of witnessing the sham fights of Whig and Tory—both Aristocrats!—the only real difference between them being that apple of discord—Office! Admitting a little distinction in favour of the last tried party—the Whigs, who, to steady themselves for a time, were necessitated to ballast their vessel with the People—a dead weight, I fear, by them considered and which they have shewn but too much disposition to cast out of their hold, as soon as it may be done without upsetting the said vessel.

There is nothing new, it may be said, in what I have advanced. It is but a statement of facts.

But it matters not—the more the subject is considered the better—for things cannot, should not, and will not, remain as they are.

THE END.

NORMAN AND SKEEN, PRINTERS, MAIDEN LANE, COVENT GARDEN.

CORN LAWS.

SPEECH

IN THE

HOUSE OF COMMONS,

FRIDAY, APRIL 3, 1840.

PRINTED FOR PRIVATE CIRCULATION ONLY.

LONDON:

JAMES RIDGWAY, PICCADILLY.

Robert Hyde Greg (1795–1875), and William Rathbone Greg (1809–81)[1]

Robert H. Greg and William R. Greg were sons of Samuel Greg (1758–1834) successful mill owner and merchant, and Hannah, daughter and coheiress of Adam Lightbody of Liverpool. Like all the Greg sons (there were six, and six daughters), they were educated at Unitarian schools in Bristol and Nottingham, and at Edinburgh University, following which they travelled in Europe as the respresentatives of Samuel Greg and Company before joining the firm. After serving their business apprenticeship Robert concentrated on the mill at Quarry Bank and the mercantile side of the firm, William was made manager of Hudcar Mill at Bury. Although each son was given a mill to run, profits were divided between them all according to age, experience, and contribution to the firm, while Samuel Greg retained overall control until 1832 when responsibility was passed on to Robert. Samuel Greg had also invested in land, creating an estate in Reddish, near Stockport, which was valued in 1814 at £3,000.

The decade 1825–1835 were a difficult time for Quarry Bank mill. Competition forced reduction in prices and subsequent drop in profit margins. Rather than reduce production, Robert chose to diversify, adding power weaving to spinning, thereby increasing output and profitability. Robert's successful strategy may have served as proof of William's argument that the problem of industry during the 1830s was not over production but under-consumption. in 1841 the family firm was dissolved each brother receiving ownership of the mill he managed. In 1844 Robert took over sole control of the family's trading firm in Manchester renaming it R. H. Greg and Company. William eventually sold Hudcar Mill in 1850 for a price well below what his father had paid for it, and left the cotton business. He spent some time writing in the Lake District before moving to London to become a civil servant, first as a Commissioner of the Board of Customs, and then from 1864 to his retirement in 1877, as Comptroller of the Stationery Office.

The Greg brothers had shown early signs of political ambition. Robert stood unsuccessfully in 1830 and in 1837, and William in 1837. Robert was eventually elected in a Manchester by-election in September 1839, while absent from England. But it would seem that by then business precluded an active political career and he sat only until the elections of 1841. Robert was active in the Manchester Chamber of Commerce, and was one of the main supporters of the Anti Corn Law League. Both brothers were in favour of parliamentary reform in the 1830s and remained supporters of the ballot, universal education, and the abolition of rotten boroughs, but in time their position on further extension of the franchise became distinctly undemocratic. Robert was also active in organizing industrialists' resistance to factory legislation in the form of the National Association of Factory Occupiers.

[The bibliographies of the Greg brothers are printed on p. 330.]

[1] See article on R. H. Greg by Charles William Sutton and on W. R, Greg by Richard Garnett in *D.N.B.* vol. 8, pp. 530–2, 'W. R. Greg: A Sketch', in John Morley, *Critical Miscellanies*, vol. 3, London: Macmillan, 1892, pp. 213–59, and Mary B. Rose, *The Gregs of Quarry Bank Mill. The rise and decline of a family firm 1750–1914*, Cambridge: Cambridge University Press, 1986. See also Anthony Howe, *The Cotton Masters 1830–1860*, Oxford: Oxford University Press, 1984.

SPEECH,

ETC.

Mr. Speaker,

Sir,—On so hacknied a subject as the Corn-laws, it is not easy to produce any new argument, it is almost equally difficult to dress up an old one in a new garment; and indeed, when I see the determination of a small, but powerful party, interested in the continuance of these Laws, to resist the slightest relaxation of them, I am inclined to doubt the efficacy of any argument but one, which is, that of Agitation.

Agitation prevailed in procuring freedom for the Negroes; *agitation* gave emancipation to the Catholics; *agitation* gave us the Reform Bill; and I much fear that a Repeal of the Corn-laws will be yielded to no other argument. That this will, however, be finally successful in securing a total Repeal of these obnoxious laws, I feel perfectly confident.

Nothing can prevent such result, unless our opponents come forward, at once, with proposals for a moderate, fixed duty; in which case they may, possibly, succeed in breaking the ranks of the agitators and scattering their forces.

In the few observations I shall address to the house, it is not my intention to weary it with details of distress, so prevalent in the manufacturing districts, the depth and extent of which no one has called in question, nor shall I do more than allude to the fact, that the master manufacturers have now, for a period of three years, been suffering a gradual diminution of their capitals. We do not attribute the *whole* of this suffering to the *Corn-laws*, but we do attribute to them its origin and its long continuance; we believe that a Repeal of them would bring present relief, and prevent a recurrence of much future mischief; we believe, moreover, that these laws are seriously undermining the permanent prosperity of our manufactures.

In the admirable "Report on the Prussian League," by Dr. Bowring, which has just been laid upon the table of the House, will be found, fully established, those facts, which certain petitioners, including myself, were so anxious to have proved at your bar about twelve months ago.

In this Report we find, distinctly established,

1. The rapid growth and formidable extent of Continental manufactures.

2. The gradual exclusion of English goods from the Continental markets, particularly from those of the German league.

3. That this exclusion owes its origin and its continuance to our Corn-laws.

4. That a Repeal, or modification of these laws, offers the only chance of checking so great an evil.

5. That the Prussian Government is, at this moment, anxious and willing to enter into treaties with us, founded on the principle of mutually lowering our respective tariffs.

To this Report I anxiously solicit the serious attention of every member of this House, and with a few brief quotations I shall, for the present, quit the subject.

Dr. Bowring states, page 19 of the Report,—

"The progress of the COTTON MANUFACTURE in the States "of the League is most striking; for the whole of the League "imported a smaller quantity of foreign manufactured cottons in "1836, than Prussia, alone, imported, in 1832. In 1829 to "1831, the excess of cotton manufactures exported, over the "amount imported, was, only, 6272 cwt., whilst, in 1836, the "excess had increased more than eleven fold, being 70,766 cwt.

"It will be seen by the following table, that, while, notwith-"standing the increase of population, the import of foreign ma-"nufactured cottons has been stationary, the exports have gone "on increasing in rapid progression."

Thus, our cotton manufacturers have not only lost their customers, but have to meet a competition in third markets, to an extent of 70,766 *cwt. annually*.

Then, again, with respect to WOOLLENS, he remarks, page 22, that—

"Whilst the imports of woollens, and woollen yarns, "have continued without any considerable fluctuations, but, "with rather a tendency to diminish, notwithstanding the in-"crease of population, the amount exported, of woollens and "yarns, has been augmented, in the proportion of seven to five, "or forty per cent.

" In 1832 the difference between imported and exported wool-
" lens amounted to 32,613 cwt., while, in 1836, the difference
" was 54,056 cwt., and in 1837, 49,967 cwt."

Thus, our woollen manufactures are exposed to a competition, in third markets, of 50,000 cwt. annually.

Page 39.—" At the Easter Fair, Franckfort, of 1839, the sale
" of English cotton goods had diminished one-third, as compared
" with the sales effected at the corresponding fair of 1838."

This, our minister, Mr. Abercrombie, attributes to the progress made by German manufacturers.

Page 39.—" Of CUTLERY, some of the superior British articles
" hold their ground; but, of ordinary ware, the demand is wholly
" supplied by German articles, and the same may be stated ge-
" nerally of articles of HARDWARE."

So much for the effects of the Prussian League, comprising twenty-six millions of people, more allied to us, in taste and blood, than any others!

Page 58.—" I have obtained repeated official assurances, and
" they will be confirmed by the Report of Her Majesty's Minis-
" ters, at the Court of Berlin, that the Prussian government, not
" only consents, but desires to enter upon formal negociations,
" the object of which shall be the mutual and progressive lower-
" ing of the tariffs of both countries, with a view to more ex-
" tended and beneficial commercial intercourse."

Page 51,—" The re, in fact, only one course to be adopted,
" unless it is intended that a trade of many millions sterling shall
" be finally sacrificed. The tariffs of Great Britain must be mo-
" dified *pari passu*, with the tariffs of the Commercial League.

" Such modifications are so obviously, so essentially, so per-
" manently, to the interest of the fifty millions of Britons and
" Germans, whom such modifications would bring more closely,
" and unite more firmly, together, that I cannot but persuade my-

" self, the Parliament and Government, looking on the one side, " to the dangers with which we are all menaced, by the enormous " diminution of our trade, and, on the other, to the blessings " which we may communicate by its larger extension, I cannot " but persuade myself, that important changes will be made on " both sides."

Sir, the manufacturers have been accused of seeking a repeal of the Corn-laws, to enable them to *reduce the wages* of their work-people. They do no such thing; they do not believe that a repeal of the Corn-laws would reduce the price of labour, either manufacturing or agricultural, for the price of labour depends upon the demand. They seek, by means of a free interchange of their productions with those of other countries, a fair remuneration for their capital and labour, and an increase of food and comforts to the people they employ; and should *natural circumstances*, over which there is no control, forbid any *extension* of their trade, they desire, at least, to remove those *artificial restrictions*, which threaten to deprive them of their *present markets*. But, so far from the price of labour being reduced by opening our ports to the admission of foreign corn, it does not necessarily follow that the price of corn itself should decline in consequence.

What followed a reduction from 6*d*. per lb. to a 1*d*. in the import duty of FOREIGN WOOL? Not a fall, but a rise of 6*d*. per lb. in the price of ENGLISH WOOL.

Why should not the same effect be produced by

the free admission of foreign corn? One half of our population could certainly consume double the quantity of food it now consumes. *Open the ports*, and you give people the means of paying, not only for the food which comes in from abroad, *but for a larger portion of what is grown at* HOME.

Sir, the prohibition, instituted by the Corn-laws, of exchanging freely for the food produced by other countries, the manufactures produced by this country, (which, permit me to observe, is the most beneficial exchange, *one necessary of life for another*,) has an action of a peculiarly mischievous character upon the manufacturing interests; and one, which it seems to me, has not attracted sufficient observation.

It compels the manufacturers at all times, to exchange for the same, or, *nearly the same quantity of food*, namely, *that produced in the United Kingdom, the whole value of their industry, however great, and however rapidly increasing.*

It is true, that the production of food in the United Kingdom increases also, but it increases slowly, and on a limited surface, where the best land has long since been appropriated, it increases *very slowly*; but population, capital, and manufactures have a tendency to increase in a more rapid ratio; and if this rapidly increasing production of manufactures must be exchanged, although, perhaps, indirectly and remotely, yet *ultimately and substantially, against this same quantity and value of* FOOD, a great injustice is committed, and great suffering must frequently be the consequence.

Suppose, for example, our manufactured produce could, by a kind of magic, be doubled in a single year, how would this benefit the producers, should they be in want of food?

The quantity of food at home, be it remembered, is, at any given time, of a fixed and limited amount.

The manufacturers would, in the case proposed, first exchange a part of their production for food in the market at home, and export the remainder. With the portion exported they would purchase an increased quantity of silk, or wool, or cotton; but these are only raw materials of manufacture, and could only be worked up again with fresh labour, into new manufactured articles.

They would also import an increased quantity of diamonds and gold, and luxuries, the consumption of which, is chiefly confined to the *rich, but if they wanted* FOOD, *how could they obtain it?*

They would have no resource but to take this quantity of precious metals, or foreign luxuries into the home market, where they took the first portion, and where only a limited and fixed amount exists, with which they could exchange it, and there they might bid against one another, and against the agricultural labourer, until the price was driven up to a famine point, when at last, and not until then, the *actual quantity* would be increased by importations from abroad. Whether limited to a direct exchange of their produce for food, or for food and its *equivalent* conjointly, the injustice is much the same. It is in both cases giving a large quantity for a small one, an increasing quantity for a stationary one.

To the same cause, the necessity of exchanging ultimately, the whole amount of our manufactured productions, for the *same, or more slowly increasing quantity of agricultural produce, namely, that of the United Kingdom*, must, I think, be attributed, the remarkable and constantly growing discrepancy between the *official and declared value of our exports*, that is between the quantity and value of such exports.

The *quantity* of our manufactures exported increases most rapidly, whilst the *value* of these exports increases very slowly, or remains for a time quite stationary.

Take, as an example, the Exports of Cotton Manufactures, during the last ten years.

	COTTON MANUFACTURES.		COTTON TWIST.	
Years.	Official Value.	Declared Value.	Official Value.	Declared Value.
	£	£	£	£
1830	35,661,380	15,294,942	5,656,467	4,133,740
1831	33,903,118	13,284,036	5,674,616	3,975,018
1832	37,206,480	12,675,622	6,726,562	4,722,759
1833	40,133,343	13,782,375	6,279,076	4,704,024
1834	44,266,902	15,302,571	6,802,237	5,211,014
1835	44,933,399	16,421,745	7,309,879	5,706,589
1836	50,733,587	18,511,692	7,844,855	6,120,366
1837	41,918,547	13,640,181	9,211,743	6,955,942
1838	54,610,501	16,715,856	10,202,027	7,431,870
1839	58,516,096	17,692,183	9,400,925	6,858,193

Thus we see that, whilst the *quantity*, or official value of exported manufactured cottons has increased £22,854,716. in ten years, the *real value*, or value of what this great additional quantity exchanged for, increased by only £2,397,241.

A similar discrepancy, though smaller in degree, is observable in the table of cotton twist, and that it is smaller is owing, merely, to the circumstance of the *raw material* forming in that, a larger proportion of the whole value.

I believe I am correct in saying, that the same facts are observable in every branch of manufacture whatsoever. Now, making ample allowance for cheaper processes of manufacture of late years, though this is more than balanced by the greater quantity consumed of the raw material, it is obvious, from the above tables, and these facts, that *something is wanting, which we cannot obtain, with which to exchange the increasing produce of our manufacturing industry*, and that something is FOOD.

Can any person suppose, if FOOD might have been freely purchased in foreign countries, in return for an extra production and export of £22,854,716., that the *value* of those exports would only have increased by £2,397,241?

But when we reflect, that all which is returned to us, in exchange for our manufactures, or nearly so, from foreign countries, must *ultimately be bartered against the same number of quarters of wheat, or their equivalent*, we can understand how the value remains so nearly at the same amount, whilst the quantity rapidly increases.

Sir, the "LANDED INTEREST" claims "*protection*," or, rather, the *landowners* insist that they have a right to "protection." From those, however, who make this demand, may surely be deducted the landowners of the Highlands, and a large part of the lowlands of Scotland, those of nearly the whole of Wales, of the mountainous and grazing districts of Ireland, of the mining districts of England, and all owners of land within a certain distance of large towns, none of whom can show any interest in the continuance of the Corn-laws.

A certain number of landowners, however, insist upon their "*right to protection*." So also have the twenty-five millions of consumers a right to protection. They have a right to protection against a monopoly in the first necessary of life, against a monopoly of the very means of existence, against being compelled, contrary to inclination, and their obvious interest, to buy their food in no market but one, namely, that of the English landowner.

What, let me ask, is the meaning of "*protection*" in such matters as this?

It means *power given to a few to supply a dear or bad article to the many*. It means a withdrawing from the producer every proper controul and stimulus, and from the consumer every security, which controul and which security can only be found in *free competition*.

A free importation of Foreign corn would do more to stimulate and improve English agriculture, than all the Agricultural Societies will effect in twenty years.

But it is argued that manufactures enjoy a protection from Foreign competition, and that agriculture has an equal claim. Certainly it has, but not *more* than an equal claim.

The protection granted to most of our manufactures, however, it must be remembered, is little more than *nominal*, as must be the case wherever a surplus is produced and exported; and this protection, such as it is, the manufacturers have expressed their willingness to abandon.

The silk manufacture, indeed, forms an exception, on which there is a protecting duty of twenty-five to thirty per cent. But supposing it were determined to give to all articles of British industry a protection equal to that enjoyed by the silk trade, still, I contend, we have a right to a free trade in corn, because the *charges alone incident on its importation*, amounting to fully thirty per cent., the home producer would in such case enjoy the same protection against Foreign competition, as that now granted to the silk manufacture.

Such a protection, one so guaranteed to them by nature, which no *fiscal* regulations could reduce, and no popular tumult destroy, ought surely to satisfy the English landowner!

What class, allow me to enquire, would benefit

so largely by an increase of population, such as would accompany a Repeal of the Corn-laws, as that of the landowner?

Having a monopoly of the land, every additional birth must increase the value of his monopoly.

Suppose we had an additional population of ten millions of people, and that these were to eat no bread but what was made from Foreign corn, these ten millions of people would be so many additional customers for butcher's meat, milk, butter, and for various agricultural produce, as also for land itself, for many purposes. They would also share, and thus diminish, the burden of taxation. They would be a benefit to all, but chiefly to the landowner, and they would be so, without consuming one single quarter of English wheat.

Sir, the only argument against the free importation of Foreign corn, deserving, as it seems to me, a moment's consideration, is that derived from the supposed impolicy of rendering one country dependant upon others for so essential an article as food.

The futility of this specious argument has been so often exposed, I will not enter upon it now. What I would remark is, that if the objection be valid, and if the *state* be determined to act upon the principle of never permitting the population to grow beyond what the country can, in all ordinary seasons support (*for the principle means this, if it means anything*), then the value of the monopoly in land, thus artificially created, *belongs to the state*, not to the landowner, and the state would have the undoubted right to impose a direct tax upon the owners of that kind of property, equal in amount to the additional value so created.

If, by reason of such monopoly, land acquired an additional annual value of £20,000,000, the state would have a right to tax it to that annual amount.

Sir, before sitting down, I should wish to bear my testimony, more particularly, against the principle of a *fluctuating duty.*

The mischiefs of our Corn-laws have been extremely aggravated by this system. A very high *fixed duty* would have been less injurious.

A fluctuating duty, even smaller in amount, and less violent in its changes, is attended with these inconveniences.

1. It prevents importations, whilst prices are rising, and pours them in upon a declining market, thereby aggravating the extremes of price, and making those changes more sudden in time, as well as greater in degree.

2. It introduces an uncertainty into the operations of the importer, which is unnecessary and mischievous, and which ought not to be allowed to exist, when we consider, that to his care– an interested care, if you please—is committed the supply of food, in time of need, to a hungry people.

This uncertainty, too, tends still further to increase the price paid by the nation for the food it finds it requisite to import, as well as to render the supply, in periods of famine, more precarious.

3. A fluctuating duty is fatal to the regular growth of corn abroad, as a regular medium of exchange for our manufactured productions, and *this*, I believe, *is the great recommendation of it to the "landed interest."*

If a moderate fluctuating duty then be thus objectionable in its operation, what must be the operation of one so extreme in its fluctuations, and connected with such high duties as in our present system of Corn-laws!

Now, let me enquire, are these mischievous laws to *continue for ever?*

Is it intended, that population should continue to swell through long convulsive struggles, till the price of wheat shall permanently acquire a limit of 73*s*. the quarter, and thus an opening be made for regular supplies from abroad? I would ask, is such a state of things compatible with our being a *manufacturing and exporting country?* Or, is the working population to become *wholly*, as it has become in part, a *potatoe fed people*, and to be liable to the periodical famines incident upon the failure of a crop, which can neither be easily transported from a distance, nor the surplus be kept over to another season?

Population *will increase*, how is it *to be fed?* Why are such alternatives to be forced upon the nation? What right have the few thousand owners of land, to say to twenty-five millions of consumers, you shall pay us a high price for your food, and frequent no shop but ours? To say to the manufacturing population, you shall continue to pay us an increasing quantity of your productions for the same quantity of ours? What right have the *owners of land*, I repeat, to say to the *owners of every other kind of property*, we demand a preference over you? To the *Capitalist*, you shall be restricted in the use of your capital, and obtain only three per cent. for your money? To the *Master Manufacturer*, you shall not extend your market? To the *Operative*, you shall be allowed only a limited competition for your labour? To the *Retailer and Shopkeeper*, you shall not increase the number of your customers? What excuse can they frame, for checking by an *artificial and forced limitation of food*, the natural expansion of population; and thus, whilst they render difficult the means of livelihood to the present generation, prevent millions from coming into existence at all?

Sir, to sum up my sentiments in a few words, our Corn-laws, as they now exist, with their *high duty and fluctuating scale*, aggravate the extremes of price, and make food scarce, cripple commerce, endanger our manufacturing prosperity, derange our currency, are a ***curse at home,*** and a ***nuisance to all Europe.***

END.

NOT

OVER-PRODUCTION,

BUT

DEFICIENT CONSUMPTION,

THE SOURCE OF OUR SUFFERINGS.

BY

W. R. GREG.

JANUARY, 1842.

LONDON:

HENRY HOOPER, PALL MALL EAST.

Robert Hyde Greg (1795–1875), and William Rathbone Greg (1809–81)

Works on economics and related subjects by R. H. Greg:

The Factory Question, considered in relation to its effects on the health and morals of those employed in Factories: and "The Ten Hours Bill," in relation to its effects upon the manufactures of England, and those of foreign countries, London: Ridgway, 1837.

A letter to H. Labouchere, on the pressure of the Corn Laws and Sliding Scale more especially upon the manufacturing interests and productive classes, London: Ridgway, 1841. 2nd edition, 1842.

Scotch Farming in the Lothians. A letter addressed to the Editor of the Manchester Guardian, 2nd edition, London: Ridgway, 1842. 3rd edition, 1842.

Scotch Farming in England. A second Letter addressed to the Editor of the Manchester Guardian, London: Ridgway, 1842.

Works by W. R. Greg:

An Enquiry into the State of the Manufacturing Population, and the causes and cures of the evils therein existing, London: Ridgway, 1831.

Social statistics of the Netherlands, Manchester: Harrison and Crosfield, 1835.

Agriculture and the Corn Law. Prize essay, Manchester: J. Wilson, [1842].

Not over-production, but deficient consumption, the sources of our suffering, London and Manchester: H. Hooper, 1842. 2nd edition, London, 1842.

Essays on Political and Social Science, contributed chiefly to the Edinburgh Review, 2 vols. London: Longman, 1853.

The one thing needful, 2nd edition, London: Ridgway, 1855.

Real cost of collecting the revenue, with reference to Sir Morton Peto's strictures, London: H. Bale, 1863.

Literary and Social Judgments, London: Trubner, 1868. 2nd edition, London, Bungay, 1869. 4th edition, enlarged, London, Edinburgh, 1877.

Rocks ahead; or, the warnings of Cassandra, London: Trubner, 1874. 2nd edition, 1874. 2nd edition with a reply to objectors, 1879.

Miscellanous essays, London: Trubner, 1882. *2nd series*, 1884.

"THAT there has been more cloth produced than could be sold to a profit, I admit;—but *why* could it not be sold?—First, *because the Landowners have taken all the People's money for food*, and left them nothing to *buy clothing with*;—and, secondly, because in order to keep up Rents, the Landowners have made a law *to prevent us selling our cloth to those Countries which have nothing but food to pay with.*

"So long as God has made the sea a highway for our merchants, recognising the brotherhood of a common world,—*so long as there is one bare back, or one uncovered bed*, in the universe, belonging to a human being who wishes for English goods on terms of fair exchange, *there cannot be an over-production of cotton and woollen cloth.*"

NOT OVER-PRODUCTION

BUT DEFICIENT CONSUMPTION,

THE SOURCE OF OUR SUFFERINGS.

In the recent discussions with regard to the extent and origin of the deplorable distress now prevalent in the manufacturing districts of England and Scotland, much has been said of "overproduction," "overtrading," "unnatural increase," and the like. Some have attributed the whole of the existing misery to the reaction consequent upon too rapid an extension of our manufactures; while others have urgently demanded a legislative "limitation of production," as the sole means of extricating the country from its present sufferings, and preventing a recurrence of them for the future.

Now as these notions have been, to a certain extent, sanctioned by Lord Stanley and Sir Robert Peel, and are much harped upon by politicians of the school of Lord Ashley and the Duke of Buckingham, it may be worth while to devote a few pages to the examination of them; and to an exposure of the consequences which any attempt to act upon them would inevitably produce, both to the manufacturing and the agricultural interests of Britain. That such notions should ever have obtained currency, is one of many examples daily before our eyes, of the facility with which men substitute words for ideas, and make use of expressions without any strict analysis of their meaning.

When Sir Robert Peel and the Short-time Deputation charge the manufacturers with "over-production," they appear to mean, that production has been unwarrantably extended; i. e. that we have increased our exchangeable produce in a greater ratio than the number or the capacity of our customers: that in consequence the demand for our goods is insufficient, and employment for those who produce them insufficient also.

There can be no doubt whatever that our present distress arises, in great part, from want of employment for our Poor; that this want of employment arises from the want of a remunerative demand for manufactured goods; and that this want of demand arises from production and consumption not having maintained the same relative rate of progress. Thus much may be safely conceded; but no conclusion can be drawn from these concessions, till we have first enquired, *whether the derangement of the relation between production and consumption has arisen from the "unnatural augmentation" of the former, or the "unnatural" diminution of the latter.*

It is certain, that manufacturers, both from the nature of things, and from the experience of the past, are fairly entitled to count upon a yearly increase in the demand for their productions,—that increase varying in its rate according to a variety of circumstances. The increase of population, both in our own Islands and in foreign countries, fairly justifies this expectation. The advancing wealth of this and other nations, and their consequently increased capacity of purchasing, further justifies this expectation. Let us examine whether the increase in our Manufactures has greatly exceeded the rate which these considerations rendered legitimate. We will take the Cotton Manufacture as an example, both as that which is most important and most suffering, and as that which is said to have increased most inordinately.*

	Number of Bales Manufactured.	Increase in four Years.	Increase per Annum.
From 1821 to 1824 inclusive	2,208,000	....	....
„ 1825—1828 „	2,516,000	14 per cent	3½ per cent
„ 1829—1832 „	3,310,000	31½ do.	8 „
„ 1833—1836 „	3,763,000	14 do.	3½ „

Now, considering that the production had increased at the rate of 8 per cent annually from 1829 to 1832, (and the demand had increased in an equal ratio, for the trade was prosperous in those

* The following table does not confirm the idea of any unprecedented or inordinate increase.

	Total official value of Manufactures Exported.	Annual increase per cent.
1821 to 1824..............	£164,700,000	....
1825 — 1828..............	186,100,000	3.25
1829 — 1832..............	228,100,000	5.50
1832 — 1836..............	275,600,000	5.25

years); and remembering also, that, during the twelve years from 1821 to 1832, the annual increase had averaged 6 per cent:—the Manufacturers surely cannot be accused of any rash or unwarranted extension, because in the four following years, from 1832 to 1836, they increased their production at the rate of 3½ per cent annually. Now, up to 1836, trade was in a prosperous condition; *and it is to the alleged undue increase previous to that year, that the glutting of foreign markets, and the depression which has since prevailed, are attributed by those who complain of "over-production."*

So far then from there having been any unfounded or excessive extension of our manufactures previous to the commencement of distress, it is clear, that had the demand continued to increase at its former ratio, the production would have been inadequate to supply it. Let us now, therefore, turn our attention to the progress of demand.

In the ordinary healthy course of trade, we supply our own population before we export to foreigners. We sell at home whatever we can, and send the residue elsewhere. We often send abroad what is not wanted abroad, but we never sell at home what is not wanted at home. Our exports, therefore, are no accurate measure of the foreign demand. Our home sales *are* an accurate measure of the home demand. Let us enquire, therefore, what proportion of our manufactures has, for a series of years, been retained for the home supply.

	Cotton Manufactured, deducting 1-10th for waste.	Cotton Exported in Goods and Yarn.	Cotton Consumed by the Home Demand.	Per Centage of the whole quantity consumed at Home.
	lbs.	lbs.	lbs.	
1824...	148,700,000	84,100,000	64,600,000	43
1825...	150,200,000	81,900,000	78,300,000	52
1826...	135,200,000	80,200,000	55,000,000	40
1827...	177,500,000	99,200,000	78,300,000	44
1828...	196,200,000	102,600,000	93,600,000	48
1829...	197,300,000	118,100,000	79,200,000	40
1830...	222,900,000	127,300,000	95,600,000	43
1831...	236,500,000	124,000,000	112,500,000	47
1832...	249,300,000	141,200,000	108,100,000	43
1833...	259,000,000	142,900,000	116,100,000	45
1834...	265,000,000	156,500,000	108,500,000	41
1835...	284,600,000	163,500,000	121,100,000	43
1836...	310,900,000	179,600,000	131,300,000	42
1837...	330,200,000	176,000,000	154,200,000	46
1838...	384,600,000	211,000,000	173,600,000	45
1839...	327,900,000	210,900,000	117,000,000	36
1840...	405,400,000	230,000,000	175,400,000	43
1841...	362,300,000	258,800,000	103,500,000	28

I do not pretend to give this table as one of more than approximate accuracy; but it is perfectly valid for the purpose of a comparison of years, and is as exact as existing documents will enable us to render it. From this it will be seen, that while the production of the manufactured article has increased pretty steadily through all vicissitudes, *the proportion of our manufacture consumed at home, has of late rapidly diminished.* While for the fifteen years from 1824 to 1838, the home demand absorbed regularly from 40 to 50 per cent. (average 44) of the whole production, during the last three years it has only averaged 36 per cent., and in the last disastrous year only 28 per cent. Nay, more, in spite of a large increase in our population, the actual *quantity* of Cotton manufactures consumed at home, is less in the *last* three years than in the *preceding* three, by 14½ per cent.; and the quantity consumed in 1841, less than at any period since 1830, notwithstanding an augmented population of more than two millions.*

We have thus shown that the home demand, which had so steadily increased for so long a series of years, as amply to justify the least sanguine Manufacturers in anticipating a similar annual progress for the future, has during the last three years alarmingly diminished, so as to render futile all their calculations. We will now endeavour to show the cause, and the extent of this diminution.

Hunger is the most imperative of all wants. A man must be fed before he is either clothed or lodged, and whether he is clothed and lodged, or not. By examining, therefore, the sum which the people have had to pay for food in different years, we

---

* It will be objected that, during the whole of this period our exports have increased. True, they have;—but these goods have to a great extent been sent abroad, because it was impossible to dispose of them at home; they have not been shipped in regular execution of orders received, but have been *consigned* for the chance of forcing a sale, by excessive lowness of price.

shall arrive at a knowledge of the relative amounts which they will have had remaining to expend in manufactured articles. It is very difficult to estimate the consumption of grain in Great Britain; but if we take the following, as the quantities annually consumed by *man alone*, we shall certainly not err on the side of exaggeration:—Wheat, 12,000,000 quarters, Oats, 3,000,000, Barley, &c. 9,000,000.

Now in 1835, the amount paid for grain food, would stand thus:—

Wheat,	12,000,000 qrs.	× 40*s*. =	£24,000,000
Oats,	3,000,000 ..	× 22*s*. =	3,300,000
Barley, &c.	9,000,000 ..	× 30*s*. =	13,500,000
			£40,800,000

In 1839, 40, and 41, Prices had risen, and the case stood thus:—

Wheat,	12,000,000 qrs.	× 68*s*. =	£40,800,000
Oats,	3,000,000 ..	× 25*s*. =	3,750,000
Barley, &c.	9,000,000 ..	× 37*s*. =	16,650,000
			£61,200,000

Annually withdrawn from the purchase of clothing, to that of food, in the article of grain alone £20,400,000

This however will give but a very imperfect impression of the total amount which was formerly spent in clothing, and which is now spent in food; for the prices of meat, milk, butter, sugar, and coffee, have all experienced a similar advance; and £35,000,000 would certainly not be too high an estimate for the amount which has been annually withdrawn since 1838, from the purchase of manufactured goods.*

The following statement will more fully exemplify this operation. It is the summary of a series of tables, prepared with the most scrupulous care, by Mr. Neild, the Mayor of Manchester,† shewing the income and expenditure of twelve of the best paid families of artizans, in Manchester, and seven in Dukinfield, in 1836, and in 1841. The total income of the twelve families in Manchester, was the same in the two years, viz. £22 4s. 2d. a week. Their weekly household expenditure, in 1836, was £14 15s. 11d.; leaving a surplus of £7 8s. 3d. for education, saving, and the purchase of manufactured articles. In 1841, their weekly expenditure was £17 9s. 8d.; leaving only £4 14s. 6d. for education, saving, and the purchase of manufactured articles. In the former year, *food* formed 54 per cent of their expenditure; in the latter year, 70 per cent.

The total weekly income of the seven families

* The above estimate proceeds upon the supposition that the earnings of the people were as great in the latter period as in the former. This, however, is notoriously not the case; for not only have considerable numbers been partially or wholly unemployed during the last three years, but throughout the manufacturing districts, extensive reductions of wages have taken place; and the slight advance which has, in many cases been obtained by agricultural labourers, has been too trifling and partial to have had much countervailing operation.

† Statistical Journal, January 1842.

in Dukinfield, was, in 1836, £8 0s. 0d. Their household expenditure was £5. 12s. 3d.; leaving a surplus of £2 7s. 9d. for education, saving, and clothing. In 1841, their aggregate income was reduced to £5 6s. 8d. while their necessary expenditure increased to £6 8s. 1d.; leaving not only no surplus for clothing, but a heavy debt instead. In the former year, *food* formed 46 per cent. of their expenditure; in the latter year, 89 per cent.

We find, then, that the *home* demand for manufactured goods, instead of having increased, since 1836, as the analogy of all previous years would have led us to expect, has greatly diminished; the high price of food absorbing almost the entire earnings of the people, and diverting into a different channel at least £35,000,000 annually, which was formerly expended mainly in articles of clothing. The diminution in the *foreign* demand we have not the same means of tracing; but thus much is beyond a doubt,—*that* it has not increased (if it has increased at all,) in the ratio which the augmentation in our exported quantity would lead us to imagine; as is clear, both from the rapid fall in the price of all articles of export, and the great difficulty which our merchants, in all parts of the world, experience in disposing of their cargoes;—*that* our exports to our best customer—the United States—which, from 1831 to 1836 inclusive, averaged £8,600,000, have since only averaged

£6,500,000;*—and *that* the demand for our goods from Norway, Russia, Prussia, Brazil, Buenos Ayres, and North America, is "artificially and unnaturally" diminished by our refusal to receive, in payment, the Corn, Timber, Beef, Sugar, and Coffee, which these Countries have respectively to offer.

The present excess, then, of the production of manufactured goods over the consumption of them, and the consequent sufferings of the People, are to be traced not to OVER-PRODUCTION, *but to* UNDER-CONSUMPTION,—*not to an "artificial and unnatural" increase in the* SUPPLY, *but to an "artificial and unnatural" limitation of the* DEMAND.

But there is another point of view from which this singular charge of over-production requires to be considered. *Increased production involves and implies increased employment.* If Manufacturers have increased their quantity produced, they must also have increased the number of their labourers. The more goods they fabricate, the more people

* There were in 1831.......... £9,000,000 declared value.

....	1832.........	5,400,000	......
....	1833.........	7,500,000	......
....	1834.........	6,800,000	......
....	1835.........	10,500,000	......
....	1836.........	12,400,000	......
....	1837.........	4,600,000	......
....	1838.........	7,500,000	......
....	1839.........	8,800,000	......
....	1840.........	5,200,000	......

do they employ. Yet we are told in the same breath that the sufferings of the poor are caused by want of employment, and that they arise from that increased production which could only have taken place by giving increased employment. Want of employment, they would persuade us, is caused by the too rapid increase of employment. "The People are starving" say the Newspapers "from want of employment." "That arises," says Sir Robt. Peel, "from employing too many of them!"

We will, however, do this statesman the justice to suppose that his meaning is more definite, and less startling than it at first appears;—and that he intends to affirm, that in 1834, 5, and 6, the Manufacturers called into existence, or summoned around them, a larger population than they had any reasonable prospect of finding permanent employment for;—and that the amount of employment having now receded to its former limits, this surplus population is thrown out of work.

Now we have already shown that the rate of progress (in that branch of industry, at least, which is charged with having increased the fastest) was only the same from 1833 to 1836, as it had been from 1825 to 1828, and not half as rapid as from 1829 to 1832. But there is no doubt that a considerable increase *did* take place both in population and production in the manufacturing districts in the period referred to. *Where did this extra Population spring from?* No one can affect to believe that it has been actually *created*—called into existence by the sudden demand for it ;—for not only has there been no time for such a process,—but we learn on the first authority,* that of Mr. Finlaison, that during the last ten years, both births and marriages have been proportionally on the decrease. The extra population must therefore have been drawn from the agricultural districts, or from some other less fortunate branch of industry. If drawn from the agricultural counties, the demand must either have absorbed the surplus inhabitants who were supported by the Poor Rates,—in which case a signal benefit was conferred upon the district, and especially upon the Rate Payers and Landlords ;—or it must have enticed away some portion of the employed labourers ; and in that case, by diminishing competition in the labour-market, must have raised the wages, and improved the condition of those who remained. If it removed Paupers, it benefitted the rich ;—if it removed independent labourers, it benefitted the poor. If again the required population were drawn from some depressed branch of industry, such as hand-weaving, much misery must have been alleviated in two ways ; those withdrawn were placed in a condition of comfort, arising from ample wages and full employment ; while those who remained were placed in an improved position by

* See his letter to the Registrar General. First Annual Report, p. 62. The marriages he estimates to have decreased from one in 123, to one in 132 ; and the births from one in 27.7 to one in 27.9.

a diminution of their numbers. In any case, and on any supposition, the condition of the labouring poor must have been amended.

We will now suppose for a moment, (as Sir Robert Peel seems to fancy) that the effect of the present depression has been to reduce manufacturing production to its former extent, and consequently to replace all this extra population in its former condition of non-employment, or partial employment. Even in that case, the increase so much blamed would at least have employed for three years a large number who would otherwise have been supported in idleness, or have preyed upon their fellow labourers by competing with them for employment. The benefit to the country would have been temporary, but it would still have been great; and the Manufacturers would still deserve gratitude, rather than reproach, for affording a short relief from a heavy burden.

But this supposition (so for at least as the Cotton Manufacture is concerned) is the very reverse of the truth, as will be seen by a glance at the table in page 7. In the four years ending 1837, the quantity of Cotton worked up was 1,190,000,000lbs. In the four years ending 1841, it was 1,480,000,000lbs. Now with every reasonable allowance for the known fact, that the pressure of the times has compelled manufacturers so to economise in labour as to produce equal quantities with fewer hands, we can scarcely doubt that more persons were employed during the latter period than during the former.

Whence then come the deplorable distress prevailing throughout the manufacturing districts, and the complaints which reach us from all sides, of thousands perishing for want of work? Simply from this cause:—In spite of commercial convulsion and depression, the demand for labour has increased, *but not so rapidly as the supply.* Employment has increased, but population has increased still faster. In England and Wales alone, the population increases at the rate of 150,000* a year, on the lowest estimate; and at this rate it will continue to increase, (unless the mortality should be fearfully augmented.) How then are these 150,000 annually added mouths provided for? The country districts afford them no resource, for farming occupations require few, if any, additional labourers;—they therefore flock to the great centres of manufacturing industry in search of employment; many of them find it;—but in periods of depression, like the last few years, it is impossible to furnish it to all. We do not know the exact amount of migration from rural to industrial districts,† but we do know that it must have been immense; for while the *natural* increase of the Population (i. e. the excess of births above deaths) during the last ten years, has been much the

* In 1840, the Births were 501,589, and the Deaths 350,101.

† It would be well if those landed Proprietors, who are at no pains to conceal their hostility to Manufactures, were to consider what would be the effect upon the value of their own property were the tide to ebb, and the vast multitudes who now

greatest in the former, the *actual* increase has been much the greatest in the latter.* A careful examination of the table given below, coupled with the annual increase of the Population above-mentioned, will leave little room for doubt, that since 1836, the manufacturing districts have had to find employment and subsistence for at least 400,000 additional persons. With this fact before us, we need not be surprised at the prevalent outcry of deficient employment and severe distress. The

reside in the manufacturing districts but really *belong* to the agricultural ones, to be cast back upon their birth-place, and claim support from their native parishes. Yet, this will assuredly take place, if trade should ever be permanently depressed. It is perfectly certain that any decided check to our commercial and manufacturing progress will raise the Poor Rates (throughout England, in country as in town districts,) to an amount never dreamed of in the worst days of their abuse,—to an amount which would speedily absorb the whole rental of the land.

AGRICULTURAL COUNTIES.	Increase per cent in the Population from 1831 to 1841.	Births to Population, in 1830.	Deaths to Population in 1840.	MANUFACTURING COUNTIES.	Increase per cent of Population from 1831 to 1841.	Births to Population, in 1830.	Deaths to Population in 1840.
		one in	one in			one in	one in
Hereford	2.9	37	63	Lancaster....	25	38	32
Cumberland..	4.8	36	51	Durham	27	35	43
Norfolk	5.7	33	51	Warwick.....	19	36	45
Oxford	6.1	32	50	Stafford	24	32	51
Suffolk	6.3	37	52	York, W. R..	18	38	43
Buckingham..	6.4	36	52	Chester	19	43	42
Average..	5.4	35	52	Average...	22	37	43

N. B.—The year 1830 is the last for which we have any calculation of the births.

evil has been, not that manufactures have increased too fast, but that they have not increased fast enough.

What then are we to think of the diagnosis and the nostrum of those grave Physicians who, finding the source of our sufferings in "over-production," propose as their remedy a "limitation of production." *Limitation of production means and implies limitation of employment;* and no language can sufficiently describe the varied forms of misery which are involved in those three words. Let us pause for a moment and look upon the facts before us. One hundred and fifty thousand souls are annually added to our population. These* 150,000 have to be fed, clothed, and lodged; for by the laws of England no man is allowed to starve. How then are they to be provided for? There are but three ways,—Emigration, Employment, or Pauperism. We must either ship them to the Colonies, support them in idleness, or provide them with profitable occupation.

I. Now I am far from being unfriendly to emigration, even on a large scale, if considerately and judiciously conducted. It is a natural and legitimate mode of relief for an old and densely-peopled country. But in this case, if it is to act as an

* I assume that this rate of increase will continue; for any idea of diminishing the progress of population, unless by improving the condition and habits of the people, or *by an excessive increase of mortality*, has been fully proved to be chimerical.

effectual remedy, it must be annually renewed, and must be conducted on a scale, the magnitude of which seems, I confess, a little startling. Including Scotland and Ireland, we should require to expatriate at least 250,000 persons every year; most of them to very distant quarters;—and where are we to find the vessels to convey them, the money to defray the cost of their passage and their outfit, or the colonies prepared to find employment and subsistence for so vast a multitude? Government may, and we hope do, intend to afford all possible facilities for emigration; but such a project as this is, we think, on too enormous a scale to be seriously entertained. Moreover, unless the emigration were compulsory, (a system not to be thought of for a moment) it would be impossible to persuade such numbers to leave their homes, and trust themselves to all the magnified perils of distant and untried adventure. Misery will not compel them to it;* and education must be further advanced among them before they will perceive that their own interest counsels it. A further objection to this scheme may be found in the reflection, that emigration never relieves a country of that class whose absence would be a benefit;—it invariably removes the *useful*, not the *redundant* portion of the Population.

II. The second alternative, that of supporting the

---

* See the Reports of the Hand-loom Weavers' Commission, especially that of Mr. Symons.

added numbers in idleness at home, will scarcely find favour with the Landed Proprietors, upon whom the burden of their maintenance must mainly and ultimately fall. And even those who have been loudest in their outcry against "over-production," will not dispute that, since we *must* support them, it will be more profitable to support them in occupation than in inactivity.

III. The third alternative is thus inevitably forced upon us. We must provide increasing employment for the increasing population. Allowing that some will emigrate, we must find sufficient and remunerative occupation for at least 150,000 additional pair of hands annually. We are bound to this, under penalty of intense and aggravated suffering to our people, of impoverishment to our wealthy classes, and of certain, speedy, inevitable ruin to our country. Where and how is this increase of employment to be found? The cultivation of the soil, we know, cannot furnish it. *It can be furnished only by a regular and continued augmentation in our manufacturing industry; and this can only result from a regular and continued augmentation in the demand for manufactured articles.*

The conclusion appears to me logical, and beyond dispute. It is impossible to escape from it. Hate manufactures as we will—traduce them as we may—the certainty is not the less cogent, that *in their extension,—steady, progressive, and unchecked—lies our only hope of safety as a nation.*

This brings me to the last branch of my remarks.

How is this necessary extension of our manufactures to be insured? There are but two ways;—either by increasing the demand for their produce, or by supplying a larger proportion than we now do, of the existing demand. Either by extending our markets, or by underselling our competitors.

Of the practicability of the latter of these methods, I confess I entertain very slight hopes. Into this discussion I shall not enter at any length, for the subject has been already pretty fully argued, and the facts necessary to form a correct judgment are for the most part before the public. I will only briefly state the grounds of my opinion. At present we are undersold by Foreigners in neutral markets, in all the staple articles of English manufacture, with the single exception of Machinery, *which we are forbidden to export.* In the articles Cotton, Woollen, Hosiery, and Cutlery, which amount together to *three-fifths* of our whole export, this is notoriously the case. In Cotton fabrics, the Swiss undersell us in several markets, and the Americans in those of Smyrna, China, Brazil, Buenos Ayres, and others.* In Woollen cloths the Belgians have beaten us in every market, especially those of China and Brazil.† In Cutlery,

* See Mr. Graham's Pamphlet on the Impolicy of a Tax on Cotton. Evidence before the Committee of Commerce and Manufactures, in 1833.—The Factory System, by R. H. Greg.

† Committee on Commerce and Manufactures. Art and Artisans, by Mr. Symons.—The goods for China and Brazil, are made 20 to 25 per cent. cheaper in Belgium than in Yorkshire.

Sheffield is immensely undersold by the Alsace, and our exports are yearly decreasing.* In Hosiery, the case is still worse ;—Saxony is driving us not only out of foreign markets, *but out of our own.*†

How far, under a perfectly free system, with cheaper food, no taxes on the raw material, and no duties but for the sake of revenue, we might yet recover our lost superiority, is a matter for grave consideration. I do not believe we could, either in Woollens, or in Hosiery; and even in the Cutlery and Cotton trade I think it very doubtful. My reasons are briefly these. The cost of the manufactured article consists of *five* items ;—the raw material; the wear and tear of machinery; the interest of capital employed; the oil, coal, and other current expenses; and the wages of labour. Now under a free commercial system, the raw material would be nearly the same in all Countries, and the advantage, where there was one, would

---

* The English Manufacturer pays 2s. 6d. for the same amount of work, which the French Manufacturer gets done for 2½d. The American Cutlery market, the most important of all, has been wrested from us :—and our exports of that article to all the world have fallen from £1,620,000. in 1831, to £1,345,000. in 1841.

† In Hosiery, we formerly supplied three-fourths of the American demand; we now scarcely supply any. Saxon Hosiery, after paying a duty of 20 per cent. is sold *in London,* 25 to 30 per cent. cheaper than the produce of the Leicester and Nottingham looms.

In Leicestershire, the Stocking Frames have *diminished* from 16,000 in 1815, to 14,000 in 1840; while in Saxony, in the same time, they have increased from 4,500 to 25,000.

be generally on the side of foreigners ;*—the current expenses would also be nearly equal, though perhaps here again the advantage would be slightly against England,†—for Belgium has coal of her own besides the facility of importing it from this country, and Switzerland and America have unlimited supplies of water, the cheapest of all motive powers ;—the machinery of foreign nations is even now not very inferior to our own, and is daily and rapidly improving; and in fact the removal of the unwise prohibition on its exportation, will probably soon place them entirely on a level with us in this respect ;—their capital is fast accumulating, and the interest of it of course yearly approximating to our own rate. In the only remaining item of the cost of production, i. e. the wages of labour, foreign nations have at present a decided advantage; and although a free trade in provisions, by lowering the price of subsistence here, and raising it abroad, would tend ultimately to *reduce* this advantage, I doubt if it can be ever *entirely* removed. Better education, more sober habits, more general frugality and forethought, united with cheaper food, will no doubt enable our people to live in much greater comfort than at present, upon considerably smaller earnings; yet I do not believe that wages will ever be *as* low in England, as on the Continent;

* France and Italy would have an advantage in Silk, and America, in Cotton.

† In the article of carriage, or transport, however, the advantage would be on the side of England.

for not only must food and rent* be always *somewhat* more expensive here, but even were these equalised, the same sum which maintains a Frenchman or a Saxon in comfort and abundance, according to their standard, will still be insufficient for an Englishman's support.† His wants are more numerous, his constitution requires more solid nutriment, and the climate alone, by rendering necessary a better habitation and ampler clothing, will probably always render the English labourer a more costly machine than his Continental rival.

These considerations lead me reluctantly to the conclusion, that the hope of being able, even under an amended system of commercial policy, to undersell our competitors, is at best slight and dubious. I fear that our exports for the future will be merely *supplemental* to those of our Rivals, and will increase less rapidly than theirs; that we shall only supply that portion of the demand of foreign nations which they are unable to supply; that in fact

---

* *Rent*, from the density of the Population, and the consequent high value of land; and *food* from the effect of climate on home grown food, and of freight on that imported from abroad.

† Wages paid for certain articles of Hosiery in 1841.

In Nottingham,	5s. 9d.,	7s. 9d.,	14s. 6d.,	19s.	per dozen.
In Saxony	3s. 0d.,	4s. 0d.,	7s. 0d.,	9s.	....

Upon these wages the Saxon lived in decency and comfort;—upon double the amount the Nottingham labourers suffered severe distress. It may well be doubted whether, with such a discrepancy as this, any alteration in our provision laws will suffice to recover the hosiery trade for this country.

we shall every year, furnish a less and less proportion of the aggregate wants of the Globe.*

If this opinion be correct, it will follow that our only prospect of continued prosperity lies in the aggregate demand of the world for manufactured articles increasing faster than our foreign rivals can increase their production.† In this case there will be trade enough for both.—If this can be effected, we may still experience a progressive augmentation of our commerce, sufficient to employ our progressively augmented population. *To encourage the consumption of all nations, should therefore be the great aim of our policy;—to remove all artificial stimuli to production on the part of our Competitors, should be another, but a very secondary object.* Happily for us, both purposes will be obtained by the same series of measures.

The demand for manufactured articles in all civilized nations is only limited by their population, and their means of purchase; and increases

* This process is already going on, as is seen by the following statement:—Proportion of the Cotton crop of America, taken by.

	Great Britain.	Continent of Europe.	United States.	
In 1827	64	25	11	per cent.
1841	51	31	18	....
Increase in consumption from 1827-8 to 1840-1	101	189	165	....

† Under the stimulus of an adequate demand, I have little doubt that the skill of our artisans, the density of our Population, and the concentration and abundance of our capital, added to our unlimited coal fields, will enable us to increase our manufactures in a faster ratio than other nations.

as these increase.* Now the population of all nations, without exception, we believe is rapidly advancing. Their means of purchase are the fruits of their soil, and the products of their industry; and these, if left to the natural operation of exciting causes, and unchecked in their development by officious interference, will, we know, increase as rapidly as their population. So far then, if we do not mar it, we have solid groundwork for the most golden expectations. But it will be of no service to us that other nations should increase their means of purchase, *if we object to their mode of payment.* We cannot supply their increased demand if we refuse the only articles they have to offer in exchange. In a word, *they cannot buy, and we cannot sell, unless we will accept their coin in payment of he purchase.*

Perfect freedom of interchange, therefore,—willing and unburdened admission of the products of other countries,—must form the sole basis of our future prosperity, *because it is the sole condition on which we can obtain extended markets for our goods, and increased employment for our people.*

---

* The vast opening which exists for increased consumption may be imperfectly guessed at from the following table, showing what our Eastern customers *do,* and what they *might* consume of our manufactures.

	Yards of Plain and Printed Callicoes Exported on an average from 1837 to 1841.	Population.	Yards per Head.
British West Indies	29.200.000	800.000	36.50
India and China	97.200.000	285.000.000	0.35

The same measures—complete commercial freedom—will, by reducing the price of the necessaries of life in England, (and still more by preventing those extreme fluctuations which have been so ruinous to all) enable the mass of our citizens again to become extensive purchasers of articles of clothing, and thus restore the home demand to its natural and healthy state, and give us a right to anticipate its steady annual increase.

The same measures will, by raising the price of food abroad, tend to assimilate the wages of the Continent to those of England. They will diminish the cost of manufacturing production at home, and augment it abroad;—and by lowering the rate of profit in Continental manufactures, will lessen the inducement to invest capital therein;—while, by creating a demand for agricultural produce, they will divert capital, enterprise, and labour into that channel; *and thus employ in feeding us, those who are now busily occupied in ruining us.*

I might proceed much further, and enter into much more detail; but this little pamphlet only professes to be an argument on one branch of a vast question, and I shall therefore conclude with a recapitulation of the points which I consider have been proved.

I. That we have no ground whatever for charging Manufacturers with any excessive or unwarranted increase of production, but great ground for charging Statesmen with excessive and unwarrantable limitation of consumption.

II That the diminution of the home demand, arising from the high price of food, is of itself sufficient to account for the distressed condition both of capitalists and artisans.

III. That the regular annual increase of our Population will *compel* a corresponding annual increase of our manufacturers, in order to provide employment and subsistence for our augmented numbers.

IV. That the progressive demand for manufactured articles, which alone can render such increase of production safe or practicable, must take its origin from the adoption of a system of perfect commercial freedom.

THE END.

THE

PITT-PEEL INCOME TAX,

AND THE

NECESSITY

OF

COMPLETE SUFFRAGE.

BY

ARCHIBALD PRENTICE, Esq.

MANCHESTER:
J. GADSBY, NEWALL'S-BUILDINGS, MARKET-STREET.
LONDON:
R. GROOMBRIDGE, PANYER-ALLEY, PATERNOSTER-ROW
SOLD BY THE BOOKSE LLERS
Price One Penny.

Archibald Prentice (1792–1857)[1]

Archibald Prentice was born in Covington Maines, Lanarkshire. He was educated at the local school, and at the age of twelve was apprenticed to a baker in Edinburgh. In 1805 he changed masters and trade to a woollen draper, and after three years removed to Glasgow as a clerk in the warehouse of Thomas Grahame. After two years he was appointed traveller to the firm in England, and in 1815 Grahame followed Prentice's advice and moved the firm to Manchester, making Prentice a partner.

Prentice had contributed to the *Cowdroy's Gazette* which he purchased in June 1824 and published as the *Manchester Gazette*, a radical alternative to the Whiggish *Manchester Guardian* (est. 1821). The *Gazette* went bankrupt in 1826 and was incorporated with the *Manchester Times* with Prentice as sole manager. The first number of the *Manchester Times and Lancashire and Cheshire Examiner* was published on 17 October 1828. The paper was published weekly on Saturday, and in 1839 reached an average circulation of 2,884.[2]

Prentice took an active part in founding in September 1838 the Manchester Anti Corn Law Association and placed his paper at the service of the League which was founded a year later. In 1845 the *Manchester Examiner* was founded which competed with the *Times* forcing Prentice to sell his share in the *Times* in 1847 and to the incorporation of the two papers in 1848.

Prentice was described by the League's historian Norman McCord as 'the moving spirit of an extreme group [in the League's Council] small in number but strong in its contribution of hard work for the League, and vociferous in its advocacy of extreme and often rash courses.'[3] The line between radicalism and Chartism was described by Prentice when he answered a question put to him at a lecture he gave in Ardwick in January 1842 'If you advocate the principles of the charter, why are you not a chartist?' To which Prentice answered: 'Because I like most of the principles of the charter, but there are many of the chartists that I do not like.'[4]

Prentice visited the U.S. in 1848 and upon his return was given a position in the Manchester gas office which left him ample leisure for literary work which included his *History of the Anti Corn Law League*, first published in 1853.

Prentice's published works include:

Opinions on the currency question, with a review of Mr. Cobbet's Lectures, being an article in the Manchester Times, of January 16th and 23rd, 1830, Manchester, [1830?].

Report of the Trial of Archibald Prentice for an alleged Libel on Captain Grimshaw, Salford Quarter Sessions 1831, Manchester: Archibald Prentice, [1831].

Organic changes necessary to complete the system of representation partially amended by the reform bill, London: E. Wilson, 1839.

The *Pitt-Peel income tax, and the necessity of complete suffrage*, Manchester: J. Gadsby, [1842].

An address to farmers, on the way in which their families are to be provided for, Manchester: J. Gadsby, [1842?]. Another edition, Manchester: J. Johnson, [1843?].

Historical sketches and personal recollections of Manchester. Intended to illustrate the progress of public opinion from 1792 to 1832, London: G. Gilpin, 1851. 2nd edition, 1851.

History of the Anti Corn Law League, London: W. & F. G. Cash, 1853.

[1] Based mainly on Robert Dunlop's article in *D.N.B.* vol. 16, pp. 301–3.

[2] *Manchester as it is*, Manchester: Love and Barton, 1839, pp. 189–90.

[3] McCord, *The Anti Corn Law League*, p. 165.

[4] *Manchester Times* 29 January 1842.

LECTURE.

The ninth monthly meeting of the YOUNG MEN'S ANTI-MONOPOLY ASSOCIATION was held on Wednesday evening, at the Old Meal-House, Nicholas Croft, on which occasion Mr. PRENTICE had been invited to deliver a lecture on Complete Suffrage. There was a very numerous attendance. The proceedings commenced soon after eight o'clock, when, on the motion of Mr. Nelson, Mr. SAUL was called to the chair.

Mr. PRENTICE came forward amidst great cheering, and said:—Mr. Chairman and Gentlemen,—As a reformer of nearly thirty years' standing, you may well suppose I come forward with great pleasure on an occasion like this, when you are assembled to inquire into the safety and practicability of that which I have asserted during the whole of that time—I mean the safety and practicability of a complete representation of the people in the House of Commons. (Applause.) The object of your association is to put down monopolies, and, among the rest, that of representation. Now, gentlemen, we have measures now before Parliament, and which very forcibly show what sort of representation we now possess. In the year 1798 Mr. Pitt brought forward together, and passed through the Houses of Parliament together, hand-in-hand, like twin-brothers, an Income Tax and a bill for the suspension of the Habeus Corpus Act. (Hear, hear.) In 1842 Sir Robert Peel, in humble imitation of the "heaven born minister," has brought before Parliament two bills, twin-born, and means to pass them hand-in-hand through both houses—the one a new edition of the iniquitous sliding-scale corn bill, and the other a new income tax, by which he proposes to raise five millions of money. Gentlemen, I think it is likely Sir Robert will still further have to follow the example of Mr. Pitt, and will have to bring forward a suspension of the Habeas Corpus Act, to prevent people grumbling at the burdens which he has put upon them. (Cheers.) I am sure when it is practically known what the tax is and how it is to be raised, it will bring to your association, and others having a similar object in view, thousands of your townsmen, to join in asking for a more full, fair, free, and complete representation in what is called, but not truly called, the Commons' House of Parliament. (Loud cheers.) Gentlemen, you will allow me perhaps to illustrate my remarks upon the present representative system by reference to the new income tax brought forward by ministers, and to compare the statements brought forward by them in support of the new bill with those urged by the same parties in reference to the corn law. When we have represented the injustice done to the commercial, the manufacturing, and the labouring classes by those other monopolies of which you complain, and which you are associated to put down—the monopolies which restrict the importation, and enhance the price of food—in answer to these remonstrances the cry has always been that we must not damage the agricultural and farming interests; that there was a rental of £40,000,000 per annum paid by farmers; that theirs was a great national interest which could not be properly or with justice interfered with; that great and vested interests were at stake; that it would interfere with their leases, and that though it might be desirable to give some degree of relief to the manufacturing and trading community, it was difficult and dangerous to touch interests greater than both the manufacturing and trading interests put together. It was represented then that the trading interests were a mere fraction of the community. You have heard it said that they were only a third; and that therefore to give up the interests of two-thirds for the sake of benefiting the one-third, would be to injure the many for the sake of the few. That was the cry when the object was to tax the whole community for the benefit of the landowners; but no sooner was the intention entertained to tax the whole community for the sake of revenue, than you have an illustration of what I want to show you, the necessity of a more full, fair, and complete representation. When they wanted to tax the whole they suddenly discover that this farming interest, which was greater than any other in the state, and to which none of the other interests would bear comparison, is not quite so great as they had taken it to be. How much do you suppose they discover that the farming interest is able to pay? You would suppose that an interest representing £40,000,000 of rental per annum would be thought to be upon a footing with any interest in the state, and taxed like any other. But look at the beauty of the £50 tenant-at-will clause! Look at the beauty of a system of partial and unequal representation, and the consequence of an absence of the ballot. The landlords have obtained a great majority of the people in the House of Commons, and their first act is to declare that this great farming interest, which was so important when put in contrast with the commercial interest, is so poor that it can contribute no more than one twenty-fifth of the taxes they are going to propose. (Hear, hear.) Well might Lord John Russell say that it was intended that the landed interest should predominate in the House of Commons! It has been proved by their acts that they do predominate—that they are all-powerful; and that though it might suit them to represent the manufacturing interest as but a drop in the bucket when legislating upon the corn tax, the moment they are going to tax income they discover that the farming interest is only equal to one twenty-fifth of the community, and when they are going to lay a tax of £3,700,000 on the country, all they discover the farming interest is able to pay is £150,000. Now I should think this enough to shew you that the present system of representation is not one that ought to satisfy the people—(cheers)—that you need a further extension of the suffrage—(hear, hear, hear)—that in fact you need a complete suffrage that will render the Commons' House of Parliament what it purports it to be, a house which really represents the opinions and interests of the whole of the people. (Cheers.) And it must convince you, that until the people are fully, fairly, and individually represented, we shall never have an end to these specimens of class legislation. (Cheers.) But it is not merely the fact that out of all this amount of taxation to be imposed, you can only raise £150,000 from the farmers, who have been so exceedingly well protected, but it happens there is a special exemption, that unless the rent of a farm amounts to £300 a year, they shall not be taxed at all. The young men who are clerks, collectors, and cash keepers, in our counting houses, and who have £40,000, £50,000, or £60,000 passing through their hands in the course of the year, salesmen with large stocks of goods placed in their hands, travellers entrusted by their employers with the negociation of important sales, dissenting ministers, young surgeons, young lawyers—all who are rising in the world, all who contrive by their industry, ingenuity, and ability, to become possessed of an income of £150 a year, they are all to be taxed to the amount of three per cent.; and the farmers are not to be taxed if they pay anything less than a rent of £300 a year! (Hear, hear, and shame.) Now you know when the Reform Bill was passing through the House of Commons, the Marquis of Chandos introduced a clause giving a vote to every £50 tenant-at-will. These gentlemen were so respectable that they could not be left out of the representation in the new scheme—they were so intelligent—had such an important stake in the country, paying £50 a year, and being respectable, just as Thurtell the thief was respectable, because he kept a gig—(laughter)—that, forsooth, they had votes for the counties conferred on them. But when they come to prepare a fresh system of taxation, all this noise about respectability and intelligence, and the high stake in the country is forgotten—(hear)—and we are told that the farmers must be exempt unless they pay £300 a year rent! (Cheers.) Now I should recommend this association, as it is an association to protest against monopolies,—I would ask them, before the bill passes into a law, that they should send a representation to the house shewing these facts, and representing that whereas the £50 tenants-at-will are not considered respectable enough to pay taxes, they shall not be considered respectable enough to have county votes—(hear)—and that whereas the young men having salaries of £150 a year, being thought respectable enough to pay a tax upon their income, shall be also thought respectable enough to have county votes. (Cheers.) But gentlemen, it is not merely that every farmer who occupies to the amount of £50 is thought to be respectable enough to have a vote for the county, while a respectable man in Manchester having £150 or £300, or any other sum a year, is not, if he happens to be a lodger, but it happens that every man occupying land in the county to the amount of £300 a year, can not only vote himself, but if he have as many sons, can make six votes for the county from one farm. (Hear, hear, hear.) But, gentlemen, this is not the greatest injustice of the proposition; there is another far more important than the one I have pointed out. It is that £150 derived from the labour of a man's head or hands should be taxed three per cent., while the man who derives £150 from land pays no more. The man who by the labour of his head, the exercise of his ingenuity and experience, realizes an income of £150, and the man who has a capital of £4000 invested in land, from which he derives £150 annually during his life, are to pay the same amount of tax; while there is this difference between them—that the clerk, or salesman, or small tradesman of £150 a year, at the caprice of his employer, or through the loss of health, the change of trade, or a thousand circumstances over which he has no control, may be penniless to-morrow, and his widow and family at his death may be cast upon the world; while the man who is taxed for the £150 derived from land is subject to no such chances, and when he dies his wife and children will still have the £4000 worth of property from which his income was derived, and be in as comfortable circumstances as before. (Hear, hear.) Now, gentlemen, under a fair and complete representation of the working classes, do you suppose that we could have such an extraordinary system of taxation as this? (Hear, hear, hear.) Then there is the inquisitorial and prying examination into a man's means and affairs that such a system will lead to—(hear, hear)—and this of itself is a thing which never could have evolved from any but a landlords' parliament. (Applause.) We talk about an Englishman's house being his castle; and that the winds of Heaven may whistle round it, and may come into it, but that the king dare not enter; and the other things which our fondness of self-laudation lead us to think unknown to other countries; but here is an inquisitorial plan—a system by which informers and spies will be placed at every man's door and come into his house to ask how much his salary is and what are his means of living. But "Oh," they say, "we do not mean to compel any man to produce his books or shew the state of his affairs!" Gentlemen, Mr. Pitt said so, in 1798. He said, "We do not compel a man to produce his books, or be examined in the presence of an informer or spy who is called a surveyor: he has the option of refusing to do so." Oh yes, he has the option it is true; but then they have the option of surcharging him to double the amount of his real income. (Hear, hear, hear.) Now could such an insulting, unequal, inequitable measure ever have proceeded from any house elected by the free choice of the people? ("No," and cheers.) Some of my friends the chartists taunt me about the workings of the middle-classes' representation. I say —Would to heaven we had one! (Hear, hear, hear.) Our present representation is one purely of the aristocracy and landowners; and therefore don't talk of middle class representation. (Cheers.) Even a representation of the middle classes, defective, unequal, and unfair as it would be—because I hold that we could not have a good system of representation that did not give the suffrage to the people—(loud cheers) —but I say if we had had a representation of even the middle classes, they would not have framed a tax that would send the tax gatherer, the informer, the spy, into every man's house to see how he lives, or which would have the effect of dragging him before a number of gentlemen commissioners—(Mr. Fleming, I think, is one)—and if they say your income is double what it really is, oblige you to produce your books, and place you in the humiliating condition of shewing that you have only so much; that the fine house which they have given you credit for is under such and such mortgages—(Hear, hear)—or that though you seemed to have a good trade, it is clogged with such and such debts, and such and such conditions which prevent you from deriving the full benefit—(hear, hear)—or that if certain parties should break, your whole trade will go at once—do you think, I say, that if we had had even a middle-class representation we should have had such a scheme as this brought before us? Why should we have any income tax at all? In the present parliament we have had a discussion on the corn laws. During that discussion the landowners always referred to the peculiar burdens on land, and they said so much land tax was paid that they ought to have a countervailing protection. This led to an inquiry, and it was found that when it was commuted—for land was formerly held on a military tenure by feudal chiefs who rendered military services—it was found at that commutation they contrived to have the land tax, which was then about one-third of the whole revenue, fixed at £2,000,000 per annum, and they have contrived it so well that it has continued fixed—a fixed duty in contrast with a sliding scale—(hear, hear, hear)—while all the rest of the taxes have increased; the other taxes, in fact, having slidden up to 48 millions, while this remains at two millions. (Shame.) This has been exposed by Mr. Scott, a bookseller, and a countryman of mine. He went over the assessments of several counties, and he found the assessments for land tax in those several counties was just exactly one thirtieth of what it ought to be. (Hear, hear.) Then Mr. Cobden took up the subject; and with his clear and forcible manner of putting truths he rendered the thing so convincing, that, finding a great inquiry was going on into this subject, they have instructed Sir Robert Peel, who is their humble servant—I say, finding that a great inquiry was going on as to this land tax which produces two millions whereas it ought to produce 16 millions—(hear, hear)—they instruct their servant, Sir Robert Peel, for he is their servant, this cotton spinner's son, whom they despise because he is one—this man who is always ready to do, I will not say their dirty work, but who is ready to do *all* their work, and it is *dirty enough*—(cheers and laughter)—they instruct this slavish serf of the aristocracy, this son of a cotton spinner, to come before the House of Commons and make a great parade of this plan by which they are to make great sacrifices for the good of the country—(great laughter)—and for which they are to tax themselves three per cent. for their stiff clays and splendid incomes, taking care that the young men who have £150 a year salary shall pay just the same! Do they think that we shall not find men bold enough to tell them what the country thinks of them? (Cheers.) But Sir Robert says the country is satisfied with his measure, and he will not explain the machinery by which it is to be worked, nor will he give time for the people's petitions, for they have managed to arrange that none shall be presented after Friday. We shall see whether the people are satisfied with it when the inquisitorial nature of it is known. (Hear, hear.) I do not rejoice that men should thus be made to know, but there are numbers of men who require teaching, and if we bring them up before the tax gatherer to give an account of their earnings and incomes, we shall have a great many converts to the necessity of a complete representation before the year is out. (Cheers and laughter.)—Gentlemen, the corn bill which is now carrying through the house is the strongest proof that could be given that the people are not represented. We have been told that this corn bill would effect a great amelioration in our circumstances; that it would effect a great reduction upon the duty on foreign corn; but there is this damning circumstance to prevent our belief in the statement, that Sir Robt. Peel in his new budget has nowhere mentioned the import duties upon corn. (Hear, hear.) He knows the present bill in fact is as prohibitory as the last, and he says nothing about the increase of the revenue likely to arise from it, although we well know that he would, did he not know there was likely to be none. (Hear, hear, and cheers.) Then if there is to be no revenue there is to be no increased importation; and if so, how are we to have more bread? The man has at last let the truth out. In supporting the corn bill he makes an assertion which he must know to be untrue; but when he comes to open his budget he lets out the truth by saying that the new corn bill is to give no additional revenue from the bringing in of more corn from abroad. (Hear, hear, hear.) I give him his choice: he either told that which he knew to be untrue before, or he tells what is untrue now; and whichever horn of the dilemma he sits upon, he has proved himself what I shall not call him, but what you may find a name for. (Loud cheers.) If the people had been fairly represented, do you think that this could have occurred? Do you suppose they would have had a minister at the head of the government who would have brought such a miserable, drivelling system of new duties as that now proposed? (Applause.) Do you suppose they would have wasted their time in reducing the duty on balsam copaiva—(laughter)—or upon asses,—(renewed laughter)—or upon anchovies to make toasts for those who have drunk rather too freely over night, and require something stimulating next morning. (Laughter and applause.) Do you suppose they would have fiddle-faddled over 750 articles to reduce the duties upon commodities not one of which you have scarcely ever heard of before? Why there is to be a reduction of 50 per cent. upon squirrell's tails—(great laughter)—the great amount imported last year being to the sum of £12. (Renewed laughter.) I have mentioned the importation of asses—(loud laughter): last year it amounted to *nine* asses and nine-twentieths of an ass. (Laughter.) Sir Robert Peel thinks he improves the chance by reducing the duty to 5s., and I suppose instead of nine and nine-twentieths we shall next year have an increase to eighteen and eighteen fortieths. (Great laughter.)—Gentlemen, do you suppose if the people had been represented that they would have stopped at these paltry reductions—the greater part of them in favour of our colonies? There is a fine shew of reducing the tariffs against the colonies, and he makes a parade of reducing the duty on butter from Canada, well knowing that we never have any from there. But I have gone through the whole of these reductions, and find that they are generally reductions in favour of colonies not producing the articles named. (Laughter.) If we had proper representation the people would have demanded a reduction, not on asses, but on sugar, that their wives and children might have had that comfort placed within their reach. (Loud cries of "Hear.") Don't you suppose they would have demanded cheaper bread? (Loud cheers.) And don't you suppose they would have said we cannot stand this duty you keep unmitigated upon cheese? (Hear, hear.) But here is a reduction of all that the people do not consume, except bacon and ham, and salted meats, which they know Englishmen do not like if they can get fresh provisions—(Hear, hear.)—and yet they come and say, what liberal enlightened men are we! we have reduced the duty upon 750 articles of consumption which you do not consume! (Applause and laughter.) Coming back to the income tax: they say it is a tax only upon those who are able to bear it. But I put it to any working man if he does not know that if you put any additional tax upon trade, the manufacturer cannot put a higher price upon his goods? That is a thing which does not depend upon him; it depends upon the customer, and the customer will give him no more. He cannot bring his profits any lower, the articles must be produced cheaper, and therefore the working man's wages must be reduced! (Hear, hear, hear.) Mr. Tierney, when Mr. Pitt brought forward his motion and said the income tax would be a tax upon land, observed: "On the contrary, I think it a conspiracy of the rich to cheat the poor into the designs of the aristocracy to oppress the middle classes." What does Sir R. Peel say: he makes a great profession, and says it taxes the rich; and says to the working man—"join us in taxing the middle classes"—forgetting what I mentioned before, that a tax upon trade is a tax upon wages. (Cheers.) Having gone over these points, to shew that there is nothing like a fair representation of the people—that there is not even a representation of the middle classes, but simply a representation of the breeches pocket—(hear, hear)—of the landowner, let us now proceed to examine the present system of voting, and see how it is guided by reason and principle. I have alluded to the votes of the £50 tenants-at-will, and now let us look at the absurdity of men having votes who only rent as much land as will keep a few cows, and living in a house not worth £20 a-year, while the men who have an income of £200 or £300 a-year have none. The latter, with all his respectability and superior intelligence, is considered inferior to the £50 tenant-at-will, and has no vote. Why here in Crumpsall, a township just out of the borough, the little cow-keeper who brings milk to your doors has a vote there for the county; while the gentleman who occupies a £45 house has no vote. (Hear, hear.) If property is to be the basis of representation, you see how unequal the principle is, because it excludes all respectable men and includes the far inferior rank of £50 tenants-at-will. (Hear, hear.) Now I know it has been said, if we had a complete representation, that it would throw greater power in the hands of the landowner. This is one of the fallacies of Mr. Baines, of Leeds. How does he shew it? He takes all the population of the counties, adds it up; then takes the population of represented boroughs, adds up these; and the inhabitants of all towns not represented he concludes to be agricultural population, and therefore says that an extension of the suffrage would extend the power of the agricultural interest. Now he forgets—I will not say it is dishonesty, because he is a reformer whom I have a better opinion of—but he forgets that there are such towns as Hyde, Stalybridge, Glossop, Heywood, St. Helens, and others, which, though unrepresented, are yet not to be classed as agricultural. (Hear, hear.) Gentlemen, you see that this mode is unsafe, that it is invidious, and gives to one man a vote who is not half so worthy and intelligent as his neighbour who is excluded; and, therefore, is it proper that representation should rest there? (No, and cheers.) Then you come to the representation of houses, and the reform bill says that every man with a £10 house shall have a vote. Now, what is the extraordinary virtue of a £10 house? The man who is extravagant and imprudent enough to have a £10 house before he can keep it over his head has a vote, but the man who is prudent enough to keep in lodgings until he can well furnish and provide for a house has none. (Hear.) The man in a £10 house has a vote which the man in a house at £9 19s., is excluded; and the man who is a labourer, and keeps a lodging house, has a vote, while the lodger, who is a respectable and much more intelligent man, and who pays all the rent, has none. (Hear, hear.)—Gentlemen, I need not ask a man what virtue there is in £10 more than £9, or in £9 more than £8, or if he has a house of £8, which was to be the Irish qualification, what virtue there is in that more than in £7 19s.? When you begin to move it is impossible to stop at anything short of complete, universal, individual representation. (Loud cheers.) It is said by some of those who wish to steer a half-way course between a £10 and an universal suffrage, that a *house* should give the suffrage. Now, I do not see any virtue in a house. I do not see why the man who pays 10s. a week for his lodgings is not as respectable as the Duke of Buckingham's serf, who pays 40s. a year. (Hear.) Gentlemen, I have explained my objection to the household suffrage before. I have said I would rather have a reading and writing qualification than that, because a house is no test of respectability or intelligence; but our choice is not between a reading and writing and a household qualification, and people think if they go so near to universal suffrage, they may as well "go the whole hog" at once. Now, though I think there might be a very good representation of the sort I have mentioned, I would rather have universal representation than household. (Hear, hear.) Why, look at the household system. You would have all the worst parts of universal suffrage without any of the redeeming advantages of it. You would include great masses of the peasantry—the ignorant serfs of those who are themselves only the serfs of the landowners—(hear, hear, hear,)—and you would have the great mass of the reading, intelligent, enlightened artisans excluded. (Hear.) Now, I say, if we are to have such a representation, let us have, as a counterbalancing power against the noblemen's servants, all the lodgers, the prudent and intelligent young men of the manufacturing towns. (Applause.) Gentlemen, I will not say much of what would be the consequence of such a representation; but you may be assured a House of Commons so elected would not have passed Sir Robert Peel's corn bill; that it would not have passed the new poor law bill, while the poor man's bread was taxed—(cheers)—that it would not have given £20,000,000 to the men-stealers of the West Indies—(cheers)—that such a House of Commons would not have taken the rights of the forty shilling freeholders of Ireland—(cheers)—that it would not continue the duty upon sugar (which is an article now scarcely tasted by the working man), cheese, and butter. (Cheers.) Then what would they do? Would they pass an act for the confiscation of property? What they—the working classes, under whose care all your great manufactories are placed—they who are entrusted with your property and lives, and who if a fire takes place are the first to go and assist in putting it out?—they who, if your lives were in danger would be the first to sacrifice theirs in your defence?—(cheers)—they who, by the torch and dagger, if they were so inclined, or by "large needles," could put an end to your property any day? No; it is only the shameless who could assert such fears. They know there would be no danger, but that, on the contrary, there would be greater safety. (Cheers.) Or do you suppose, under universal suffrage, the moral influence of man on man would be destroyed all at once? Is there not reason to believe it would be increased? Should we not have the power to appeal with increased force to men's sense of justice when they were no longer smarting under political grievances? No man could then say you are an enemy to me because you would not give me the suffrage. The working man would have the suffrage; he would be willing to talk with me and reason with me dispassionately and calmly; and I say it is absurd to assert that the man of station and respectability would not have as much or more influence than now. (Hear, and applause.)—Mr. Prentice spoke of the absurdity of trying to convince men that others could manage their affairs better for them than they could manage for themselves, and retired amidst loud and prolonged cheering.

After Mr. Prentice's address Mr. Pountney moved a vote of thanks to him, which was seconded by Mr. Nelson, and carried.

Mr. Holland, surgeon, proposed a petition praying that the proposed tax upon wages, incomes, or profits might not be carried into a law, and that it might be restricted to real property. The petition, which was seconded, and carried amidst great cheering, was signed before the meeting separated by a great number of persons present, and, it was understood, would be despatched by the next day's post to the borough members for presentation.—A vote of thanks was then given to the chairman, and the meeting separated.

J. GADSBY, PRINTER, NEWALL'S-BUILDINGS.

Richard Cobden (1804–65)

Richard Cobden's speech in the House of Commons on 8 July 1842 was his first major speech in Parliament.[1] It was delivered in the course of a debate started on 1 July by Robert Wallace, MP for Greenock, Scotland, on the distress of the country. Peel's defence of his financial policy led Cobden to respond by criticizing the Prime Minister's position on every point. The League's *Anti Bread Tax Circular* recommended the printed speech to its readers 'not only to keep as long as they keep anything but also for distribution. The monopolists are mere playthings in his hands.'[2]

Much has been made of the growing affinity of Cobden's and Peel's views of the economy in the summer of 1842.[3] But at the time Cobden's understanding that Peel was drifting towards free trade did not prevent him from stepping up his attack on the Prime Minister, part of which was in defence of the industrialists who were accused of responsibility for unemployment by introducing labour saving machinery, and of inciting to violence by exaggerating the workers' suffering. In a speech on 13 July to the League's delegates gathered in London for an emergency meeting to discuss, at the same time as the House of Commons, the state of the country, Cobden condemned Peel's position on machinery as tantamount to incitement to violence.

> ... the alluding to machinery in the way Sir Robert Peel had alluded to it, was as dangerous to the country as it was reprehensible in the prime minister himself. (Hear, hear.) ... – he had almost said it was especially wicked. (Hear, hear.) Now what were the effects which were being produced in this country by Sir Robert Peel's allusion to machinery? He had received a letter from a friend at Burnley, which he would read to the meeting:-
>
> 'Burnley, July 11, 1842
>
> 'Sir Robert Peel's machinery clap-trap is producing some effects. During the last week a bundle of lucifer matches was thrown into a cotton mill near Accrington; part of the matches were found consumed, fortunately they had not reached the cotton, or the mill would have been destroyed. There is a common expectation among the poor suffering labouring people that machinery is going to be done with, and they refer to the remarks of Sir R. Peel in the newspapers as authority'.
>
> These were the natural effects of the observations made by Sir R. Peel. What more natural than that the distressed and suffering people – driven to extremities by their suffering – should take up the opinion of Sir R. Peel, and attribute to

[1] John Morley, *The Life of Richard Cobden* (1879), London: T. Fisher Unwin, 1906, p. 244, Nocholas C. Edsall, *Richard Cobden Independent Radical*, Cambridge, Mass., and London: Harvard University Press, 1986, pp. 116–17, and Wendy Hinde, *Richard Cobden A Victorian Outsider*, New Haven and London: Yale University Press, 1987, p. 108.

[2] *The Anti Bread Tax Circular*, 14 July 1842.

[3] E.g. Edsall, *Cobden*, pp. 117–18.

machinery all the miseries which they endured. They were told that the manufacturers were incendiaries. Now, he apprehended that they were the last men in the world, circumstanced as they were, to do anything likely to lead to violence of any kind. When a lucifer match would destroy not merely the produce of their industry, but would destroy the capital also, was it likely that they would provoke violence in the manufacturing districts, ... The real incendiaries were not to be found in that body, but in the House of Commons and the Cabinet (Cheers).[1]

[1] *Manchester Times*, 16 July 1842.

ALARMING DISTRESS.

SPEECH

OF

RICHD. COBDEN, ESQ.

IN THE HOUSE OF COMMONS

ON FRIDAY EVENING, JULY 8, 1842.

PRICE ONE PENNY.

Mr. COBDEN: Notwithstanding the many statements which had been made during the present session, and notwithstanding all that had been said in the course of this debate, he still really entertained serious doubts whether honourable gentlemen on the ministerial side of the house were at all convinced of the actual existence of distress amongst the people. After listening to the speeches which had been delivered by members on the opposition side of the house, and observing the silence that had been kept by honourable gentlemen who supported her Majesty's government, he certainly did entertain serious doubts whether, after all the complaints made of the great and grievous distress that prevailed throughout the country, those complaints were not considered by hon. gentlemen on the other side of the house as mere party statements, and the question of distress itself a mere party question. For, he would ask, were there really no hon. gentlemen on the ministerial benches who represented any portion of the community that were afflicted by distress? (Hear, hear.) Where was the honourable member for Leeds? (Cheers.) Where were the two honourable members for the West Riding of Yorkshire? (Hear, hear.) Was there no distress prevalent in that vast and populous district of the north? (Hear.) They were silent. Why was it left to members on the opposition benches to carry on this debate? He could account for it on one ground only—either they did not believe in the existence of distress, or, though believing it, they were willing to hush up all the facts connected with it for the sake of party purposes; (hear, hear;) and he must say that he thought her Majesty's government had in some degree lent themselves to the first persuasion; for he had not heard from the right hon. bart. any sufficient acknowledgment of the general distress of the country. (Hear.) The right hon. baronet's remarks went merely to consider the distress of the cotton trade in the districts surrounding Manchester, and his observations were calculated to impress the minds of his supporters with the conviction that things were not so bad there as they had been represented. The right hon. baronet brought forward a statement of which he (Mr. Cobden) had just right to complain, because it was calculated to mislead his (Sir R. Peel's) followers as to the state of trade in Lancashire. The right hon. baronet told the house that during the first half of the present year, 74,000 bales of cotton more had been taken out for home consumption than were taken out for the first half of last year. True, the fact was so; but if the right honourable baronet had instituted a comparison between the first half of this year with the last half of last year, he would have found that there had been a diminution of 145,000 bales; or if he had made a comparison between the first half of this year and the two half years of 1840, he would have found a deficiency of 105,000 bales; or if he had established a comparison between the first half year of this year, with the average of the last ten half years, he would have found a diminution of 35,000 bales. There were reasons well known to all who were conversant with the cotton manufactures why the quantity of cotton taken out for home consumption during the first half of last year was less than usual. But why did the right honourable baronet go through all the statistics of the Board of Trade for the purpose of finding out the state of the cotton trade? Was it to give consolation to those honourable gentlemen who were ever ready to give him their support? Was it worthy of him, who was the Prime Minister of this great country, to stoop to such an expediency as that? (Cheers.) Was there not danger in the adoption of such a course on the part of a Prime Minister? Might not those who looked to him as their authority, and who knew little of these matters themselves, say, "So long as we find the right hon. baronet buoyed up with confidence in the state of the trade of the country we need not be much alarmed about it?" It was true that the imports of raw cotton had not much diminished since last year, but what had been the fact? The consumption of cotton had been from the spinning of the coarsest description of yarn. Looms had been thrown out of employment, and the spinners had been employed just to spin the coarsest yarn, by which the manufacturers were saved from a great loss which they would have otherwise incurred. But did this give relief to the people? Did it give wages to the country? (Hear.) He did think that it would have been more becoming of the Prime Minister of this great country to look the matter fairly in the face, and to tell his followers and the country what was the condition in which we were really placed. The right hon. baronet went into no inquiry as to the cause or causes of the distress which prevailed, except as to the condition of one branch—the cotton manufacture. And in reference to that branch, the right hon. bart. said that we were suffering in consequence of alterations in the construction of machinery. The remark of the right honourable baronet was, that sudden improvements in machinery threw great masses of the people out of employment; that while new inventions gave employment to women and children, they always displaced the labour of large masses of the adult population. "I agree with you," said the right hon. baronet, "that ultimately, improved machinery must give additional employment to those whose business it would be to make it; but in the interval the introduction of that improved machinery threw large masses of the manufacturing population out of labour." Now, he (Mr. Cobden) denied the fact. (Cheers.) The proposition was not true. He (Mr. Cobden) denied the proposition that machinery threw great bodies of the people out of employment. It was well known that improvements in machinery were very slow and gradual. It took a long time to bring them into work, and their introduction was so occasional and gradual, that they never could have the effect which the right honourable baronet had attributed to them. Capitalists resisted the improvement of machinery as far as they could. Every body knew what difficulties patentees had to get capitalists to take up an invention. Every body knew the loss which the capitalist sustained by a new invention superseding existing machinery. The right honourable baronet had evidently been misled by what took place during the riots of the Luddites; but he might as well argue, that because men went about and burnt wheat ricks, therefore wheat ricks were the cause of agricultural suffering. It was true that stocking machinery was destroyed in Leicester and Nottingham, in the years 1811 and 1812, but was the stocking machinery a new invention at that time? No; it had been in use many years. It was also true that many power looms were destroyed. But were those looms a new invention? On the contrary they had been in use upwards of forty years. The cause of this destruction of machinery was not that improvements had superseded the labour of large masses of the people, but because of the well-known orders in council. The spinning machine was invented by Arkwright, in 1767, long before it was brought into use. The power loom was invented by a clergyman in 1787, and in 1817 only 2000 power looms were in existence in Lancashire, and only one half of those were employed. The right honourable baronet admitted that ultimately machinery might give immense employment to the people, by adding vastly to the demand for labour. What was the history of the cotton trade? Arkwright's machine was invented, as he had said. in 1767, and only 30,000 persons were engaged in the cotton manufacture; now, more than a million and a half subsisted by it. When had there been an instance of any craft carried on by hand labour, in which the growth was so rapid? What was the history of agriculture? No man could justly accuse the proprietors of estates of being too ready to adopt improvements in implements of husbandry. In many parts of the country they still used the plough that Cincinnatus followed. (Laughter.) Did agriculturists give employment to increased numbers of the people? No; they annually sent thousands to the towns where machinery was in use. What were Manchester Bolton, Stockport, and other towns but the creation of labour-saving machines? (Hear.) They were towns filled by persons who had abandoned their ploughs and spades for the spindles, shuttles, and hammers of a former generation. (Hear. hear.) Pandering to the prejudices of the working classes on the one side, and soothing the ignorance of the upper class by fallacies on the other, was surely unworthy of the prime minister of this country. He did not complain of the honourable member for Macclesfield, (Mr. Grimsditch,) he was only following his vocation. (Hear.) But he did complain of the right honourable baronet, and he sincerely hoped that he would indulge in no more tirades against the employment of machinery. (Cheers.) How, then, continued the honourable member, ought we to be engaged now? Instead of looking out for something to cover and conceal the mischief, we ought to do what we can to uncover and disclose it, in order that we may apply a remedy. What can restore your trade and give employment to your people? That is the question. You talk of over-production. What a charge to bring against a people, that they are over-industrious. (Cheers.) I can imagine a case of a person going to a foreign country, barbarous and unimproved, and bringing word back that the inhabitants were idle, vicious, ignorant, and deficient in forecast; but what a tale would it be for such a man to speak of a distant people, and to complain that they were over-industrious, that they had accumulated too much, and that their fault was over-production! (Hear, hear.) I do not ask either of the honourable members for Macclesfield—they are privileged men—but I do ask the right honourable baronet what is the meaning of over-production? It means that too much is produced; and what can be thought of a country which produces so much, and where the great mass of the people possess so little? Does it not show that there is some mal-distribution of production? It is because we have lost sight of that science which teaches the right distribution of wealth. We have adopted the steam engine, and have employed it in every possible way, but we have lost sight of the great philosopher who was contemporary with Watt, and who told us how the wealth to be acquired by the steam engine was to be distributed. Because we have lost sight of that discovery, the great mass of the people is at this moment so wretched. Those who are so fond of laughing at political economy, forget that they have a political economy of their own; and what is it? That they will monopolise to themselves the fruits of the industry of the great body of the community; that they allow the productions of the spindle and the loom to go abroad to furnish them with luxuries from the farthest corners of the world, but refuse to permit to be brought back in exchange what would minister to the wants and comforts of the lower orders. (Cheers.) This, in one word, is the true reason why the mass of the people is at this time so wretchedly clothed and so miserably fed. As legislators, you have the charge of giving employment and sustenance to the people. Fault has been found with the wording of the motion. I can only say, that my honourable friend is willing to change it, in order that no man may have a pretext for voting against it. All he wants is, that this house, before it separates, should pledge itself to inquire, that it may devise measures for the relief of the suffering population. You cannot give that relief by charitable contributions, by preaching, by collections, and I will prove it. You have heard from my honourable colleague (Mr. Marsland) a pathetic statement of the present condition of the borough of Stockport; the population were formerly paid £6,000 a-week in wages. How will you make up that sum by charitable contributions? How will you supply the vacuum, if the whole cotton trade is to follow the fate of Stockport? Twenty millions were annually spent in the cotton trade. Does not this fact show the prodigious importance of finding employment for the people, as the only means of putting an end to the present distress? How many men are engaged in the cultivation of wheat? Six millions a-year would pay them all; not one-third of the sum paid in wages in the cotton trade. Open your eyes, then, to the real condition of the country; knowing that your own permanent interests are as one with the manufacturers, you will see the necessity of looking the difficulty in the face, and dealing with it not as a party question, but as a matter in which the welfare of the whole state is concerned. This might be said to be a Manchester question three years ago, but it is not so now. I see the honourable member for Leeds in his place, and I challenge him to say whether the condition of Leeds at this moment is not worse than that of Stockport. We have not 40,000 utterly unemployed; our poor rates are not so high; his borough must be one vast poorhouse. I ask him whether charitable contributions will be sufficient, or whether something else must not be done to meet the growing evil? You may talk of machinery, but go into districts where machinery has not been improved for the last two hundred years. I ask the honourable member for Nottingham, where there are no tall chimneys, no change of modes of working, but where they pursue the plan pursued 240 years ago, what is the condition of that town? There has been no change of fashion to make a difference, for there has been no change of fashion in stockings, excepting that it has become the fashion to wear them all over the world. (Cheers and laughter.) Yet the condition of Nottinghamshire is worse than the condition of Lancashire. But if I were to point to one place, which is in the most deplorable—the most hopeless state—I would say it is Hinckley: there are 1,500 stocking frames, and only 21 fully employed. Benefit clubs and associations of every kind have been broken down, and the place has been given up to pauperism. The locust swarms are spreading even over the land, and the poor-rates in the neighbourhood, I am told, are £1 per acre. Let country gentlemen take this as a warning. (Hear.) The locust swarms will spread rapidly; and the land will have to maintain them. I tell you that I believe before we meet again, several other large towns will be given over to pauperism, and the people must be fed by the surrounding districts. Let us look, then, at the pottery districts. The honourable member for Macclesfield will rejoice *to* hear that they there work with the same machine which was in use in the reign of the Pharaohs. (Laughter.) It is as old as the time of Moses; and let that console him. I apprehend that at no period of its history was the pottery trade so severely depressed as at present; its prospects are not only cheerless, but hopeless. Go into your mines—your collieries; you have heard how they work them; there has been no great improvement of machinery in them; and what is the state of the mines of Staffordshire? There are 25,000 utterly destitute of employment. I am informed that in the time of the orders in council they were prosperous, compared with their present condition. Go to the glasscutters of Stourbridge and Warrington, or to the glovers of Yeovil, and you will find the same. If there be one part of the country better off than another, it is where the best machinery is in use; I mean Lancashire, where the working classes have, for several years, been living at the expense of their employers. (Hear, hear, from Sir R. Peel.) The right honourable baronet cheers me; why, then, did he make such indirect allusions to machinery? True it is that he invests his remarks in honied phrases, very satisfactory to those who are sitting behind him; but, on the one hand, he panders to the working classes, and, on the other, the tail-end of his party rejoices in the delusive consolation he affords them. I know at this time a place where a hundred wedding-rings were pawned in one week, to provide the owners with bread. (Hear, hear.) Men and women have subsisted only upon boiled nettles; and in the neighbourhood with which I was originally connected in business, Burnley, the starving people dug up the putrid carcase of a cow, rather than die of hunger. (Hear, hear, hear, and cries of "Oh, oh.") I know by that groan that gentlemen do not believe it. (Cheers.) I wrote to a trusty man, a schoolmaster, to ask if the report were true, and he sent me not only his own attestation, but that of many of his neighbours. The multitude dug it up, carried part of it away for food, and the farmer was obliged immediately to bury the remainder, in order to get rid of the effluvia. Another case occurred, in which the carcase of a dead calf was carried away for food. ("Oh, oh.") You may well cry "Oh, oh," and groan. If you believe these statements, why do you sit here and refuse to apply a remedy? (Loud cheers.) From these individual cases you may picture the condition of the whole mass of your suffering fellow-creatures. You may tell me that the people have the poor law. So they have; but thanks to their spirit, they would rather live on nettles and on garbage, than go into a union workhouse. Is this state of things to be left till the winter? We want inquiry, that gentleman on both sides may know the truth, and apply a remedy. I do not wish to mix up the corn laws with this question. I care nothing for the corn laws, if you can provide me with a better remedy. The noble lord, the member for North Lancashire, might reasonably be expected to show some sympathy for such suffering, but he doubted whether the repeal of the corn laws would afford the expected benefit. He told us that the Americans took as much again from us in the last three years as formerly.

Lord STANLEY: I beg pardon; I said no such thing.

Mr. COBDEN: Perhaps I am reversing what fell from the noble lord; (cheers;) but his commercial views, I own, are rather embarrassing to me. He said that the Americans sent over two millions more than they took from us. Their difficulty was not in sending commodities to us, but in taking returns from us. The noble lord has yet to understand that foreign trade is reciprocity—that it consists of nothing but barter; and before he indulges again in a speech, (to the eloquence and logical reasoning of which all must listen with pleasure,) I advise him to make himself practically acquainted with the subject on which he talks.

As a statesman, he could not be better employed than improving himself in practical information. I have heard him both at Lancaster and here, and on both occasions he showed himself pre-eminently ignorant on commercial matters. He told us the other night that we must excuse him on such topics, as he was not accustomed to address the house upon them; this is certainly true, and I think the right hon. baronet exercised a sound descretion in undertaking to speak for him on various occasions. (Cheers and laughter.) The noble member for North Lancashire, where distress is so severe that the people are subsisting on nettles and carrion, ought to know whether the people can or can not be supplied with food from America. From an acquaintance with the trade on both sides of the water, I may state, as my firm belief, that when a repeal of the corn laws does take place, the tidings of such a happy event will be instantly followed by a revival of trade. It would at least be the beginning of a new era in which employment would be found for the people. I know no other means for producing such a result, and it seems to me that all members for manufacturing places have an important duty to discharge before the house separates. I cannot give a stronger proof of the perils which I think surround us, than to say that I shall feel it my duty to stop the wheels of government if I can, in a way which can only be justified by an extraordinary crisis. Nothing can warrant a member in stopping the supplies, but such a conviction as weighs at this moment upon my mind. I wish to compel government to enter into the question with a full conviction of its importance. At present it is my solemn persuasion that they have not their eyes open to the truth. What was said yesterday by the Mayor of Stockport?—that he could not be responsible for the peace of the place; and what said the chairman of the guardians of the poor?—that he would not undertake to support the starving people beyond three months. The right hon. baronet knows that the state of Stockport is only a type of the fast approaching condition of Bolton and many other places. I do not mean to threaten outbreaks—that the starving masses will come and pull down your mansions; but I say that you are drifting on to confusion without rudder or compass. (Loud cheers.) It is my firm belief, that, within six months, we shall have populous districts in the north in a state of social dissolution. (Hear, hear.) You may talk of repressing the people by the military; but what military force would be equal to such an emergency. (Cheers.) Imagine the case of Stockport destroyed, and eaten up by its poor, what are you to do with 60,000 starving people? How are you to deal with a population formerly earning £500,000 a-year? The military will not avail. I do not believe that the people will break out, unless they are absolutely deprived of food; if you are not prepared with a remedy, they will be justified in taking food for themselves and their families. I do not threaten you with this state of things. (Cheers.) I do not know whether I understand that cheer; but I do not mean to tell you anything in a menacing manner. (Hear, hear.) I tell you what is the present state of Stockport, and I call upon you to realise in your minds the consequences of a refusal to inquire. Will you tell me, in reply, that the 60,000 people in Stockport are to lie down and die? If they do, their deaths will lie at the doors of the government; but, as Englishmen, they ought not to be permitted to starve. Is it not important for members for manufacturing districts, on both sides, to consider what they are about? We are going down to our several residences to face this miserable state of things; and selfishness, and a mere instinctive love of life, ought to make us cautious. Others may visit the continent, or take shelter in rural districts, but the peril will, ere long, reach them even there. Will you, then, do what we require, or will you compel us to do it ourselves? This is the question you must answer. The inhabitants of Stockport come here with clean hands; for what does Commissioner Twisselton, in his report, say of their condition? "We find in connection with the large earnings of the operatives engaged in the cotton trade, industrious habits of no common stamp, regulated and secured, in great measure, by the peculiar nature of their employment; and a degree of intelligence already much in advance of other classes of the working people, and still growing with the general growth of popular education. It appears, also, that when in the enjoyment of prosperity, they avail themselves to a great extent of the advantages of provident institutions, and that partly through this, and partly through other circumstances, equally creditable to their character as a working people, they avoid almost altogether dependence upon poor-rates. On the occurrence of general distress, we find them neither a pauperised mass nor readily admitting pauperism amongst them; but struggling against adversity, beating far and wide for employment, and, in many cases, leaving their country for foreign climates rather than depend upon any other resources for subsistence than their own industry and skill. Those among them who have not been able or willing to leave a place where at present their labour is of little or no value, have been found enduring distress with patience, and abstaining, sometimes to the injury of health, from making any application for relief." Such was the population which came to the house and made this claim at his hands. And what do they ask? They do not ask for charity. (Cheers.) They do not ask me to come here to obtain a mitigation of the poor law. I gained the popular support in Stockport without pledging myself upon the poor law. (Hear, hear.) What the people want, is the means of exercising their industry. They abhorred pauperism as much as any honourable gentleman in this house. They simply said, "Leave us alone." And I say, sir, that whatever misfortune befals such a people lies at the door of the government and of this house, and the people are not responsible for it. (Cheers.) I am therefore entitled to ask and to insist upon an answer from the government to the question, "What do they intend to do for the people?" I am entitled to ask whether they are to be satisfied with no better report than the one given by the right honourable baronet, that he expects a good harvest. It is true, sir, that some of our best workmen are going abroad. If the best go, they leave the worst behind. The manufacturers are going also, increasing the burden for those who remain. Have hon. gentlemen considered what must be the effect of this emigration upon the country? I can see a remedy for all other evils, but I can see no remedy for this. We are sowing the seeds broadcast for a plentiful harvest of workmen in the western world. Thousands of workmen are delving in the mines of the western continent, where coal can be raised and sold at 1s. a ton. We are sending there the labourers from our cotton manufactories, from our woollen, and from our silk. They are not going by dozens or by scores to teach the people of other countries the work they have learnt—they are going in hundreds and thousands to those states to open works against our own machines, and to bring this country to a worse state than it now is. There is nothing to atone for the system which leads to this, and if I were to seek for a parallel, it would be only in the revocation of the edict of Nantes by Louis XIV., or the decree of the Duke of Alva in Belgium, where the best men were banished from their country. (Hear, hear.) I see nothing why we should not take good measures from the right hon. baronet, or why we should prefer those of the noble lord the member for London. The noble lord is called the leader on this side of the house, and I confess that when I first came into the house I was inclined to look upon him as a leader; but from what I have seen, I believe the right hon. baronet to be as liberal as the noble lord. If the noble lord is my leader, I can only say that I believe that in four out of five divisions I have voted against him. He must be an odd kind of leader who thus votes against those he leads. (Hear.) I say this to show that I am actuated by no party spirit. I will take measures of relief from the right honourable baronet, as well as from the noble lord; but upon some measures of relief I will insist. I do not believe that any one would ask this of the right honourable baronet from any wish to supplant him; (Hear, hear;) no rational man would wish to supplant him. (Hear, hear, hear.) Seeing the position in which he is placed, I do not know any one who would wish to jump into his seat, even if he had the power. I give him credit for the difficulties of his situation; but this question must be met, and met fully; it must not be quibbled away; it must not be looked upon as a Manchester question; the whole condition of the country must be looked at and faced; and it must be done before we separate this session. (The honourable member sat down amid loud cheers.)

J. GADSBY, PRINTER, MARKET-STREET, MANCHESTER.

Richard Cobden (1804–65)

Cobden's speech was delivered to the Manchester Anti-Corn Law Association and registration committee on 1 September 1842.[1] His emphasis on reasoning with the farmers as the way of winning them over to the free trade was not quite representative of neither the lecturers' technique nor the *Circular*'s recommendations for the most effective means of approaching the farmers. An editorial in the 22 September 1842 issue of the *Circular* suggested scare tactics as more likely to impress farmers.

Can it be imagined that whenever the feeling shall have taken possession of the minds of our agricultural labourers, that they are the victims of oppression and injustice, they will long continue willing or passive victims? ... It is our firm conviction, that whenever the ignorance, and with it the forbearance, of the rural population shall cease, this country will have to pass through the horrors of a revolution, and that nothing can avert this dreadful calamity but a more equitable distribution than is at present made in this country of the gifts of Providence. To this end, then, are no means so certain as the repeal of the corn and provision laws – a measure which might, to some extent, prevent heaping together of the overgrown fortunes of our great landowners, but which would bring comfort and contentment to the cottage of the husbandman provide employment for our increasing numbers, and avert from the possessors of property the dangers by which they are now so fearfully threatened.

May they be wise while it is yet time!

Free trade then was offered to the farmers as a survival strategy which will prevent the farm labourers from rising up in arms and seizing their property, a far cry from Cobden's appeal to calm reasoning which did not seem to include playing on fears of rural violence.

[1] *The Anti Bread Tax Circular*, 8 September 1842.

SPEECH

OF

R. COBDEN, ESQ., M.P.,

TO THE

ANTI-CORN-LAW LEAGUE,

IN REFERENCE TO

THE DISTURBANCES

IN THE

MANUFACTURING DISTRICTS.

One of the most crowded meetings of the members of the Anti-Corn Law Association and the registration committee of the League took place on Thursday evening, at the rooms in Newall's Buildings, that has been held for some time.—After the routine business of the evening, the secretary reported the registering of 421 new members in Manchester, and 600 in Liverpool, in addition to the 1800 names received a week since.—Mr. Murray, one of the lecturers of the League, gave a short and interesting account of his visit to the midland counties.—During the address of Mr. Murray, Richard Cobden, Esq., M.P. for Stockport, entered the room, and was received with loud cheers. At the conclusion of Mr. Murray's speech,—

Mr. George Wilson, the chairman, rose and briefly introduced Mr. Cobden to the meeting.

Mr. Cobden presented himself, and was received with great cheering. He said—Mr. Chairman and gentlemen, I feel very much obliged to you for the kindness of this reception. Certainly, since we had last the pleasure of meeting in this room, very important changes have taken place in reference to our question both here and elsewhere. I come recently from the House of Commons, and I dare say you have had the opportunity of observing that in that arena we have not been without making some progress. (Hear, hear.) I may say that, so far as discussion can result in the success of any question, the question of the corn law is settled in the House of Commons—(applause)—for discussion is at an end;—(applause)—we had a month all to ourselves. (Applause and laughter.) The corn law was brought on again and again; and nobody could be found, although the *Post* and other organs of the bread-taxers were rallying them severely for their pusillanimity, no one could be found on the side of the monopolists to answer the arguments that were adduced in favour of repeal. (Applause.) Now, I say, gentlemen, unless it is intended to rule this country by means of a physical force majority in that house, the question is settled. (Applause.) We shall see whether that will be the policy which will be pursued in the next session. (Hear, hear.) With regard to the proceedings here, lamentable and deplorable as they are, I consider them to be a natural corollary from the proceedings in the House of Commons. (Loud applause.) I told you this question of the corn laws was settled in the House of Commons so far as argument and discussion went. The country saw this; but when the country saw that truth and justice, though established in the House of Commons, had no effect upon the measures of that house, what was the conviction which was naturally begot in the minds of the people,—eminently addicted—eminently attached to the principles of truth and justice? (Applause.) I say it has struck the public with despair at the conduct of the last session of parliament. (Applause.) I don't speak merely of the working classes; I speak of

the middle classes also; and I say it behoves the aristocracy of this country to mark well the effect of our last session of parliament upon the minds of the middle classes of this country—(hear, hear)—and I will adduce as a proof the three elections which took place at Nottingham, Southampton, and Ipswich, at the close of the last session of parliament. What were the astounding circumstances connected with those elections? In Nottingham upwards of 1800 electors voted for a chartist! (Hear.) In Southampton upwards of 500 of the electors of that borough—a borough not situated in the centre of an agitating, manufacturing district—but a borough dependent mainly upon the aristocracy,—I say in that borough upwards of 500 of the electors of the middle class voted for a chartist! (Hear, hear.) And if you go to Ipswich, where the candidate was a stranger, avowedly without influence, avowedly without substance, possessing no recommendation but the advocacy of the material points of the charter—there a chartist polled upwards of 400 votes of the middle class. (Hear, hear.) Now I say these are circumstances which prove that the proceedings of the last session of parliament have gone far to strike with despair the minds of the middle as well as of the working classes of this country; and for the conduct of the working classes, whatever it may have been, I arraign the House of Commons and the government as being the guilty causes of that conduct, however deplorable it may have been. (Applause.) What was our conduct in the House of Commons? We met there in February; the people starving for want of bread; a million and a half of petitioners praying to be allowed freedom of access to the corn of other countries. What was the first measure proposed by the prime minister? A bill having for its avowed object (for he did not conceal it) to secure to the landowners from 54s. to 58s. a quarter for their corn. That was the avowed object of his corn law, without consulting for a moment the condition of the consumers of corn, without pausing for an instant to ask how the starving wretches of this country should pay for their corn, without condescending for a moment to regard any question but the question of price to the corn grower, the rent holder, he proposed a law which should take from the people a price of from 54s. to 58s. a quarter for their corn. (Applause.) And when it was proposed to that house by myself that the price of labour should be considered—that the rate of wages should be considered, as well as the price of corn,—when I showed them from their own records that they had passed votes in that house declaring that they had no power to regulate the rate of wages, and when I called upon them to consider that, before they passed a law to fix the price of bread, they actually negatived my motion. (Hear, hear.) I moved that before passing a law to fix the price of corn, the house ought to consider how far it was in their power to pass a law which should regulate the rate of wages; but they actually rejected my motion, and still determined that they would pass a law, the avowed object of which was to regulate the price of corn. That was the first act of the session—the prime minister's first new law. And what was all the rest but a lamentable disregard of the best interests of the country,—the whole being mixed up with such disgraceful disclosures of bribery and intimidation as were enough to sicken and disgust any civilised and Christian community. (Applause.) Why, gentlemen, I have blue books, of which some day I will take the measurement in feet and inches—(I have not done so yet, but they are as high as this, said the honourable member, holding his hands about two feet apart)—blue books disclosing bribery—I will not say in how many boroughs, for I forget the number—but almost every other day we were getting a blue book from a committee, disclosing scenes of corruption which would make any Christian man shudder; and yet when these disclosures were brought before the house they were met with jeers and laughter. (Hear, hear.) Now I mention these facts, not with reference to any political change, but to show you that the conduct of the House of Commons and the government has smitten with despair the people of the country, and has been the guilty cause of the long-suffering body of working men in this district having done that which I deeply deplore, and which I am sure you all join me in deeply deploring. Well, gentlemen, in the midst of these lamentable circumstances, the effect of the conduct of parliament, what do we hear from the guilty authors and abettors of this confusion? Why that the Anti-Corn-Law League has produced it; yes, that we, who have been incessantly advocating the repeal of the corn laws, in order to give the people bread and employment, are the guilty cause of the people rising in insurrection for want of food and wages. This is the charge that is brought against us. Now, gentlemen, so gratuitous a display of profligacy as has been manifested by the London press, and a portionof our press in this town, on this subject,—such a specimen of profligacy I believe never was equalled in the annals of the press. (Applause, and "It never was.") Why, I should not, for the sake of meeting our opponents condescend to allude to it at all; but when you do see charges like this made against a body like the Anti-Corn-Law League, reiterated day after day simultaneously by a dozen newspapers; why our friends, even our dearest friends, might naturally say—"Surely after so many reiterated accusations there must be something in it." And it is because I believe that some of our friends elsewhere, in spite of their experience of our conduct here, may by these reiterated accusations be led to doubt whether we are not to blame in this matter—it is therefore, and therefore only, that I condescend to notice these attacks. (Applause.) And it is to satisfy them—it is to convince those ministers of religion, those ladies, and that numerous body of the moral and religious portion of the middle classes of this country who have lent us their assistance,—it is to convince them that we are not unworthy of their aid, that I alone would condescend to notice these charges. (Applause.) Now, gentlemen, I would venture to say, and if nothing else that fell from me should go forth to the public, I hope that this at least will do so—I will venture to say in the name of the Council of the Anti-Corn-Law League, that not only did not the members of that body know or dream of anything of the kind such as has now taken place,—I mean the turn-out for wages—not only did they not know, concoct, wish for, or contemplate such things, but I believe the very last thing which the body of our subscribers would have wished for or desired, is the suspension of their business, and the confusion which has taken place in this district. (Loud applause.) And I pledge my honour as a man, and my reputation as a public man and a private citizen, that there is not the shadow of the shade of a ground for the accusation which has been made against us. (Loud cheers.) I know the charge has been made by men in this town; I believe it has been credited by men in this town; I challenge every man who has entertained such belief to the proof; and I will pledge myself to give the worst enemy we have in this town £1,000 if he will substantiate the charge against us. (Loud cheers.) Gentlemen, I say so much for the satisfaction of any of our friends who might by possibility be misled by such a continued reiteration of this charge. But now for the authors of these charges; and I only wish to say that I believe there is not one of them that for a moment believes what he states—(hear, hear);—there is not one of these newspaper editors in London—there is not one of these newspaper editors in Manchester who make these charges, who believes them for a moment to be true. (Loud applause.) Not one of them. They know better. Why then do they write it? I'll tell you why. It is with the desperate hope that they will inflict a moral taint upon the Anti-Corn Law League. They cannot oppose our principles; for their own political chief has given up the whole question, he has avowed himself to be with us in principle; they cannot therefore denounce our principles; and from the moment that the prime minister declared himself a free trader—from the moment that he said it was not only best to buy in the cheapest markets where others took goods from us, but that it was best to do so whether reciprocity existed or not—(laughter and cheers)—from the moment he went that "whole hog" in free trade, their mouths were closed; but still they had their dirty work to do; they must say something, and what so natural and so politic as that these miserable tools of a beaten, a vanquished party should commence immediately to attack the Anti-Corn Law League? Their only hope, their only chance now, is in impairing our moral influence with the country. That is the game. (Applause.) Why the prime minister himself gave them the cue at the end of the session, for, with unparalleled meanness, when he knew that nobody could follow (Mr. Villiers wanted but five minutes, but he could not get it) Sir Robert Peel talked against time; he looked at the clock; he knew the time when the Usher of the Black Rod would come to summon us to the House of Lords; he sat still until he thought he could talk the whole of the remaining time; and then he occupied it in throwing a stigma on the men upon whose principles he had been acting. (Applause.) He gave the cue to the press, and the press took it up certainly in a most willing manner. (Applause.) But, gentlemen, there is something in the one in which we are assailed, coupled with our being mixed up with this lamentable transaction (I mean with the lamentable proceedings of the working classes in this district,) which indicates that our enemies may possibly be disposed to try to prevent the future operations of the Anti-Corn Law League. (Loud applause.) They would be very glad if they could so far excite public opinion against us that their myrmidons in the agricultural districts should feel warranted in preventing our lecturers from preaching the doctrines of truth to their serfs. That is what, in my opinion, these furious tirades against the Anti-Corn Law League are leading to. Now I predict that they won't dare to do anything of the kind. (Loud applause.) They would if they could; but you may depend upon it they won't meddle with the Anti Corn Law League in that way. (Loud applause.) If they could succeed in prejudicing us with the great body of the middle classes in this country, they would do it immediately; but we are too strong for them, and they know it. (Applause.) The Anti-Corn Law League is much stronger now than ever it was, and it will be infinitely stronger next February, at the meeting of parliament, than ever it has been before. (Loud cheers.) And there is nothing which can prevent our moral influence from becoming irresistible in this country, except any indiscretion on our own part, which should give our enemies the opportunity of impairing our influence with the moral and religious part of the community. (Loud applause.)

And, gentlemen, we have been lately charged with being in collusion with the chartist party. Now the parties who are charging this are labouring under the disadvantage of having themselves been working for the last three years to excite the chartist party against us—(hear),—and by means not over-creditable, as we shall by and by perhaps have the opportunity of demonstrating to the world. I will not say a word upon that at present; but, by means which may meet the light, they have succeeded in deluding a considerable portion of the working classes upon the subject of the corn laws. And I have no objection in admitting here, as I have admitted frankly before, that these artifices and manœuvres have, to a considerable extent, compelled us to make our agitation a middle-class agitation. I don't deny that the working classes generally have attended our lectures and signed our petitions; but I will admit, that so far as the fervour and efficiency of our agitation has gone, it has eminently been a middle-class agitation. (Applause.) We have carried it on by those means by which the middle class usually carries on its movements. We have had our meetings of dissenting ministers; we have obtained the co-operation of the ladies; we have resorted to tea parties, and taken those pacific means for carrying out our views which mark us rather as a middle class set of agitators. Now the parties who, by their manœuvres, their unprincipled tricks, their hiring of traitors, have, I will say, compelled us in some degree to make our agitation a middle class agitation, have unfortunately drawn their own teeth in this matter, and cannot now charge us with being chartists. (Applause, and laughter.)

We are no political body; we have refused to be bought by the tories; we have kept aloof from the whigs; and we will not join partnership with either radicals or chartists; but we hold out our hand ready to give it to all parties who are willing to advocate the total and immediate repeal of the corn and provision laws. (Loud cheers.) Being, therefore, wholly unconnected with political parties, whatever indiscretion may be committed by political parties, no blame can fairly be attached to our body. (Applause.)

Now it is necessary, at the present moment, gentlemen, when it is attempted to make us responsible for the conduct of other parties — it is especially necessary that we should take up our own independent position, and not let our enemies thrust us from it. With regard to the present lamentable movement in this part of the country, I have said that we are not the authors or abettors of this movement; but don't let us for a moment be put upon the defensive, don't let us waste another moment in defending ourselves, but let us take care to reiterate it to the world, that it is the measures of the legislature that are justly responsible for the present state of things. (Loud applause.) It is not this or that political party—it is not this or that agitation which accounts for the present tumultuous state of the north of England; it is long existing causes, which are to be found in our own statute book. (Loud cheers.) There we must go for the causes of all the misgovernment and wretchedness found amongst the working classes; and we must pin them to this, gentlemen; we must reiterate this, and not let them get us on the wrong scent, and persuade the world that it is this or that temporary cause which has led to this state of things; we must go back to the great cause—the mischievous legislation under which we are suffering. (Loud cheers.) There is no doubt the object of our opponents is to divert attention from that cause; that one of their great objects is, if possible, to prevent us going on discussing the corn law, its objects and effects; and to put us on our defence for our supposed connection with these proceedings. Now, I say that I will never open my mouth in defence of the League on this ground after what I have said to-day. Let the League go on in their own course, agitating—agitating—agitating incessantly for the repeal of the corn laws. (Loud applause.)

Gentlemen, you are strong in the country; you are stronger than you think in London. The middle classes in London are almost to a man for the repeal of the corn laws. (Applause.) You are stronger than you think in the south of England; you have strength in the rural boroughs that you are not aware of; and I will tell you now what I did not venture to say on a former occasion—that I don't think Manchester will carry the repeal of the corn laws, but that we shall carry it only by making it a national question. (Loud cheers.) Therefore don't let the enemy make it be believed that this is a mere manufacturers' or cotton spinners' question: that is one of the enemy's manœuvres to make it appear that you are treating the whole country as if it consisted only of 250,000 manufacturers; there is not a man, woman or child who is not as directly interested in the repeal of the corn laws as any cotton spinner in Lancashire. (Loud applause.) And it is by their consciousness of that, and by the aid they will give us when they come to know that—which they are fast coming to know,—that you will carry the repeal of the corn law, and not by your own unaided and isolated efforts.

But, gentlemen, the present occasion is a very seasonable one for drawing closer the bonds of union between the employers and the employed in this district. The present disastrous commotion arises clearly out of a dispute about wages, there is no doubt about that; every body, not blinded by prejudice must see that. It began in Staffordshire, with Mr. Sparrow, whom I know personally to be a tory iron master. The disturbance broke out there; it has extended through the country; and it is a question which must be settled by masters and men.

Now our business is, first to show the working men that the question of wages is a question depending altogether on principles apart from party politics,—that the question of wages is one which depends on the same principle in England as it does in America, Switzerland, Russia, and everywhere else; and that if we had the charter to-morrow, the principles which govern the relations between masters and men would be precisely the same as they are now. (Applause.) I believe that many of our friends of the working classes have a notion that if they could get some great and sweeping political change, it would have the effect of altering their position in society, that in fact every man would become a master,—and that there would be no masters owning great cotton mills then, and employing a number of men to work in them. (Hear, hear.) Why what is the case in Switzerland? what is the case in America? I have seen as great cotton mills there as we have in England; and though those countries are republics, and every man has a vote, yet wages depend there precisely on the same principle as they do here, as they have done from all time, and as they must do to all time. (Loud applause.) Therefore, gentlemen, the first thing to do will be to separate in the minds of the workmen, the question about wages from the question of party politics; and I believe they are just now in a right mind to take up the question upon right grounds; I believe that the working classes here generally are of opinion that the intrusion of the Chartist question has not been of any service to them in the question about wages. (Applause.) I believe they are quite disposed to discuss and settle this question apart from party politics. Then what will enable the master to give better wages? By getting a better price for his goods. And how is he to get a better price for his goods? By extending the markets. (Loud applause.) How can he sell more goods and thus give more employment to labour, except he can get an enlarged market, and thus meet the wants of the increasing population of the country? There is no other way. (Loud applause.) Our business is not to alter constitutions; we don't seek for chartism, whiggism, radicalism or republicanism—we simply ask for an enlarged market to enable the capitalist to extend the sale of his goods and thereby to increase the demand for labour and augment the rate of wages. (Applause.) This is a time, gentlemen, when I hope masters and men will meet and discuss this subject apart from party politics. (Applause). The time is peculiarly favourable for this, and I think, notwithstanding the lamentable circumstances, the state of the public mind in this country, both with masters and men, will settle down into a more rational disposition to view this question apart from passion and prejudice, than ever it did before,—for I do think, gentlemen, that the present disturbances will leave less of the traces of prejudice or of resentment in the minds of the middle classes in this part of the country than any former tumults ever did before. (Applause.)

I remember in 1839, when they attempted to stop the mills, and when I believe upwards of 600 persons found themselves in prison—I remember quite well that the feeling on the part of the middle class was one of unanimous indignation at that movement; and we all remember that when those unfortunate men were brought to trial, they were generally convicted by middle class juries with very great celerity. (Hear, hear.) Gentlemen, I believe that the last three years' endurance and suffering on the part of the working class has very much altered the feeling with which the middle class generally in this part of the country view this movement on the part of the working class. Their patience and endurance in the course of the last three years has been admired by all; it has been extolled by the prime minister himself; for he said, in his closing speech, "I give them credit for the utmost patience and quietness"—(and I ventured to interject, across the floor of the House, "and you have given them nothing but credit.") (Cheers, and laughter.) But I venture to say there will be fewer differences between the middle classes and the working classes than on the occasion of any former tumults which have unfortunately visited this part of the country. Well, now is the time, then, I say, for masters and men to draw closer the bonds of union between them, and to see and understand that they have but one common interest; now is the time. (Applause.) And I think that our business and our efforts should be directed to show to the working classes, and to show to some of their masters—(hear, hear)—what are the principles which regulate the rate of wages in this country. It is lamentable to see how little these principles are understood by persons whose daily business they affect, and who ought to understand them before they understood anything else. (Applause.) They go and study astronomy, and botany, and heaven knows what; and are all the while utterly ignorant of that principle which governs as infallibly their daily concerns as do the laws of nature the motions of the heavenly bodies. (Loud applause.) Of this they are utterly ignorant. Now, if we would produce a sound and healthy tone here, we must give these persons to understand what it is that regulates the rate of wages; it is necessary that we should exert ourselves, each in his own locality, to inform the public mind on this subject, and to detach the question of employment, and keep it altogether separate from these party questions with which it is attempted constantly to be involved. (Loud applause.) Some allusion has been made here to certain parties in this district who still uphold the system of corn laws. We have parties here —I won't mention their party names—but there is a particular political party here who think that they ought to uphold these corn laws. (Hear, hear.) Now, I would give that party a little bit of advice. I have seen something of the state of feeling on the part of the high aristocratic party in the House of Commons; and I tell the conservative party of Manchester, that if they don't look sharp, they will actually be left behind by their own party of the landed aristocracy. (Applause, and laughter.) I positively believe that there are large numbers in the House of Commons, who believe that they should make a sacrifice of some thousands a year by repealing the corn laws,—there are scores of them sitting on the conservative side of the House of Commons—who would be willing to go further than our own conservative manufacturers in the repeal of the corn laws. (Great applause.) And I declare that the thing of all others which I found most difficult to explain to men in the House of Commons, in private conversation, was how men who are engaged here in manufacturing and spinning could possibly be in favour of the corn laws. (Applause, and laughter.) They positively cannot understand it; and why? They themselves give up the whole question as regards the manufacturers; they begin by admitting that the repeal of the corn laws would give a vast impulse to your prosperity; even

Mr. Melville, who preaches in favour of the corn laws—(hear, hear)—begun his sermon by admitting that the change would immensely increase your manufacturing prosperity, but he says it would add so much to the population of the manufacturing districts that the interests of morality and religion would be endangered thereby. (Great laughter.) But they don't deny for a moment that it would vastly increase your prosperity, and give a great impulse to the industry and population of this district; and when they find that there are men here, and numbers of them too, largely interested in manufactures and spinning, having great numbers of the working classes dependent on them, who are nevertheless advocating this system, which checks, controls, and cripples their own pursuits, I may well excuse the honest consistency of the rational landowner, who looks through the mist of early prejudices, and ignorance, and interest, which is the worst mist of all to see through—(applause),—if he cannot understand how the manufacturers here can be in favour of the corn laws. (Loud applause.) There is but one argument which I would refer to in connexion with our agitation. I believe, gentlemen, that at the present moment, the government of this country, and the aristocracy of this country, are very anxious indeed to see the people employed, for they don't like that state of things when men of property cannot go to bed with perfect safety in this country—(hear, hear),—and they are therefore very anxious to see the people employed. Now, the argument which we have to address ourselves to at this moment, is to show the government, and to show the country, that *instant* relief would be afforded to the manufacturers and to the working people from a repeal of the corn laws. (Applause.) Now, I believe it would be perfectly easy to demonstrate that, at the present moment. If I were called upon to do so, I would only take into consideration the case of America. In the United States, you have at this moment the market open to you; you have only 20 per cent. duty laid on your goods; you may take your manufactures of every kind there at a duty of 20 per cent. *ad valorem*. When we argue for a free trade with Austria, they tell us we can have no reciprocity, we can get no relief there; and if we point to Russia, France, or Spain, they tell us the same story. But here is the case of America, in which our largest customer has thrown open her ports to you, and is wishing to receive your goods to any extent. (Applause.) And, now, as to her means of paying for them, we have just as ample proof. Not a letter comes from America which does not state that they are overburdened with bread stuffs, that they have had a most bountiful harvest, and that they have a surplus of three million quarters of wheat, all of which might be sent to this country before next June. I received this intelligence in a personal interview which I had in London with one of the largest American merchants; and I saw one in this town to-day, who said that he was really thinking of letting his warehouse, or giving the landlord notice that he should leave it, but he added that he had a letter from his partner in America, by the last steamer, which said, "If you could only get the corn laws repealed in England, we could send you plenty of orders." (Applause.) There is this American merchant in England, his warehouses empty, and his presses standing idle: those presses could be kept going packing your goods for America, and the docks at Liverpool might be kept in activity in receiving corn from America, which might reach the starving mill-hands of our No. 1 district here, and infuse gladness and contentment into their bosoms. (Loud applause.)

Gentlemen, our strong case at this moment is America; we must urge this on all occasions; if you meet with a sceptical, incredulous neighbour, who doubts that we could get *instant* benefit from the repeal of the corn laws, take up the case of America. (Applause.) It is no use, gentlemen, America opening her ports to us at a low duty; we cannot get any more trade from them unless we will take what they have to give. (Applause.) For the last ten years they have been reducing their duties every year; ten years ago they passed a law reducing their duty every year, until it reached, in 1842, 20 per cent. *ad valorem*. Yet what is the effect? The *bonâ fide* legitimate trade with America is less now than it was ten years ago—(hear, hear);—for you have lent them thirty or forty millions sterling, the interest of which to the extent of about £1,500,000 has now to be deducted from the cotton and the rice which they send you, and you only send back the difference in goods. (Applause.) What use, then, is there in sending out ambassadors to ask them to reduce their tariff on your goods? If they were to reduce it to one per cent. you could have no trade with them, unless you would take back the goods they have to give you. (Applause.) Gentlemen, the case of America answers all the difficulties, and shows, clearly and indisputably, that you have instant relief at hand the moment you pass a repeal of the corn laws, even so far as America is concerned. (Applause.) Now, gentlemen, I have trespassed a long time on your attention. (Applause, and "Go on, go on.") I was going to make one remark with regard to the policy that has been pursued by Sir Robert Peel in the house this last session. I think it has been apparent, throughout the whole of the discussions, that Sir Robert Peel, who is a tyro as a free-trader, has lost sight of the most important object which we seek in free trade. He has constantly told us, in reference to the tariff, and in reference to the corn laws, and in every measure which he has brought forward, he has constantly told us of the cheapness of commodities which he had in view. He has told us how his measures will reduce the price of beef, and timber, and other articles; but he has lost sight of that more important object which we have in view,—the giving of employment to the people. (Applause.) He thought, very likely, that he should alarm the monopolists if he told them that he was going to open up a new continent, where we should find a supply of food for our labourers in an indefinite extent. Therefore he points to the cheapness of foreign stock on one side of the house; and then, to allay the fears of the other, he says it is not probable that we can get much beef from Holstein. (Applause and laughter.) Still, gentlemen, Sir Robert has constantly harped upon cheapness. Now I think we have heard a great deal too much about cheapness. Low-priced articles may come from two causes,—from the inability of the people to consume, or from an abundant supply of the article of consumption. Now, I predict that we shall have low prices very soon—(hear, hear);—an abundant harvest may give us wheat as low as 40s. a quarter; but will an abundant harvest, and the consequent low prices, give us employment for the people? (Hear, hear.) Now it is an object which every government and every body in the country has the greatest interest in, to give employment to the people; and that can only be accomplished by enabling the manufacturers to exchange their productions for those of other countries. (Applause.) And, mind you, they are now dealing only with the germ of the difficulty, when they are trying to put down, by force of arms, the people who have been lately tumultuously uprising in consequence of their severe distress. When they have put down the people, they will still have the far greater task to perform of finding them employment and good wages. (Applause.) I say it is their duty; and why? I would not say of a government like that of Switzerland, which has no Custom-houses, that it was the duty of the government to find employment for the people; but I say it is the duty of our government, who have undertaken to meddle by law with every branch of commerce and every pursuit of industry in the country. (Applause.) They cannot complain, therefore, that they are bound to find employment for the people. There is not a single article in which we deal that is not wrapped up, like a mummy almost, with acts of parliament—(applause and laughter);—we cannot move a hand or foot in commercial transactions without being hampered with customs' laws; nor can we take any step towards exchanging the articles we produce for those of other countries without coming in contact with protective laws and prohibitory duties. (Applause.) I say, therefore, it is the duty of the government to find employment for the people; and when they have put down these tumults, I say it is as nothing compared with the duty which they still owe, with the magnitude of the task which they still have to undertake, of finding employment and subsistence for the people. (Loud cheers.) That must be done. For, let me tell you, this tumult is not a mere question about the rate of wages with the people. I admit that this insurrection, as it is called, did begin with a dispute between masters and men about wages; but what was it which swelled the numbers of the turn-outs,—what caused these multitudes to roam over the country, stopping manufacturing pursuits, but because they immediately met with a sympathising body of thousands and tens of thousands of people who had no employment at all?

Let the masters who were employing these people three weeks ago all agree to give the wages of 1840; and still you will not get over the difficulty at all. What is to become of that mass of pauperism which is still existing in Stockport, Paisley, Carlisle, Manchester, and elsewhere? How are these people to be employed? They are fast eating up the resources of the middle classes, and bringing them down to pauperism themselves: is that to go on? Can it go on in Stockport for another year, without transferring the whole of the property to the paupers? (Hear, hear.) I know they are giving great assistance from government to these boroughs. I know that, in the case of Paisley, the Provost went up to London, and said that he must have £600 a-week, or he would not be answerable for the peace of that borough. (Hear, hear.) But this cannot go on. If the government is to feed the people, who is to feed the government? (Loud applause.) Turn this matter in any way you please, and the difficulty still is, how to find employment and subsistence for the people. (Hear, hear.) The difficulty does not lie merely on the manufacturing districts; it is touching them to the quick in the agricultural parts of the country. I heard that it was stated by one of the members for a borough in Essex, that he never knew that county in so bad a state for employing its poor as it is now in the midst of harvest; and he says that the prospect for the winter is more dismal than anything he ever saw before. And, gentlemen, they have stopped up the outlets for their rural population; the tide that used to set into the manufacturing towns is not merely checked, but is rolling back upon them—a desolating tide of pauperism. (Hear, hear.) So that the difficulty is not merely how the manufacturing population shall be employed, but how they are to be provided for in the agricultural districts. The question must be met. (Applause.) It is not enough for government to say that they have put down the people here by the military; it is not enough for them to say that they have got thousands of poor wretches in prison—a larger number, I believe, than was ever known to be in the prisons of this country for any public delinquency since the days of Henry the Eighth—(loud applause);—I say it is not enough for them to say that they have quelled the disturbances by imprisoning or shooting the people; the duty lies with government still—and we must urge it upon them—TO FIND EMPLOYMENT AND SUBSISTENCE FOR THE PEOPLE. (Loud applause.) We have told them—the manufacturers and traders of this part of the country have told the government and the aristocracy—"If you'll allow us, we will find employment and subsistence for the people." (Hear, hear.) And what has been the answer? "You have incited them to insurrection!" "Very well, then," we say, "having put it down in your own way, tell us how you are to find them employment; and you shall never have peace or rest from us until you do find employment, and give content to the people of this country." (Loud cheers.) Gentlemen, with regard to our future tactics, as we are rather a practical body, I should most certainly recommend that we pay a visit, as soon as the harvest is over, to the agricultural districts. (Hear, hear.) We shall be very unwelcome visitors, but no matter about that; we must go into the rural districts, and we must teach the people there that they have a common interest with ourselves in getting rid of these monopolies. (Applause.) We must tell them, gentlemen, that they have to pay an income-tax in order to ensure the continuance of these monopolies; and you'll find that that income-tax is a blister which has been drawing for some weeks, and by the time you get there, I have no doubt you will find the patient so very *im*patient under the infliction, that he will be quite disposed to listen to some other doctor than the one that installed himself at Tamworth. (Applause and laughter.) Let us tell the agriculturists that if the State-doctor will only come and take a larger dose from our medicine-chest than he took last session—(laughter),—if he will only come to our pharmacopœia for a larger prescription than he took before (and he borrowed it, or rather stole it from us, and never made any acknowledgment)—(laughter)—if he will only give us a larger measure of free-trade, we of the manufacturing districts will enable the government to dispense with the income tax on the rural districts altogether. (Applause.) Now I think that will be a very good bribe to offer our agricultural brethren. (Applause.) The income tax is clearly put on to keep up these monopolies. It is proposed that it shall be remitted to three years. If the corn laws are repealed, it is possible it may; but if they keep on the monopolies on sugar and corn, I promise you it will be raised from sevenpence to a shilling in the pound. (Applause.) Gentlemen, we shall find enlightened friends in the agricultural districts in all directions; let us cultivate their acquaintance; and don't let us look upon this as a manufacturers' question. Low prices of corn are coming upon them; high rents, contemporaneously with low prices, will make them ready listeners to our lectures. (Applause.) Let us show them that, with a repea of the corn laws, though they might no longer obtain high prices for their produce, the landowners would not have the power of extorting from them their present enormous rents when corn had jumped down to 40s. a quarter. (Applause.) Let us explain this to the farmers: and let us show the labourers that they were better off with corn at 40s. a quarter, than they have been during the last three years, when it was 70s. Let us teach them these things, and let us do it in the spirit of kindness and conciliation. Let us, above all things, show that we are the peace-makers in the community, not the peace-breakers, as our false opponents would allege—(loud applause);—and I have no doubt, I feel morally convinced that if we do our duty for the next six months, Sir Robert Peel will not meet us in the next session of parliament, without bringing with him a bill which he believes will be one that will annihilate our agitation. (Applause.) He'll never meet the House of Commons again, with the country in anything like its present state, but with a new corn bill in his hands, gentlemen, I'll guarantee to you. (Loud applause.) And upon the exertions made by the advocates of free trade, during the interval between this and the time when parliament meets, will depend altogether the character of that corn bill. (Applause.) It will altogether depend upon the exertions of the league. Let us then unite ourselves with every class of the community as fast as we can. Let us endeavour, when we meet again in parliament, to present one unbroken rank of middle classes and working classes, to denounce that monopoly which is uprooting our commerce, which is ruining the working classes, and which is bringing upon the country a continuance of the miserable spectacles which we now behold. (Applause.) Let us do our duty, gentlemen, one six months longer; let us exert ourselves with tenfold energy; and call upon the people to unite, as they will unite with us; and I engage that when parliament meets again, the Prime Minister will not dare to face us without bringing a corn bill such as he believes will demolish the agitation about the corn laws. (Loud and prolonged cheers.)

The Rev. OWEN OWENS, from the Principality of Wales, briefly addressed the meeting, expressing his own conviction of the necessity of a repeal of the corn-laws, both for the interest of the farmers and the labourers.—His address was received with great approbation, and at its termination the meeting separated.

PRENTICE AND CATHRALL, TIMES OFFICE, MANCHESTER.

Q in a Corner

Possibly by John Harris (1784–1858), a Quaker from Kingston-on-Thames. Harris published in 1853 *Tit for tat: for juvenile minds, with large additions of prose and verse for more mature intellects, in advocacy of peace principles*. An earlier edition, published in 1830, was signed 'Q in a corner'.

A LITTLE COMMON SENSE,

AND

A FEW FACTS,

IN ANSWER TO A LETTER ADDRESSED TO THE ELECTORS OF LANCASTER BY "OLD ENGLAND,"

ON

FAIR PRICES AND FAIR WAGES;

OR,

OLD ENGLAND'S INTERESTS CONSIDERED.

BY Q IN A CORNER.

A letter signed "*Old England*," addressed to the electors of Lancaster, on "Fair Prices and Fair Wages, or Old England's Interests Considered," has been sent to each elector. This silly production, under ordinary circumstances, would be unworthy of notice; but as it is understood that Messrs. Green and Marton, the present representatives of the Borough, have each subscribed £5 towards the expenses of the publication, it follows that the sentiments it contains coincide with their views, and embody their opinions. As such it may fairly be taken as the address of the said members to their constituents on the important question of the corn laws, and therefore requires some comment.

"*Old England*" sets out with complaining of the "plentiful abuse of landlords and agriculturists by the well-fed, sleek-looking lecturers, paid by the League," whilst with admirable consistency, he attributes to "that band of conspirators," the members of the League, the most base, selfish, and revolutionary objects.

"*Old England*," himself a political partisan, wishes to impress you with the belief that the corn-law question is a political party question, and he quotes Alison's History of Europe to show "the danger of political innovations." As well might he call astronomy a political question. About three hundred years ago, the great astronomer, Galileo, for maintaining the then new doctrine that the earth moved round the sun, which all the world now acknowledge to be true, was accused, as the League is now accused by "*Old England*," as a dangerous innovator, and imprisoned as an enemy to religion and the state. Every new discovery is an innovation. Adam Smith discovered, seventy years ago, the folly and impolicy of corn laws and restrictions on trade, and these great truths are now acknowledged by statesmen of all parties—aye, even by statesmen who have not the courage to carry them into practice. Sir James Graham said in parliament last year that "*the principles of free trade are the principles of common sense,*" and Sir Robert Peel declared that "it is for the interest of the country to buy in the cheapest and sell in the dearest markets of the world." These are the doctrines of the League, and because they endeavour to propagate them by "liberally supplying you with tracts and pamphlets," "*Old England*" wishes to persuade you that the members of the League are revolutionists, and disaffected to the institutions of the country.

Talk of dangerous innovation indeed! Let us see who have been the greatest innovators, the landowners or the League? In 1773 the law allowed the free importation of foreign wheat at 6d. per quarter duty, whenever the home price was at or above 48s. per quarter! Now the innovating landowners passed a law in 1815 prohibiting foreign wheat altogether, until the home price reached 80s. per quarter! The people at that time denounced this innovation as a monstrous injustice, and assembled round the houses of parliament, beseeching members not to pass so cruel a law. Soldiers were ordered to disperse the multitude, and to guard the parliament while they passed this inhuman statute to beggar and starve the people. This was the first law parliament ever passed surrounded with soldiers. *Was not this a dangerous innovation?* In 1828 the landlords passed the sliding scale law, by which foreign wheat, when the home price was 48s. per quarter, was charged with a duty, not of 6d. per quarter, as in 1773, but with a duty of 38s. 8d. per quarter! Was not this innovation? Again, in 1842, Sir R. Peel's corn law, instead of 6d. per quarter, as in 1773, charges foreign wheat with 20s. per quarter duty! Thus it seems *the landowners have been the innovators*, and because the League complains of these innovations, and ventures to show the people how they have been plundered, by referring them to the corn laws of past days, "*Old England*" insinuates that the League are "enemies of peace and order, and upholders of confusion, disorder, and revolutionary movements."

But to return to "*Old England's*" letter. After calling in question the motives of the manufacturers, and abusing the lecturers of the League, he very consistently adds, "*Let us calmly discuss this question.* I maintain that the members of the Anti-Corn-Law League are seeking to sacrifice this great and once happy country for their own selfish purposes. But assertion without argument is nothing, therefore I proceed to the proof." Now what is the first fact he proposes to prove?

He says, "Free trade is now the cry; that means, free trade in everything *except what they themselves sell.*" How does this assertion comport with the truth? Why, in 1839, when the anti-corn-law delegates, from all the principal manufacturing towns in England and Scotland first assembled in London, they unanimously passed a resolution declaring "that whilst they demanded, as an act of justice, the repeal of the corn and provision laws, *they sought no protection for themselves,* but on the contrary desired to see protection to manufactures and agriculture abolished together."

"*Old England*" further says that individuals, members of the League, ask for protection for themselves, and he very properly observes, "If manufacturers are to be at liberty to purchase agricultural produce at the lowest market, why should not the landowners be at liberty to buy their clothes at the lowest market also? *But no, cries Mr. George Wilson, chairman of that band of agitators calling themselves the National Anti-Corn-Law League, don't take off the duty on starch, for I deal in starch.* O! exclaims the celebrated John Brooks, another Leaguer, *pray don't reduce the duty on foreign coffee, for I have been speculating in coffee.*" Now if there be one word of truth in the allegation that Leaguers wish to retain protection on their own respective trades, whilst they ask that it shall be taken away from others, let the electors of Lancaster treat such with the contempt which they deserve. But what are the facts? When the government, in 1842, altered the tariff, they proposed, in mistake, a lower duty on foreign starch than existed on foreign wheat. The starch makers very properly remonstrated, saying, we have no objection that the duty on foreign starch shall be altogether abolished, provided you also abolish the duty on foreign wheat and flour, from which starch is made, but so long as you *continue* the duty on foreign wheat, it is but fair that you should lay the *same duty* on foreign starch. The proposition was so just that government at once rectified the mistake. And this is what "*Old England*" calls seeking "free trade in everything except what they themselves sell." The story of Mr. Brooks and the coffee duty is an equal perversion of the truth. The facts are as follow. The duty on British coffee, before the late alteration in the tariff, was 6d. per lb., and on foreign coffee, 9d. per lb. By the new tariff, British coffee was reduced to 4d. per lb., and foreign coffee to 8d. per lb. The reader will see that under the old tariff the duty on foreign coffee was 50 per cent. higher than the duty on British coffee, but under the new tariff the difference was increased to 100 per cent. Mr. Brooks, with other holders of foreign coffee, applied to the government (not as falsely stated to *raise*, but) to lower the duty charged by the new tariff, from 8d. to 6d., which reduction, if made, would have saved 2d. per lb. to the consumer, and still have left the greedy monopolists 50 per cent. preferential duty, the same which they enjoyed under the old tariff. But the government refused to listen to the proposition, and actually increased the monopoly duty on coffee from 50 per cent. to 100 per cent., which increase you now pay. So much for the misrepresentations of "*Old England*."

Your would-be instructor then proceeds to warn you. "Beware (says he) of the present cry for cheap bread. Beware, I say, for there lurks under it the *real* object of the manufacturers, *low wages*." This nonsense about cheap bread and low wages has been answered a hundred times. It is only necessary for every man to refer to his own experience to prove that wages do not rise and fall with the price of bread. During the years 1839, 1840, 1841, 1842, whilst the price of bread was so high, did any of you receive higher wages than you had before, or pay higher wages than you paid before bread rose? "*Old England*," tauntingly asks, "Has not bread been cheap enough for the last two years?" True, but is the working man worse off with cheap bread? Have his wages been reduced in consequence? Why, "*Old England*" most unwittingly answers these questions. He tells you that "trade is acknowledged on all hands to be in a flourishing state," notwithstanding this mischievous cheap bread; employment is more plentiful; that "there may be a few instances in which wages have lately advanced!" What! wages advancing with cheap bread! Why, only a few sentences before he told you to "beware of the cry for *cheap bread*," which only meant *low wages!* But he further tells us that "wages have been lately advanced, not from the generosity of the masters, but from the urgent clamours, and even turn-out of the workpeople, whose wages were so low that they were sunk in destitution and misery." Now, *when* were wages so low that workpeople were sunk in destitution? Why, from 1839 to 1842. And was this period of low wages also a period when bread was cheap? *No, just the contrary; during all these years bread was very dear.* But no sooner does bread become, as "*Old England*" says, "cheap enough," than, according to his own statement, wages rise, and workpeople turn out to get more wages still! Verily "*Old England*" must be a sorry simpleton, or he must take you to be great simpletons.

"*Old England*" next turns prophet. "Assuming," says he, "a total repeal of the corn laws, probably one third of the land in this kingdom, now under the plough, would be thrown out of tillage. The produce under reduced prices would not pay the expense of cultivation, and rates, and taxes, leaving rent out of the question." Now, this is not the first time we have heard prophecies like these. In the report of the committee of the House of Commons on the corn laws, in 1814, the farmers and land agents from various parts of the country, declared that unless wheat could be maintained at 80s. to 100s. per quarter, heavy land must be thrown out of cultivation. The land agents also stated that they were valuing the rents, calculating wheat to sell at those prices. It is curious enough that since the date of these predictions, now thirty years ago, the average price of wheat has never reached 80s. per quarter, except in the years 1817 and 1818. For several years it has been below 50s. per quarter, and during one year it was below 40s. per quarter. Did the land, as these prophets foretold, go out of cultivation, even at this low price of wheat? But has any body ever heard of a million labourers being thrown out of employment, even when wheat was under 40s. per quarter, as "*Old England*" tells you would be the case if the corn laws were repealed? ***Why, there are not a million agricultural labourers in all England, Wales, and Scotland.*** According to the population returns of 1831, (see Porter's Progress of the Nation, section 1, page 53,) the number of males, twenty years of age and upwards, employed in agriculture, are as follows:

England	744,407
Wales	55,468
Scotland	87,292
	887,167

Poor "*Old England!*" What a specimen of monopolist wisdom!

Ah! but there's Ireland to be taken into the account! Why, only a few days ago, the leading Conservative journal observed, "The great evil of Ireland is, that the people are *fighting* for the land." Would Paddy be ruined, think you, if he had half an acre instead of a rood? And if he could obtain it at £2 or £3 an acre, instead of £5 or £6 an acre, which he now pays, would it be worse for him? And does any body suppose that wheat would fall below 40s. per quarter, if the corn laws were repealed, seeing that the average price of wheat in Jersey, where there are no corn laws, for the ten years from 1832 to 1841, was 48s. 4d. per quarter? Not only have all the predictions about land going out of cultivation been falsified, but, from 1816 to 1835, there have been no less than 453 acts of parliament for inclosing waste lands, and under these acts there have actually been inclosed the enormous quantity of 10,348,612 acres of new land!

It may be well to remind monopolist prophets that the above

is not the only case in which their forebodings have proved erroneous. In 1819 landowners made a great outcry for protection to British wool, and accordingly a duty of 6d per lb. was imposed on foreign wool, the effect of which was to destroy a large portion of our manufactures, which required an admixture of foreign and British wool, and to bring great distress and ruin upon the woollen manufacturers.

It is a remarkable fact that the price of British wool, *instead of advancing*, from the high and prohibitory duty imposed on foreign wool, *continued to decline*, until it reached a lower price than had been known for a century. In 1825, Mr. Huskisson proposed to reduce the duty on foreign wool to ½d. and 1d. per lb. But notwithstanding the experience of the effects of protection, the landowners *again predicted* that the British wool growers could not compete with foreign wool-growers, and if foreign wool were admitted the farmers would be ruined, sheep would cease to be bred, and the most fearful consequences would ensue. In spite, however, of these dreadful forebodings of ruin, the reduction of the duty on foreign wool was carried out, and mark the results.

The imports of foreign wool in 1820, the year after the duty of 6d. per lb. was imposed, were 9,775,605 lbs.; after the duty was reduced in 1825, the imports gradually increased, and in 1839 they reached 57,364,772 lbs. The benefits of the reduction of the duty on foreign wool were not confined to the woollen manufacturer, the British wool grower equally shared the advantage. Notwithstanding the enormous increase in the imports of foreign wool, the prices of British wool recovered from their previous depression, *and maintained higher rates than during the protective system.*

It is not a little amusing to see this boaster of "loyalty to the Queen, and attachment to the Protestant Church established in these realms," at one moment reminding the electors of Lancaster "that no Radical had ever been returned as member for Lancaster at a contested election," and the next bringing to his aid "*an American republican!*" Now if a Free Trader had ventured to quote in favour of free trade the authority of one who forswears all kings, princes, and potentates, one who considers the union of church and state unholy, who holds the Chartist doctrine of short parliaments, universal suffrage, and vote by ballot, doubtless it would have been urged by so loyal a personage as "*Old England*" that free trade and republicanism were associated together, and that it was evident that the object of free traders was "to attack," as he says, "every institution in this country most dear to Englishmen, and to bring the crown of our beloved Queen into the most imminent danger."

"Listen" says "*Old England*," "what Mr. Clay, an *American republican*, but yet a celebrated statesman, thinks of free trade. In a letter, dated in April, 1843, he writes, 'Free trade is a beautiful vision, existing only in the imagination of philosophers and theorists, and practically repudiated by all nations.'" Now since "*Old England*" has set the example of quoting republican authority *against* free trade, we may also venture, without fear of incurring the charge of disloyalty, to quote the authority of *an American republican in favour* of free trade, and our authority shall be a statesman who ranks higher and is more distinguished by his countrymen than even Mr. Clay. We allude to Mr. Calhoun, who has been invited to offer himself as a candidate for the presidency at the next vacancy, and who, in a letter dated in January last, declining to stand, says, in reference to the question of free trade, "*I hold protection to be another name for a system of monopoly and plunder.*" Again, he says, "I who upheld free trade against monopoly and plunder in the worst of times, and braved the menaces of administration and opposition when backed but by a single state (South Carolina), will not, cannot abandon the glorious cause now when its banner waves in proud triumph over the metropolis of the commercial world. *No. I shall maintain immoveably the ground I have so long occupied until I have witnessed its great and final victory, if it shall please the Disposer of all events to spare my life so long. It will indeed be a victory; the harbinger of a new, a brighter, and higher civilization.*"

But, proceeds "*Old England*," with a degree of gravity befitting so much wisdom: "Seriously, free trade, carried out to its fullest extent is a thing impossible, not only because it would ruin three-fourths of our tradesmen, but because the government of the country could not be carried on, if such an amount of duties were repealed." Now *free trade* is only another term for *more trade*, and "three fourths of our tradesmen" are not likely to be ruined by an *increase* of trade. We have already seen that free trade in wool increased the consumption of foreign wool from 9,775,605lbs. to 57,364,772lbs, thereby giving employment to six times as many people as were previously employed in working foreign wool. The additional number of people thus employed would be furnished with the means of buying food and clothing of our shopkeepers and tradesmen, who otherwise would not have been able to purchase at all, and this would seem an odd way of ruining tradesmen to any but such reasoners as "*Old England*."

But it is not in wool alone that free trade has increased the demand for employment, and consequently an increase to the business of our tradesmen. In every instance, without exception, where monopoly has been relaxed or abolished, it has uniformly been attended with an increase of trade, and we dare "*Old England*," or any one else, to *prove* the contrary. Our trade with India and China in 1814, during the East India Company's monopoly, amounted to £1,374,690; under free trade it had increased, in 1839, to £5,600,576.

The silk monopoly shows similar results. In 1824 foreign silks were allowed to be imported at a duty of 30 per cent. The monopolist manufacturers predicted then, as the corn monopolists do now, that "by the end of two years, which it was proposed to allow before the prohibition should finally cease, the silk trade would be destroyed." But mark the results. The average consumption of raw and thrown silk in the ten years *preceding* 1824, under the *monopoly* system was 1,940,902lbs.; but the average consumption in the twelve years *following* 1824, under the partial *free trade* system was 5,020,034lbs.

The success of the abolition of the linen monopoly is not less remarkable. Previously to 1825 the linen manufacture was protected by duties amounting to from 40 to 180 per cent., and bounties were granted on all linens exported. These were all abolished in 1825, and the duties on foreign linen reduced to 25 per cent. No sooner was the trade unshackled than enterprise and skill were directed to it, the increase of the linen manufacture in Dundee has been even more rapid than the increase of the cotton manufacture at Manchester, and, in 1833, the exports of linen from that port were as great as those from all Ireland.

But, says "*Old England*," "the government of the country could not be carried on, if such an amount of duties was repealed by free trade." Now, Free Traders do not propose to diminish duties on articles which now afford revenue to the Queen's exchequer, and therefore, if free trade were to be enacted to-morrow there would be nothing to prevent the government being carried on just as at present. What Free Traders seek is, the abolition of all monopolies; *but monopolies bring no revenue to the Queen's exchequer;* they only put revenue into the pockets of the monopolists.

Take for example, sugar. Foreign sugar is selling, without duty, at 2d. per lb.; British West India sugar, of similar quality, sells at 4d. per lb. Why is this? Because foreign sugar pays a duty of 7d. per lb., and British West India, or monopoly sugar, only pays 2¼d. per lb. The object of this duty of 7d. per lb. on foreign sugar is *not to raise revenue for the Queen's exchequer*, because not one pound of foreign sugar is consumed in England, but it is to keep out foreign sugar, and thus to give an artificial price to British West India sugar; and this object it has accomplished, as we have seen that the sugar monopolists are enabled to get double the price for their sugar that foreign sugar can be bought at. If we had free trade the duty on foreign sugar would be the same as that on British West India sugar, viz., 2¼d. per lb. instead of 7d. The duty on coffee is levied on the same principle as sugar. Foreign coffee pays a duty of 8d. per lb., monopoly coffee a duty of only 4d. per lb.

Now, every increase in price, in consequence of protection, amounts to a tax. If we are made to pay 4d. per lb. for sugar, which in the absence of monopoly laws we could buy for 2d. per lb., the extra 2d. per lb. is a tax, but it is *a tax which is not paid to the revenue of the country*, it goes into the pocket of the monopolist, who gets 2d. per lb. more for his sugar than it is worth, and so both the people and the Queen are defrauded. The consumption of sugar last year was 4,045,181 cwts., which, at 2d. per lb. amounts to the enormous sum of £3,775,500, and this is the sum of which the people were plundered last year by the sugar monopolists. Free Traders want to put a stop to this plunder, but that Solomon, "*Old England*," tells you that "if free trade is carried out the government of the country cannot be carried on."

But the view we have taken is only a small part of the mischief arising from the continuance of monopoly. A large portion of the working classes are deprived of the means of buying sugar and coffee, in consequence of the prices being raised double what they ought to be by the prohibition of foreign sugar and coffee. If foreign coffee and sugar were admitted at the same rates of duty as British West India, (and this is all the Free Traders ask for,) there is little doubt the consumption and the revenue would both in a short time be doubled, as was the case with coffee when the duty was reduced 20 years ago. The consumption of coffee in 1824, when the duty was 1s. per lb., was 7,993,041 lbs., the following year the duty was reduced to 6d. per lb., and in 1831, the consumption had increased to 23,704,627lbs., yielding at the low rate of duty a greater revenue by 40 per cent. per annum than at the high rate of duty.

The sugar monopoly is destroying both the sugar trade and the revenue; for the consumption of sugar was greater fourteen years ago than at present. In 1830 the consumption of sugar was 4,147,350 cwts., in 1843 the consumption was only 4,051,181 cwts., although the population, in that period, has increased upwards of eight millions!

Nothing but the monopoly prevents the sugar trade from being doubled. Look, then, at the consequences of the abolition of this monopoly. Double the number of ships would be wanted, double the number of sailors, double the number of porters and carters and carriers; the business of the merchants and grocers would be doubled, and the Queen would receive double the revenue. *Free trade, then, instead of diminishing would increase the revenue.* It would enable millions to indulge in sugar who cannot now afford to use it. It would create increased demand for employment, and thus create customers to shopkeepers and tradesmen for a variety of taxable articles, which would again bring additional revenue to the exchequer.

The beneficial effects produced by the abolition of the sugar monopoly are equally applicable to all other monopolies, and therefore we need not further enlarge on corn, coffee, timber, or any other of the existing monopolies.

Here we might conclude, but we cannot pass "*Old England's*" ignorant and mischievous remarks on machinery. "Let me remind the working classes," says he, "that if trade were increased a hundred fold, they have a giant to contend with which they can never overcome. Whatever may be the extent of trade, machinery will prevent its being advantageous to the working classes generally. *Observe, I do not wish to influence their minds against machinery.* It is unfortunate for the working classes, but it is absolutely necessary, if England is to maintain its place in the front of nations."

Hear this philanthropist! He wishes to be thought the friend of the working classes. Machinery is a great evil. He commisserates their unfortunate condition, but, good man, *he would not put it down.* No; "it is absolutely necessary if England is to maintain its place in the front of nations." What! If machinery be an evil to the *working classes*, for the benefit of what class ought it to be sustained? What does he mean by maintaining our place in the front of nations? Ought not the happiness of the *working class*, that is, of the great body of the people, to be the first consideration? May not that country, where the working class are the most happy, be said to be in the front of nations? If machinery then be not good for *all*, away with it.

"*Old England*" tells you that machinery is an evil because it dispenses with labour, and this is the way men of his unreasoning class argue, without for a moment inquiring whether or not it does dispense with labour. Now let us take the cotton trade, and inquire how far his theory accords with facts. Before the wonderful inventions of Watt and Arkwright the cotton manufacture employed, in this country, about 30,000 people. From that time to the present there have been constant improvements in machinery, and if what "*Old England*" says be true, there ought now to be fewer people employed than then. But what is the fact? Why, that now about 2,000,000 people are dependent on the cotton trade for bread! Every new invention, which lessens the cost of production, increases the demand for the article produced, and brings new labour into employment. This applies not only to the cotton, but to all other manufactures. But the additional employment which machinery creates is only a small part of the benefits we derive from it. Compare the wages of those who work by the aid of machinery with those who work by hand-labour. Look at the wages paid in those agricultural districts far removed from the neighbourhood of manufactures, where able-bodied labourers earn only 6s. to 9s. per week. Look again at Ireland, "blessed country!" as "*Old England*" would exclaim, where they have no machinery, "no giant to contend with which they can never overcome;" and what are wages there? Why, Mr. O'Connell, at the League meeting, in Covent Garden Theatre, declared that thousands of men in Ireland would be glad to work for 4d. to 6d. per day, and could not get employment!!

It is difficult to calculate the benefits which the world has derived from the cotton manufacture alone. Millions in our own country are clothed with comfortable and beautiful garments, which, *but for machinery*, they could never have possessed; and millions more, in foreign lands, have also been clothed by the aid of our machinery, and millions more would be glad to get our clothing in exchange for their products, but are prevented by monopoly laws, which forbid it. The gift of invention is one of the most precious gifts the Almighty has bestowed on man; it has enabled us to supply ourselves with an amount of comforts and enjoyments which were unknown to our ancestors, and which, without machinery, we never could have possessed. See the triumphs steam is every day accomplishing; it now enables us, in a short time, and at a small expense, to traverse the country from one end to the other; it has brought distant nations within a few days' communication with us, and thus, by the constant and rapid intercourse of countries with each other, it is gradually wearing away national prejudices, antipathies, and jealousies, and drawing more closely those bonds of peace and brotherhood, which remind us that we are all children of the same great family, and that God is the Father of all. But we have not derived all the benefits from machinery which we might, and we never shall enjoy the benefits which the Almighty designed, until all those mistaken and wicked laws are abolished which prevent us from freely exchanging the products of our industry and skill with every country in the world. Suppose, for a moment, that, on the north-side of your river *Lune*, there abounded coal and iron, and that the people were distinguished above all others for their skill, and ingenuity, and mechanical inventions, by which they produced great varieties of cotton and woollen cloths, and silks and iron-wares, beyond what they needed for their own use, but of corn and other articles of food they were unable to produce sufficient for their own consumption. And, suppose that, on the south-side of the *Lune*, there was abundance of rich and fruitful land, which produced more food than the people could eat, but there being no coal and iron, they were unable to supply themselves with clothing equal to that of their neighbours. What would you think of the law-makers, who governed the north-side of the Lune, passing laws to prevent their people exchanging their manufactures, of which they had more than they could use, with their neighbours across the river for food, of which they had not enough—who thus condemned the people on the north side to short commons, those on the south side to be badly clothed? And what would you say of those who, in the language of "*Old England*," told the distressed manufacturers on the north side, in answer to their complaints, that if they were only allowed to exchange their surplus clothing with the people across the river for food, they would thereby have more employment and more food, and that both parties would be benefited? "Let us remind the working classes that if trade were increased a hundredfold, they have a giant to contend with which they can never overcome." "Machinery is the great evil, and the cause of all your distress." Substitute England for the north side of the Lune, and foreign countries for the south side, (and the only difference is a narrow and fresh water, instead of a wide and salt water division,) and then you have an exhibition of the folly and wickedness of our present system of monopoly.

The letter writer foresees a long train of evils to follow the repeal of the corn laws. "If," says he, "the rents of landowners are reduced to the extent proposed, they must reduce their establishments," &c. What is it that maintains the rents of landlords, and keeps up their establishments? Why is it that the rent of land is higher in England than in any other country on the face of the earth? Is it that the land is richer or more fruitful than in other countries? No. It is commerce and manufactures, which, in every country, and in all ages of the world, wherever they have flourished, have given increased value to land, and have left behind imperishable monuments of their glory. Has it ever occurred to "*Old England*" *to inquire into the value of land before the introduction of manufactures?* And has he ever reflected on the consequences to landowners, if manufacturers are driven to remove with their capital and skill to other countries? Bad laws and bad governments have often put industry to flight, and the desolation which marked the consequences may be seen in the ruined and deserted cities of all parts of Europe.

Hitherto our superiority in machinery has enabled us to bear a load of taxation greater than any other country in the world, as well as an equal burden of taxation, in the shape of corn and other monopolies; but the time has arrived when *this can no longer be borne without subjecting the working classes to the greatest privations.* Foreign countries have been forced to become manufacturers because we would not take their natural products in exchange for ours, and have now become powerful rivals in manufactures, and within these two years laws have been passed to enable them to import our machinery. With English machinery, therefore, and cheap food, how is the English workman to compete with foreign workmen without great privation? If landowners were not blind to their own interests, they would see that no class in the community have more to fear from the decline of manufactures than they. Our population is increasing at the rate of 1000 souls a day. *Can the land find them employment?* If not, what is to become of them? How are they to be maintained, if manufactures be destroyed? They must become paupers, and then the law says that they must be maintained by the land before the landowners can touch one farthing of rent. These are serious questions for consideration, and it is worth while for landowners to pause a while, and reflect upon them.

The letter writer has either very confused notions or he forgets how he contradicts himself, in his anxiety to establish his case. He tells you that if we export manufactures, "foreigners will not pay in money for these goods, they *will only pay in produce,*" and then he says if we want to buy corn foreigners will not take our goods in exchange, "they *will compel us to pay in money.*" Now these are points we may very well leave to be settled by the merchants who carry on the trade, for we may rest assured that the English merchant will not part with his goods for nothing, and it is as little likely that foreigners will part with their corn without an equivalent. If the trade in corn were placed on the same footing as that of all other commodities, it would be regulated by the same laws of exchange, for nothing is more evident than that trade is the barter of the products of one country for those of another, and that money is the mere instrument by which the exchange is effected. Our imports during the last twenty years amount to about £900,000,000, and it is clear that these imports must have been paid for by the export of the like value of our manufacturing products; they could not have been paid for in money, because all the gold and silver in the kingdom does not amount to £30,000,000.

"But," says "*Old England*," "foreigners will not pay in money for our exports, they will pay in produce, and *that produce chiefly articles of luxury*." What the League complains of is that *at present* foreigners do give "*chiefly articles of luxury*" in exchange for our export of manufactures, because the law prohibits them from giving any thing else, and it is for this reason that the League seek the abolition of all monopolies. They want to see the corn and provision laws abolished, and then, as well as wines, and fruits, and silks, and diamonds, and jewels, and luxuries for the aristocracy, we can as freely import corn, and beef, and bacon, and butter, for the working classes. The manufacturer does not want *money* for his goods, so long as he can get plenty of eatables in exchange for them; he will never lack customers to purchase them.

"But," says "*Old England*," "now let us look forward for half a dozen years, when (if the manufacturers carry a repeal) this country will have become dependent upon foreign nations, such as Russia, Germany, and perhaps America, for a supply of food for one-third of its population—*Does not monopoly always raise the price of an article?*" (That is the League doctrine, and perhaps it is the only thing in which they agree with "*Old England*." But what an admission from such a quarter!!) "And will not these states, when they have driven Englishmen out of the market, raise the price of corn which they sell to us?"

Now it is clear that "*Old England*" wishes to alarm you with the idea of the danger of dependance on foreign countries for corn. But what are we to do? we are already dependent on them for corn. During the last ten years, we have not grown sufficient for our own supply, and have therefore been obliged to import no less than 12,000,000 quarters from foreign countries. But where is the danger of dependance? Is it not the order of providence that we should be dependent on each other for the comforts and happiness we enjoy? Think you, if the Almighty designed that nations should be independent of each other, he would not have given to each country every variety of product, that so they might be independent of exchange with each other? But "God has made of one blood every nation of the earth." He has given to different countries varieties of soil, climate, and capacities that, so by the exchange of the productions of each with the other, peace and good will might be promoted between them, that all might taste of his goodness, and all might learn that they are children of the same great family. "Does not monopoly always raise the price of an article?" Certainly it does, and it is a serious ground of complaint against the landowners that they have passed laws securing to themselves the monopoly of feeding the people of this country with high-priced food. "Will not Russia, Germany, and America, when they have driven England out of the market, raise the price of corn which they sell to us?" There certainly is less to fear, from prices being raised by a supply from *three* countries, than when it is confined to *one* monopoly country as at present. But what idle nonsense it is to talk of any country being able to dictate to another the price of corn or any other commodity. The price must, at all times, be regulated by the supply and demand. Every individual, who has corn to sell, will send it to the best market, and nations will do the same. Whenever the English market is higher than any other, supplies of corn will naturally flow in, as well as of any other commodity. We are dependant on one country (America) for three-fourths of our supplies of cotton, and on China alone for supplies of tea, but *corn is an universal article*, it grows in nearly every country in the world. If, therefore, Russia, Germany, and America, were foolish enough to combine to raise prices, there are a hundred other places who would be glad to supply us. But the supposition is too absurd. Supplies of all articles may be safely left to the natural love of gain among all traders, and there is much more to fear from a combination amongst the tradesmen of one large town to starve the people, than there is of all the world to starve a nation. There is a remarkable instance of this in 1810. When Napoleon had shut the whole continent against us, and we were at war with all the world, we received from France itself, in that year, in spite of all his prohibitions, no less than 300,000 quarters of corn.

In conclusion, we cannot help thanking "*Old England*" for his letter, because it will be the means of exciting discussion and reflection on the most important question that can engage the attention of the electors. We earnestly entreat you, in the consideration of the corn laws, to seek for facts, not to mix it up with the party questions of Whig, Tory, or Radical, or to be frightened from the discussion by charges of innovation or disloyalty. Consult the records of your own courts, and you will find there was a time when persons were tried, at Lancaster, and executed for witchcraft. There were *then* living people like "*Old England*," who branded the first agitators against this absurd and inhuman practice as infidels, in the same way as he and other monopolists *now* accuse those who oppose the cruel and inhuman corn laws of seeking "to endanger the crown, and to destroy the institutions of the country." But the time is not distant when such charges against the League will be laughed at as equally absurd with the accusation of infidelity against those who ridiculed the folly and wickedness of burning old women as witches.

The object of the League is, by the diffusion of information, by the encouragement of discussion, and by every legal and constitutional means, to obtain the total abolition of the corn and provision laws, and every other monopoly, and thus to restore to every man his inalienable right, freely to exchange his industry with every nation under heaven. They hoist the banner of free trade, and invite all the nations of the earth to give us, of their abundance, such things as we need, in exchange for such things as we have to give, that so nations may be drawn together by mutual interests, the bond of peace and universal brotherhood. In this holy object are leagued the wise and good of all classes and parties. It embraces the highest nobles in the land, the acknowledged best stock farmers, and the best arable farmers; the richest bankers, the richest merchants, the largest shipowners, the largest and wealthiest cotton, linen, silk, woollen and worsted manufacturers, philosophers, poets and learned men, hundreds of Christian ministers of all denominations, thousands of tradesmen and shopkeepers, and millions of working men. Truth and justice is their aim, and, by the blessing of God, they will finally triumph.

Printed by J. Gadsby, Newall's-Buildings, Market-Street, Manchester.